Ingratitude ❧

Ingratitude

The Debt-Bound Daughter in
Asian American Literature

erin Khuê Ninh

NEW YORK UNIVERSITY PRESS
New York and London

NEW YORK UNIVERSITY PRESS
New York and London
www.nyupress.org

References to Internet websites (URLs) were accurate at the time of writing.
Neither the author nor New York University Press is responsible for URLs
that may have expired or changed since the manuscript was prepared.

Library of Congress Cataloging-in-Publication Data
Ninh, erin Khuê.
Ingratitude : the debt-bound daughter in
Asian American literature / erin Khuê Ninh.
p. cm.
Includes bibliographical references and index.
ISBN 978-0-8147-5844-1 (cl : alk. paper) — ISBN 978-0-8147-5845-8
(pb : alk. paper) — ISBN 978-0-8147-5885-4 (e-book)
1. American literature—Asian American authors. 2. Mothers and daughters.
3. Fathers and daughters. 4. Obedience. I. Title.
PS508.A8.N56   2010
810.9'35254—dc22   2010041362

New York University Press books are printed on acid-free paper,
and their binding materials are chosen for strength and durability.
We strive to use environmentally responsible suppliers and materials
to the greatest extent possible in publishing our books.

Manufactured in the United States of America
c   10 9 8 7 6 5 4 3 2 1
p   10 9 8 7 6 5 4 3 2 1

for my sisters ❧

Contents

Introduction

I have trouble understanding why someone so smart would drop out of school and run away from home at 14 and end up as a junkie-whore. Yes, it's hard to be the dutiful daughter of immigrant parents from China and Hong Kong, the kind who consider friends a frivolity and an 89 per cent exam mark a failure . . . But I'm a parent now. Millions of Canadians have overcome such traumas, if that is the word, without self-indulgent melt-downs.

> Canadian journalist Jan Wong, in interview
> of Evelyn Lau, *The Globe and Mail*

Too often, . . . narratives of gender and sexual awakening are accused of undermining the "serious" work that Asian American texts are expected to perform: to expose anti-Asian sentiment in the United States, to limn the trauma inflicted upon Asians by Western imperialism, to envision better worlds where Asians and Asian Americans will not be construed as foreigners in their own homes, to create a common cultural ground for pan-Asian unity, and (more recently) to apprehend Asian Americans' larger global-economic agendas and cross-border alliances. Each of these social agendas comprises a supportable priority. However, it would be a mistake to interpret the pursuit of these goals as anomalous or more important than the exposure of tyrannies within the household.

> Rachel Lee, *The Americas of Asian American Literature*

This is a book about the Asian immigrant family and intergenerational conflict—conflict that we think we know; after all, the story has been often enough told. But in order to dislodge us from our tired circuits around the immigrant family romance, this analysis deliberately brackets the (inter)personal. So *Ingratitude* will not be particularly interested in the mothers in our bones. Instead, it will conduct a reading of the immigrant nuclear family as a special form of capitalist enterprise: one invested, Gayatri Spivak might say, in obtaining "justice under capitalism." To the extent that migrating to positions of global advantage is about the hope for upward mobility, it is about the hope of profiting in the Western capitalist economy. And I do mean profit, because this project considers the Asian immigrant family a production unit—a sort of cottage industry, for a particular brand of good, capitalist subject: Get your filial child, your doctor/lawyer, your model minority here. The book also takes up the systems of that production: What is it to leverage guilt or fear, to manufacture in a subject these very useful mechanisms of ingratitude or inadequacy?

The upcoming readings of narratives such as *Fifth Chinese Daughter* (Jade Snow Wong, 1945), *The Woman Warrior* (Maxine Hong Kingston, 1976), *Oriental Girls Desire Romance* (Catherine Liu, 1997), and *Runaway: Diary of a Street Kid* (Evelyn Lau, 1995) reconstruct the processes by which diligent, docile, immigrants' daughters are produced. We attend to the means, and then the psychic costs, of this subject formation: even when it succeeds, but especially when it misses its mark. When she ran away from her parents at age 14, Evelyn Lau spent two years on and off the streets of Canada—scrambling for food and shelter in foster homes or strangers' homes, selling sex for drugs and basic necessities, risking attack and being attacked—enduring, in short, the harshest physical conditions it was in her power to choose. All this, rather than go back to being the dutiful daughter of her immigrant parents: earning straight As, cleaning the house, one day to become a doctor. What was it about that existence she found so very dreadful? Even years later, she does not know; she cannot say. Something, she thinks, about being trapped inside that house.

Such is the core conundrum of this book: how is it that young women like Evelyn may come to madness or suicide without being able to point to any legitimating personal histories of abuse or trauma in the home? Jade Snow enumerates the minutiae of her grievances against her parents, and these youthful sorrows of curfews and playmates do demonstrate a certain unfairness or disproportion in their child-rearing practices. Yet no strand of these minor episodes, however finely strung, could approximate the intensity of the "stubborn, unhappy struggle . . . between [Jade Snow] and her family" (JS Wong, 90). She is punished unreasonably, but not beyond the bounds of Chinese cultural strictures or of American senses of propriety; in response, she takes a position in a white household at the age of 16 in order to move out of her own family's home, the beginning of a course to which she later refers as a "break with her parents" (136). The "enraged struggle" (Kim, *AAL*, 66) implied by such a severing resonates with that of daughter figures in a litany of other childhoods, comparably vexed and equally mundane. Thus, despite the wealth of literary accounts we know to be generated by filial distress, there has been precious little language *even in these stories* to explain exactly what drives these young women to the desperate things they do. It is that peculiar disjunction which drives this book to look for the circuits of power and subjectification running beneath the narratives, the structural rather than inflictive violences that prove such a challenge to articulate in literary form.

∿ critical precedents: going home again

At either end of the 50 years between the publications of *Fifth Chinese Daughter* and *Runaway*, second-generation narratives of the immigrant family are joined by structural and thematic consistencies all the more uncanny for the changing conditions that Asian America has undergone. This is a period that straddles Japanese American internment, the Korean and Vietnam wars, sweeping transformations and proliferations of the ethnic and class composition of the racial demographic, the dramatic globalization of capital and of ethnicity, and midway through that span, the birth of Asian America into political sentience as a radically minded coalition. Yet the intergenerational conflict—its forms of power, its discourses of subject formation—replicates with compelling faithfulness across an era of seemingly imposing historical changes. At every interval and increasingly, this period has produced narratives by young women railing against their upbringings—to the point where such stories have become recognizable commodities, their extraordinary correspondences droning into ordinary clichés of a literary convention. Consequently, in the very motion that recognizes these narratives as forming a prominent genre of Asian American literature, scholarship has come simultaneously to dismiss them as texts partaking in a politically devalued and, thus, foreclosed project: Filial angst is cast as willing maidservant to a racial project[1] to downgrade conflict from the political and historical to the cultural and interpersonal. It is deplored that the ethnic community "is described in terms of social death, Asian parents are depicted as unfeelingly oppressive and laughably ineffectual, and Asian American youngsters are celebrated for escaping the prison of ethnicity" (Li, 129). Such accounts of parental pressures and communal expectations are said to lend undue credibility to the model minority myth, and to disable critiques of institutional racism, political disenfranchisement, and economic exploitation, by diverting blame for the iniquities produced by those social forces onto the ethnic subjects themselves, their families, or their communities (Kim, *AAL*, 60). The field has thus tended to conflate unfavorable representations of the ethnic family with model minority narratives, and forcefully to dissociate itself from both.

In posing its critique of the generational narrative, Lisa Lowe's "Heterogeneity, Hybridity, Multiplicity" begins by recognizing that the texts of Asian American literature will often frame themselves as stories centrally *about* the dynamics of generational and cultural divide. The essay then proceeds to caution against "interpreting Asian American culture *exclusively* in terms of the[se] master narratives," because doing so will yield an essentializing and reductive reading of Asian American culture: that of the timeless, personal, and familial struggle of assimilation (Lowe, 62–63; emphasis added). Granting the political pitfalls of a purely privatizing or internalizing narrative of oppression, however, it is no less problematic to deal in exclusively *externalizing* explanations, which project the locus of power (and oppression) outward—and leave ethnic communities' social institutions looking impossibly innocent of accountability.

This has been the wont of progressive scholarship, to finger the white establishment whenever the wages of intergenerational conflict have come calling. Wendy Motooka has reproached "the Asian American critical enterprise" for just such critical deflection: "We tend to think of ourselves as outside the field of power, or at least we write about 'it' as if it were 'out there,' rather than considering 'it' as *us*" (Motooka, 208). Thus, even when prompted by the makings of a crisis in Asian American mental health,[2] our scholarship has more often than not been circumscribed by the strict blinders on our politics. In "A Dialogue on Racial Melancholia," David Eng and Shinhee Han respond to what they describe as "disturbing patterns of depression that [they] have been witnessing in a significant and growing number of Asian American [college] students," who seem from the examples they provide to be specifically the children of immigrants (Eng and Han, 344). Yet as a "critical response," the essay is guilty of a harmful hermeneutical bias. Despite its earnest intent to fathom the psychological distress of their students, the essay immediately—and ultimately exclusively—attributes this distress to the psychic tolls of externally imposed racialization and stereotype: media productions of Asianness and other systemic forms of racism. That bias governs the argument, *with the exception of a brief space* in which the authors respond directly to the following explanation from one of their distressed subjects: "My parents sacrificed everything to raise me here . . . and now it's up to me to please them and to do well in school" (353). The student's reference to her parents in causal terms is neither subtle nor obscure; for the length of three paragraphs, the authors are held by her frank citing of parental martyr rhetoric and expectations, to consider that familial pressures may be a factor in her crisis. And yet, *even as* this hermeneutic possibility is posed, it is foreclosed by the authors' own curious phrasing: "are Asian American parents as completely selfless as the theme of sacrifice suggests, or is this theme a compensatory gesture that *attaches itself* to the parents' losses and failures?" (354; emphasis added). Rather than suggest that it is the parents who nurse their losses with themes of sacrifice, the argument contorts to bar its parental subjects from occupying the syntactical subject position, in order to avoid indicting them with agency: "*The loss experienced* by the parents' failure to achieve the American Dream . . . *is a loss transferred* onto and incorporated by Elaine for her to 'work out' and to repair" (353; emphasis added). In this scrupulously passive language is an exemplary, and implausible, piece of misdirection. While there is no question that the losses of immigration matter, that institutional racism and media representation figure into the second-generation experience, so too does power in the most intimate, vulnerable, and formative of social contexts—one which may demand that the subject compensate for familial losses by successfully navigating hostile social and political waters, and which may very well redouble the stakes of "racial" failure: "Those Asian Americans who do not fit into the model minority stereotype . . . are altogether erased from—not seen in—mainstream society," Eng and Han lament, then tack on, "they are often rejected by their own families as well" (351). Whereas the injury of stereotype takes the brunt of their analysis, the familial warrants from the article only that reluctant aside, as if, compared to lack of prime-time TV diversity, erasure from the family is the less devastating rejection. In its flight from the inescapable yet inadmissible implications of familial power, Eng and Han's article manifests the scholarly stance which discourages even the elaboration on intergenerational conflict, so thoroughly has it been deemed a specious and perfidious trope. In the face of real distress, this is a dangerous reticence. Disabling in advance those inquiries that discomfit "our" political collective, how will we craft but the most painfully evasive critical responses? The built-in urgencies of the situation demand much more of us—but for starters, they require a more textually and materially accountable reading, as part of owning our accountability.

Given the sophistication of reading practices at the disposal of cultural scholarship, a theoretical reappraisal of generation and family need not be guilty of ahistoricizing, dematerializing, aestheticizing, or commodifying Asian American culture; it need not accept, in other words, that the familial space is exclusively "private."[3] Thus, *Ingratitude* articulates familial dynamics through precisely the kind of cultural materialism to which that theme has long been considered antithetical, and indeed through a baldly monetary lexicon that resonates with that of other recent scholarship. With the emergence of such work as Lisa Park's *Consuming Citizenship* and Christine So's *Economic Citizens*, economic participation increasingly surfaces as a dominant and defining trope of Asian racialization. Their work makes plain that—whether intent upon entering circuits of social exchange metonymically with money (So), or with the signifying powers of conspicuous consumption (Park)—it is through economic registers that the Asian American subject finds expression in language and the Western nation-state. Where Park and So may consider the microeconomics of the family in relation to the greater labor and commodities markets, however, this project attends to the financial and operational management that goes on inside the institution itself—behind the household doors at which economic dictates do not stop. I offer an analysis of the political-economic structures of power obtaining between parents and daughters in the immigrant family. What we call intergenerational conflict is at bottom a conflict of interests, and as such, symptomatic of a social and economic unit whose agents are differentially vested in power. Such conflict appears apolitical only when its language of filiality and affect—suffering and guilt, devotion and anger, trauma and disownment—is allowed to be spoken in isolation from the politics of the family. An understanding of generational dynamics as implicated by and participating in a racializing, gendered, and material history is by no means reductive of cultural politics, but even more fully accountable to them. For even by Lowe's terms of "multiplicity," if indeed Asian Americans are subjects marked by differences (of class, gender, sexuality, etc.), then we are also marked by generation; and if we as subjects are overdetermined by multiple axes of power, then the parent-child axis must be one. We are better served by a view to the *relationality* of these axes and explanatory narratives, than by the stance that one set of accounts must supplant the other as obsolete. Read through the family's economic aspirations, or a parent's class and national investments, Asian American intimate relations reveal themselves to be profoundly ordered by a capitalist logic and ethos, their violence arranged around the production of the disciplined and profitable docile body.

Certainly it is true that, in the tradition of Jade Snow Wong, the trope of intergenerational conflict has often been applied to conservative political ends: reconciling subjects with power. This apparent correlation prompts David Palumbo-Liu to draw a political distinction between what he considers more historically materialist literary accounts of Asian American family dynamics (such as Milton Murayama's *All I asking for is my body*), and more "popular" (hegemony-friendly) texts such as *Fifth Chinese Daughter* and *The Woman Warrior,* which he believes to "lend themselves to [model minority] readings" (Palumbo-Liu, 413), by virtue of their inattention to the American sociopolitical context. However, as I hope to demonstrate presently, these latter texts may "lend themselves" equally well to a historical materialist reading of the economic, social, and political inherent to them. As both Lau and Liu's work illustrate, a narrative of intergenerational conflict need not be explicitly historical-materialist in order to "problematize" the "thematics of individual transcendence" (408) characteristic of model minority discourse. Moreover, because the critic's reading practices are not identical to the narrative she reads, even a text that may be said, by design or in effect, to "privatiz[e] social conflicts and contradictions" by "confining them to the . . . domestic sphere of family relations" (Lowe, 78) can prove to be analytically productive as a *symptomatic* reflection of that which it submerges.[4]

An easy target of scholarship and a case in point, Amy Tan's *The Joy Luck Club* assimilates its characters to an America whose systemic racial and economic discrimination it cleanly ignores. The book's manipulation of intergenerational conflict—a "recuperative project that replaces an overly critical, authoritative parental voice with that of an oppressed woman" (Bow, *Betrayal*, 94)—must be understood not as distinct from or in contrast to, but as part and parcel of such assimilationist obfuscation of power. Yet while the former recuperative move (redeeming social conflict) has met with collective censure, the latter recuperative move (redeeming familial conflict) has received considerable critical support. Regarding the latter, Patricia Chu remarks approvingly that

> The novel [*The Joy Luck Club*] is winning and persuasive when it suggests that images of the mothers as superhuman others are largely projections of the daughters' own fears and fantasies, as in the story where Waverly Jong learns to see her mother, not as a malignant adversary . . . but simply as an old woman waiting for her daughter's acceptance. (Chu, 149)

This quote refers to a moment in which an adult Waverly describes herself as "a scared child," hiding from her mother "behind my invisible barriers" and imagining "what lay on the other side: Her side attacks. Her secret weapons. Her uncanny ability to find my weakest spots"; but in her epiphany Waverly decides "I could finally see *what was really there*: an old woman, a wok for her armor, a knitting needle for her sword, getting a little crabby as she waited patiently for her daughter to invite her in" (Tan, 183; emphasis added). The passage sets up, and Chu's commentary perpetuates, a false binary: as if authority that is not malicious in intent must then be inert, indifferent to power and incapable of harm. Rather than allow that authority may be caring and yet harmful, that it may mean well and be deeply invested in power, Tan and her critic both suggest that authority is either malignant or not authority at all, "just" or "simply" an old woman: passive and helpless to the will of another, and tragically misconstrued. Scholars recognize that Tan's "mother-daughter discord eventually evaporates without a trace of historical justification" (Li, 116), because "the conflict" between them is revealed "to have been not so much related to class tension and the daughter's increasing cultural enfranchisement and mobility, but simply to childish growing pains surrounding individuation that necessitate the adult's attempt to regain self-esteem" (Bow, *Betrayal*, 109). However, "childish growing pains" is not merely an alternate explanation for conflict, unrelated to and supplanting social and cultural accounts; rather, to characterize conflict as "childish" negates it as genuine conflict at all. There is, Tan claims, no problem here. And the analysis of power is irrelevant in a universe that disavows conflict itself. Thus, a refusal to interrogate power in the familial context can also disable social critique: conflict that does not exist renders any accounts of class tension or cultural disenfranchisement moot. But alternatively, criticism that takes to task subjection within the family is well-situated to appraise its intersectionality with other apparatuses of power. For if the narrative that evacuates intergenerational conflict urges us to reconcile ourselves with a universe in which there is no authority but what we mistakenly imagine, one which *acknowledges* vested power within the family may be part and parcel of, even necessary to, a study of those powers within which the family exists.

model minority mythologies ∾

Because the Asian immigrant family has by definition entered the province of Asian American national subject, the reappraisal of one means a necessary reckoning with the other. Thus I join a recent slate of scholars in proposing that, given the ascendancy of model minority discourse in contemporary political culture, it is imperative to reassess both the discourse itself and scholarship's stance upon it. Dismissing the model minority identity as a discursive instrument, used by whiteness to discipline other non-white communities, has long represented the ideological consensus among Asian

American intellectuals and activists; this is what Viet Nguyen has termed the field's "model minority thesis," in response and rebuttal to the mainstream's "model minority paradigm." Per his synopsis of that paradigm, Asian Americans are identified with "a system of social values that prioritizes family, education, and sacrifice" and "prioritizes obedience and hierarchy"; these values incline the group to be "reluctant to blame others for any lack in their social position," "willing to accept their social position with gratitude," and guided by "self-sacrifice rather than self-interest, . . . quiet restraint rather than vocal complaint in the face of perceived or actual injustice" (Nguyen, 146). The paradigm deems that, thanks to these accommodationist virtues, Asian Americans are able to raise themselves out of poverty without public assistance or special consideration, serving thus as a silent but willing rebuke against those who would demand changes from the system rather than strive to succeed by its rules.

It is a central tenet of the model minority *thesis* that the model minority identity is a *myth*: an invention of dominant culture that bears little relation to reality. Thus, the rebuttal relies heavily on indicators of Asian American failure or deviance, statistics of poverty or criminality that attempt to demonstrate the fabricated nature of this discourse of achievement. That may be a disingenuous case to make, however, or one that partly misses the point. The heart of the issue is not whether an Asian immigrant family currently meets the socioeconomic or professional measures of the model minority. Rather, the issue is whether it aspires to do so, whether it *applies* those metrics: not resentful of the racializing discourse of Asian success as a violence imposed from without, but implementing that discourse, with ingenuity, alacrity, and pride, from within. In other words, an identity's materiality is perhaps more appropriately gauged by its fictions and active identifications (what its discourses aim *to* fabricate) than merely by its present circumstances.

By such standards, if ever that identity was only myth, certainly the model minority is mythical no longer. As Susan Koshy has forcefully argued, the aspiration "of new immigrant groups" of various Asian ethnicities for inclusion in forms of white privilege—conditional upon their complicity in an ongoing contradistinction against blackness—is a crucial element of their racial formation and agency (Koshy, 154). Likewise, Karen Su cites "post–Civil Rights economic gains as well as an influx of professional-classes in immigration" (Su, 24) as having shifted Asian American class identifications upward, and contributed to the formation of a population "more prone to accepting" the mantle of the "model minority" (25). She observes that the majority population of the community is now made up of first-generation immigrants who may cleave to the very accommodationist values "demonized within Asian American identity politics" (20); they are accompanied by young professionals who, in rapidly growing advocacy organizations, operate on principles of individual economic advancement for the voting consumer (24).[5] Though she treats these groups as distinct and doubly dismaying rather than related phenomena, Su recognizes that the turn to model minority identifications characterizes both immigrant and second generations, and asserts that it is politically unfeasible to insist on alienating or ignoring this dominant majority "as if they were 'fake' Asian Americans" (24) or embarrassing mavericks. In his overview of Asian American identity politics, Glenn Omatsu, like Su, recognizes that neoconservatives have achieved a critical mass in the population, and by virtue of their numbers that they cannot be summarily dismissed for their views. However, what he poses as an ideological enigma or disconnect from the civil rights struggles—"Where did these neoconservatives come from?" (Omatsu, 180)—can be readily explained by the intergenerational, immigrant paradigm: As "newcomers to Asian American issues" (183), the neoconservatives are likely the progeny *not* of civil rights–era activists as he supposes (178), but of the post-1965 arrivals Su and Koshy cite. The children of post-1965 immigrants have been intravenously injected into the climate of material access and economic restructuring Omatsu describes, in the immediate wake and ongoing mobilization of model minority discourse. If they recognize U.S. racism not in the lineage of social movement coalitions, but rather in terms of the glass ceiling, this is but in keeping with their parents' (neoconservative) convictions and training: that their children must excel to overcompensate for disadvantage in the racial hierarchy (Louie, xxxi, 56). Thus, these "young, middle-class professionals," graduates of "the elite universities" (Omatsu, 181), whom Omatsu calls a new breed, I call second-generation.

In recognition of the paradigm's actual currency among an increasingly professional-laden immigrant population (Koshy, 192), Koshy bids scholarship acknowledge that Asian American racial formation entails a *dialectic* of agency: not only the externally imposed "assignation" of model minority status, but also the internally driven "assertion" of that identification (158). Moreover, she bids "left and right progressive critics" achieve not only an analytical clarity on the "political embarrassment" of such assimilationist investments, but also on our own political investments in denial—our standing on the wish for the essentially subversive Asian American subject (160). In that vein, Nguyen also critiques the Asian American intellectual class (which he defines as "inclusive of academics, artists, activists, and nonacademic critics" [Nguyen, 5]) for its rigid valuation of cultural texts and practices in proportion to their oppositional politics, and its censure of texts and practices for any accommodationist tendencies; he finds such a value system limiting and dishonest in a context where, not only does the "model minority" as an identity form the mainstream of contemporary Asian American culture and politics, but those intellectuals themselves practice selective accommodation for their pragmatic institutional survival. Where it secures consideration and resources within the university, in other words, the field's leveraging of social oppression is a savvy self-marketing ploy. While I am less concerned here with scholarship's commodification of Asian American identity per se, I too would have us interrogate the animosity directed at narratives of intergenerational conflict, for self-incriminating investments scholarship may have therein. For in a very real sense, the model minority do not come from nowhere; we—academics, dissidents, activists alike—come from them. Such studied disregard as the field reserves for these stories suggests something there that it would cost too much to see. But that the model minority paradigm can hardly be articulated, even in synopsis, without resort to a language of filiality—sacrifice, obedience, hierarchy, gratitude—signals that it is time to stop skirting the obvious: The assimilationist, individualist, upwardly mobile professional class of the model minority *is*, for familial intents and purposes, Asian America's model children. An effective understanding of the Asian American subject's relation to the nation must therefore come to terms with the immigrant family as that nation's intermediary and agent.

· · ·

Ingratitude charts a model of subject formation not exclusive to, but racially and gender-specific to, second-generation Asian American daughters. Of course, to speak of subject formation is already to locate this book in a Foucauldian universe; it is to suppose the subject an effect (though not always a fully actualized effect) of the techniques of power by which her body and knowledge are ordered. It is further to take technologies of power to be contextually adaptive systems interested in the development and optimization, as opposed to merely the repression and control, of the subject. Though Foucault has been much faulted for failing to elaborate a theory of the thinking subject, the *genealogy* his work has produced (McLaren, 113) of the human subject as an effect of power, "created as the delimiting field of possibility for all thought" (Bersani, 3), is by no means antagonistic to such an endeavor. I thus choose here, borrowing from Butler and the toolbox of psychoanalysis, to extrapolate from Foucault's dissection of systems to the psychic effects these systems must produce. For disciplinary and discursive forms of modern power, the desired subject is one efficiently managed by and productive within its intersecting institutions. These institutions (the school, the office, the prison, the home) serve specialized functions and interests but a common ethos; they are most highly rewarded when they each play well with others. It stands to reason that, mechanisms of subjection being mobile across material contexts and institutions, we may find certain practices iterated across plantation owner and parent (a comparison made in chapter 1), Chicano and Asian immigrant communities (chapter 4), or even white patriarchal domesticities at the turn of an earlier century and our own patriarchal domestic spaces (a parallel that informs this argument throughout); and that subjects trained to similar technologies—debt bondage, discursive disownment, designated failure, to name a few—will adopt recognizable postures. Taken modularly, the elements of subjection I describe here are thus hardly exclusive or proprietary to the Asian immigrant family. As each of its systems emerges from a specific problematic of race, nation, class, gender, or other power differential, and adjusts as those problematics shift, the complex that is this model of Asian American daughterly subject formation may be functionally distinct, without being essentially distinctive.[6] This post-structuralist perspective on power should allow us the latitude, without having to efface particularities, to acknowledge parallels that social forms may take across immigrations (see Anzia Yezierska's *Bread Givers* for echoes of Jade Snow Wong from a Jewish immigrant's daughter from Poland), across compulsory reproductive femininities (inarticulably oppressive, "loving" relationships, in Kate Chopin's *The Awakening*), or even across the diversities of "the" Asian immigrant family, which in backgrounds and circumstances is itself by no means singular.

This brings us to perhaps the thorniest of the book's self-positioning tasks: situating its subject as "Asian American,"[7] despite its heavily Chinese American archive. *Ingratitude* selects for narratives by Asian women that detail uneventful second-generation upbringings in North America,[8] within nuclear families with Asian biological parents, and which give their extended attention to intergenerational conflict. The project's systematic construction serves, in a different manner of speaking, to isolate the dynamics of intergenerational conflict, controlling for factors such as physical abuse or interracial parentage which would complicate the analysis, and holding constant others such as immigration generation. This is not to say that the reading presented here is valid only within such very strict parameters, but to appreciate that it must be manifestly valid within them. Only very recently has publishing yielded literature from writers of South- and Southeast-Asian extractions meeting these exacting requirements, as the Afterword will note. Stories by Jhumpa Lahiri and Chitra Divakaruni do enter the argument periodically in the chapters that follow, but given the more recent arrival of these immigrant groups into the Asian American demographic and literary market, it is not surprising that the ethnic distribution of intergenerational-conflict literature is uneven. There is presently ample evidence in cultural forms *other* than the literary that these discourses of filiality and model minority operate widely across Asian immigrant ethnicities; in popular, online, and visual culture as well as journalistic media, their tropes surface plainly from the unpublished lives of non–East Asian American women.[9] With time, it may be that the intergenerational-conflict narratives running through these various communities today will surface increasingly in literary form.

It must be said, however, that literary studies will never generate a statistically adequate or demographically accurate sample of immigrant communities' varying productions of the model minority; that is not its strength. To measure the incidence of intergenerational conflict and its discourses of race and family across the mesh of ethnicity, class, immigration classification, and countless other demographic lines, we best look to the empirical methodologies of present and future social science scholarship—such as Vivian Louie's *Compelled to Excel*, Stacey Lee's *Unraveling the "Model Minority" Stereotype*, Lisa Park's *Consuming Citizenship*, Margaret Gibson's *Accommodation without Assimilation*, Miri Song's *Helping Out*, and Eliza Noh's "Asian American Women and Suicide." Such ethnographic and quantitative analyses grant access to the types of research questions that can both complicate and challenge the permutations of the current theoretical model, within material specificities: How, for instance, might the pressures for achievement compare for the daughters of immigrants such as post-1965 Indian doctors (whose visa classification allowed them to parlay their educational credentials into American professional status), versus those of immigrants who, like Korean college graduates-cum-shopkeepers, have experienced a galling downward mobility? It would hardly be prudent to look to theoretical readings and literary instruments for answers to such demographically discerning questions.

Nevertheless, without a calibration of social practice to documented history, *Ingratitude* may appear to invite charges of an essentialist characterization of the Asian American family—assuming, in effect, the beleaguered position of the authors whose narratives I recuperate. To be clear, the argument to follow *will* elaborate that these cultural discourses are inflected differently in different eras, in directions made possible by developments in economic and social policy. And yet, the project does not intend to preface its analysis with a review of the history of Asian immigration to the United States, because that body of particulars is not sufficiently integral to this theoretical model to bear repeating here. This is not to deny the direct impact of immigration legislation on familial formations and therefore the contextual relevance of those changing policies to the topic at hand. This is, however, to stand on the cultural materialist position that social structures and cultural productions are not the unilateral products of the economic and political, but that the two realms exist in a dialectic. Such a materialist reading allows that a family, community, or nation might well insist on an ideological conviction over-and-above or even in defiance of material particulars (such, in a sense, being one of the hallmarks of a hegemonic ideology), and subsequently leverage that system of belief to form and force material realities. Hence, this book will not attempt to account for the literature faithfully or mechanically along the contours of shifts in immigration. Rather, as I stated earlier, the intergenerational conflict—its forms of power, its discourses of subject formation—replicates with compelling faithfulness across an era of seemingly imposing historical changes. Thus it is my position that the paired structures of the model minority and intergenerational conflict are, like the class struggle itself, *neither ahistorical nor historically bound*. The relative autonomy and persistence of this narrative being among its more defining characteristics, to subordinate it entirely to historical explanations is to risk misconstruing it fundamentally.

This book is of the belief that, in a dialectically minded study of discursive and emergent social formations, literary methodologies are a needful antithesis to the empirical.[10] Per Raymond Williams' thesis on structures of feeling, it is at the limits of our current language for social formations—"at the very edge of semantic availability" (Williams, *Marxism*, 134)—that we diagnose experience through a complex of thought and affect, cognition and sensation, "which cannot without loss be reduced to belief-systems, institutions, or explicitly general relationships, though it may include all these as lived and experienced" (133). These structures of feeling enable us to sense and respond to new alignments of social power and meaning, regarding which we do not yet have conceptual clarity. And if they are caught at work anywhere, Williams maintains, it is via aesthetic attempts to articulate whole sensibilities that such fourth-dimensional diagnostic apparatuses will be found: in artistic and literary expression, "often the only fully available articulation" (133). It is in a culture's aesthetic production, then, that we may hope to distinguish those relations with which the subject struggles and that yet even she cannot see to explain, much less to bare to the researcher's gauge. Here we may sense the distance between claim and instantiation, and the interpellations into powerlessness and subjection that whirr silently in the gap. Differently put, what the examination of literary narratives can offer to the larger investigation into Asian American socialization is the textured wealth of a cultural product enmeshed in the symbolic, attentive to language, and self-incriminated with every word—an ideal hunting ground if one's quarry is the inconspicuous logic of power's symbols and rhetoric, and the trapped movements of the subjected mind. This pursuit I believe to be a reasonable one, even within the limitations of uneven ethnic distribution. I am committed to this project's claims to a broader applicability than it can immediately demonstrate, because I hope it will not be the numerical representativeness of primary texts but rather the explanatory power of the resulting model which decides the limits of its relevance.

narrative and structure ൟ

Narrative structure is a vexing issue for the texts included in this study; beginning with the Wong in chapter 1 and continuing into the Lau and Liu in chapter 3, *Ingratitude*'s core texts are all symptomatically devoid of plot. As we will see, regardless of what genres they claim to occupy—ranging in form from diary to memoir to novel, variously retrospective or immediate, with varying mixtures of memoir and fiction[11]—they are all piecemeal in structure, relating a day or an incident at a time without a definitive arc to unify and make sense of all their pieces. This makes for what Tomo Hattori describes as "an aimless, episodic quality . . . ; they do not conclude so much as stop" (Hattori, 239). Pacing and dramatic structure are challenges to accounts preoccupied with the ways in which nothing happens, every day. What their words do not find language for in isolation, however, emerges collectively; and like layers of a recurring dream, these texts, assembled, unfold a story with a beginning, middle, and end.[12] So it is that the four chapters of this book build upon each other in a trajectory that is both linear and hopelessly entwined—such that none of them could rightly be presented as a free-standing unit, and none of them truly makes sense alone. If this book has a structure, it is a classic plot. If it has a genre, it is biography. The collective biography of the Asian American daughterly subject, it is its own mix of memoir and fiction; it is an autobiography by indirection.

Ingratitude begins with two of the seminal texts of Asian American literature, Jade Snow Wong's *Fifth Chinese Daughter* and Maxine Hong Kingston's

The Woman Warrior, to theorize a paradigm of parental power structured by fundamental paradox and impossibility. In an analysis especially informed by Michel Foucault's theories of power, Judith Butler's theories of subjection, and feminist theories of trauma, I argue that through modes disciplinary and discursive, the second-generation daughter is perpetually produced as the unfilial subject—caught in a system of "designated failure." A keystone of familial discourse, the construct of "filial obligation" defines the parent-child relation as a debtor-creditor relation, but within this system without contract or consent, the parent-creditor brings into being a child-debtor who can never repay the debt of her own inception and rearing. Such debt is structural, a matter of position rather than payment, and places the child ever in violation.[13] Into this paradigm figures also the workings of sovereign law: rule of law which may determine its own jurisdiction, enlist or expel its own subjects, and decide the nature of transgression at will or whim because it is, itself, the very essence of judgment. Though this portion of the argument builds on Agamben's work, it takes its cue from Foucault's position in *Discipline and Punish* that the sovereign has not surrendered the field entirely to biopower in the modern era but that the two co-exist, forming in this case an "economico-legal complex" (paraphrased from Fitzpatrick, 13). Moreover, a view to both forms is imperative here, to address a Foucauldian "operation of power . . . in which life is put [so explicitly] 'in question' and where [life] can be *both protected and eliminated*" (ibid.; emphasis added): Precisely on its productive "care of life" does parental authority, with its prerogative of birth *and* banishment, base its deductive brandishing of death. Informed by the foundational work of such critics as Sau-ling Wong and Lisa Lowe, chapter 1 performs a re-reading of *Fifth Chinese Daughter* which closely critiques the logic implicit in "intergenerational conflict," and lays the groundwork of analysis for my discussion of later texts.

In turning to *The Woman Warrior*, chapter 2 traces the particular challenges to narrative form posed by the depiction of an injury which cannot be embodied or instantiated, an affliction which is partly because it "is not one." I interpret Kingston's narrative strategies, in which the imaginary is inextricable or indistinguishable from the "real," as an attempt to relate a subjectivity haunted by dire threats, but marked by no empirical harm. Maxine's daily life is one in which nothing of account "happens"; her formation as a daughter, however, is structured by the constant threat of violent disownment. That threat, conveyed in the anecdotes and legends of her childhood imaginary, deploys discourse to condition the subject. Jade Snow's attempts to relate the injustices of her upbringing, through the woefully mundane details of her interactions with her parents, suffer from an inability to justify the depths of her anger with the seeming inconsequentiality of her examples. Such powerlessness to substantiate one's suffering compounds and is itself a form of affliction. In forgoing the details of her American childhood, however, Maxine instead foregrounds its discourses, and confronts her parents' use of discursive power: through the fierce tales of her imaginary, the narrator is enabled to articulate an anger proportionate to the harm threatened, and to recognize the threat itself as a type of harm done. In regarding the discursive as a material force, I reference Anne Cheng's formulation of racial grief versus grievance, and also depart from earlier scholars like Elaine Kim and King-kok Cheung who, in order to protect an emerging identity politics, asserted between a "material reality" and a "discursive fiction" of violence in the family a distinction which is ultimately untenable.

Chapter 3 finds that between the era of Wong's *Fifth Chinese Daughter* and that of Evelyn Lau's *Runaway: Diary of a Street Kid* and Catherine Liu's *Oriental Girls Desire Romance*, economic relations within the family have evolved in response to changing opportunities for the model minority. Second-generation children become viable capital investments, raised to enter the lucrative math- and science-based professional fields now open to them, in order to repay their parents' suffering with prestigious consumer goods. In this context, I suggest, the unprofitable pursuit of literature can become an overdetermined act of self-preservation and disobedience, and an interesting precursor to other forms of masochistic rebellion: drug addictions, suicide, running away from home. Informed by psychoanalytic arguments regarding passionate attachments to power and the function of love and dependence in domination, this chapter neither valorizes nor censures masochism, but addresses both the possibilities and the limitations of such agency. In revisiting model minority discourse, the chapter asserts that because of the immigrant family's commitment to capitalist ideals, a model child is required to be a model minority, dutiful and grateful to family and nation both. In this chapter and the next, I examine the subjective costs incurred in becoming— and in failing to become—the model minority.

Drawing from each of the foregoing discussions of disciplinary and discursive power, economic investment, disownment, and resistance, chapter 4 examines the formation of the daughterly subject in relation to the family's exceptional structural investment in female chastity. Reading Chitra Divakaruni's "The Word Love" and Fae Myenne Ng's *Bone* in conjunction with each of the novels from previous chapters, I consider female sexuality as a site not only of particular concern but of particular utility for familial authority.

Anthropological work on chastity has long suggested a material basis and rationale for the cultural management of virginity, but these studies have tended to theorize the economic and social systems in which female bodies circulate without theorizing the female subject. Combining such anthropological perspectives with the techniques of literary criticism, I develop a Foucauldian analysis of the administration of sexuality but also a rendering of the young woman thereby produced: a paranoid and self-policing subject, commended to herself as object. To stand accused as a "lying, whoring, ungrateful, uncontrollable daughter" (Lau, *Inside*, 202) is not, I find, necessarily to be suspected of sexual activity so much as to be managed into obedience, as the regulation of a daughter's chastity both requires and justifies measures of extreme control which make for an especially thoroughly disciplined subject. Finally, while I am interested in this chapter to address familial standards and investments which are unmitigatedly gender-specific, and relationships to power particular to women, I tread against the traditions of both psychoanalytic and Asian American feminist scholarship in declining to idealize the mother-daughter relation as one of natural alliance. I take as my unit of analysis the parent rather than the patriarch because within the context of intergenerational dynamics, it is the parental position which determines the interests and agenda of "the family," and it is for the sake of the family—parental interests above and beyond gender differentiation—that the female docile body, guilty subject, and capital investment is produced.

1 §

The Filial Debtor

Jade Snow Wong

> To Pa, the demands he makes on Fred are coherently interlocked in an irreproachable logic. Cultural preservation, filial piety . . ., maintenance of the blood line and family name, guardianship of junior family members, attainment of degrees in higher education (preferably medical or legal), upward socio-economic mobility coupled with undying devotion to a single geographic locale (Chinatown), law-abiding citizenship, commitment to the work ethic, abolition of all unedifying sentiments, prudent expenditure of energy, respectfulness of manner, cleanliness of person—all are Necessary to the patriarch, hence one and the same. Transgression of one injunction means transgression of all.
> Sau-ling Wong, in discussion of Frank Chin's
> *The Year of the Dragon*

> There is nothing mysterious or natural about authority. It is formed, irradiated, disseminated; it is instrumental, it is persuasive; it has status, it establishes canons of taste and value; it is virtually indistinguishable from certain ideas it dignifies as true, and from traditions, perceptions, and judgments it forms, transmits, reproduces. Above all, authority can, indeed must, be analyzed.
> Edward Said, *Orientalism*

Of Jade Snow Wong's early autobiography, it is well established that the 1989 introduction invokes, from its very first sentence, an exoticizing and problematic rhetoric of Chinese cultural otherness, and introduces her childhood experiences immediately into a discourse of "cultural conflict" or (in her words) "conflicting cultural expectations." "[M]y upbringing by the nineteenth-century standards of Imperial China, which my parents deemed correct, was quite different from that enjoyed by twentieth-century Americans in San Francisco, where I had to find my identity and vocation" (JS Wong, vii). In the narrative, that which is Chinese in association is often felt to be constricting, anachronistic, or developmentally arrested, while qualities deemed "American" become synonymous with a versatile modernity and individual empowerment. This bias makes *Fifth Chinese Daughter* no less than prototype for the kind of "intergenerational conflict" narrative which scholarship has understandably censured for its self-directed essentialism, its eager adoption of Orientalist binaries:[1] "The notion of cultural conflict between the immigrant and American-born generations—the enlightened, freedom-loving son or daughter struggling to escape the clutches of backward, tyrannical parents—is one of the most powerful 'movies' ever created to serve hegemonic American ideology" (SL Wong, *Reading*, 41). And under examination, that grand narrative reveals itself indeed to be deeply self-contradictory. Jade Snow compares her own family dynamics unfavorably to those of the white middle-class home for whom she works, noting approvingly that in this (implicitly representative) Western family, "children were heard as well as seen" (JS Wong, 113)—but she fails to realize that the adage "Children are to be seen and not heard" is a bit of American, not Chinese, cultural wisdom. She learns through her exposure to Western schooling to take pride in questioning the authority and belief systems of her parents, but never notes the (twofold) irony in her unquestioning acceptance of American ideologies and cultural institutions:

> "I can now think for myself, and you and Mama should not demand unquestioning obedience from me. . . ."
> "Where," [father] demanded, "did you learn such an unfilial theory?"
> "From my teacher," Jade Snow answered triumphantly, "who you taught me is supreme after you, and whose judgment I am not to question." (128)

Does she merely fail to question the American pedagogies which, in her view, embody the very principles of philosophical interrogation and individual thought (thereby failing to challenge the injunction to challenge all injunctions)? Or does she decline to question those pedagogies at the order of parental injunctions which are themselves undermined by the Western teachings to which they defer? The shortcomings of this binary cultural opposition are clear.

Moreover, the narrator's efforts to exoticize Chinese America are unraveled time and again by telltale signs of a locally grown pragmatism. Despite advertising Chinatown as "the heart of Old China," Wong is forced, in her actual descriptions of the customs and habits of the enclave, to relate cultural modifications stride for stride alongside cultural traditions. Each modification conceded affirms the anti-essentializing insight that "Culture is not a piece of baggage that immigrants carry with them; it is not static but undergoes constant modification in a new environment" (SL Wong, *Reading*, 42). In describing a Chinatown funeral procession, for example, the narrator advertises the ethnic culture as one of imported foreignness ("then came a strange sight: Buddhist priests in flowing somber robes trailed along" the San Francisco street), but is soon compelled to report that this cultural spectacle was only "roughly patterned after the funeral processions in China": mourners in China wear white, not black; services are traditionally held in family homes, not funeral parlors; and burial days are chosen for their astrological fortuity, not by the days of the work week. "This [last] custom is rarely observed [in the U.S.] because of its inconvenience" (JS Wong, 76). Such deviations from the old-world norms attest to the fact that, as Lisa Lowe and Maxine Hong Kingston suggest, Asian American customs and relations are adaptive, organic practices. "'That wasn't a custom,' said Bak Goong [Great Grandfather]. 'We made it up. We can make up customs because we're the founding ancestors of this place'" (Kingston, *Men*, 118). Thus, as readers we witness not the "unmediated vertical transmission of culture from one generation to another," but the "making of Asian American culture" via "practices that are partly inherited, partly modified, as well as partly invented" (Lowe, 65).

Like the immigrant community's revised cultural customs, the immigrant family's child-rearing practices are responses to present realities, and native to this soil. Much as Jade Snow may wish to package her upbringing as one transplanted whole and unadulterated from an exotic context ("She was trapped in a mesh of tradition woven thousands of miles away by ancestors who had no knowledge that someday one generation of their progeny might be raised in another culture" [JS Wong, 110]), it is clear by her own admission that her parents have made fundamental adjustments to old-world parenting standards: "You expect me to work my way through college—*which would not have been possible in China*" (129; emphasis added).[2] While certainly immigrant parents' expectations emerge out of the mores of their own upbringings, uneven and selective, meaningful changes mark their adaptation of those mores to their adoptive country. Easy though it may be to fall in with Jade Snow's own accommodation of Orientalist discourses, I maintain that the immigrant family is not scripted or predicted "by the book" of ancient philosophical texts. In counterpoint to tiresome readings of the perpetual Confucian foreigner,[3] I offer a reading which sees the immigrant for the opportunist, survivalist *first-generation American* he is—one whose relentless adaptation process is driven by the pragmatics of household governance, and the demands of thriving in capitalist America. It is thus *as* adaptive "practices" and adaptively deployed discourses, rather than as alien cultural givens, that the generational dynamics of Asian immigrant families such as Wong's warrant theoretical attention. To put it another way: Wong's immigrant family operates as it does not because it thinks itself Chinese in China, but because it knows itself to be Chinese in America.

This chapter will pair its reading of the political economy of the Wong family's parent-child relations with a consideration of the formal qualities of their daughter's narrative, as the latter is shaped by the challenges of telling (the self through) the former. The structure of *Fifth Chinese Daughter* is remarkable for what Shirley Lim has called its "relentless linearity" (Lim, 257), a devotion to strict chronological order which seems to me to strive for thoroughness—and achieve instead gloss. Wong's account moves through her childhood at a rapid clip, as if reporting all the past that's fit to print. This combined superficiality and hunger for comprehensiveness reflect, I suggest, an acquiescence to traditional biographical and narrative metrics that privilege the notable event over the unexceptional hour. "Included in this story," Wong announces in her introductory note, "are the significant episodes which, insofar as I can remember, shaped my life" (JS Wong, xiii); this may prove an impracticable narrative strategy, however, for a past pronounced not so much for exceptional episodes as for its patterns—the very repetitive days cast narratively aside while the writer scans her personal history for incidents of magnitude. That search for magnitude will defy her as, unlike her parents, Jade Snow does not directly experience the uprootings or immense losses of immigration; her parents do not die unexpectedly, nor abuse her, and in fact she explicitly recognizes their treatment of her as characterized by love. Thus, the blanketing statement with which she opens her account: "Life was secure but formal, sober but quietly happy, and the few problems she had were entirely concerned with what was proper or improper in the behavior of a little Chinese girl" (2). Yet as her narrative proceeds "in spite of her parents' love" (2), it will show the strained nerves of this placid existence: the sinews of power in family life. Jade Snow's parents enact control via a merging of economic circuits and disciplinary technologies, and it is in those mundane, externally unremarkable terms that they and their fifth daughter struggle over the meaning and conditions of filiality.

∾ economic circuits

For Jade Snow, the question of filial obedience is shot through with financial considerations and structured by an economic logic. To begin with, accounting and fiscal matters enjoy a remarkable prominence in Jade Snow's chronicle of her relationship with her parents. Enumerated in what Christine So describes as "excruciating" detail are the rates of pay Jade Snow received from her mother while in junior high school for performing an "exhaustive list" (So, 44) of chores around the house: laundry, dusting and sweeping weekly, with extra polishing and scouring once a month, for 50 cents per week. While So implies that such sparse compensation is root cause for the narrator's felt injustices, however, this is not necessarily the case.[4] For one thing, the narrator here ticks off the list of her tasks not with the resentment of one exploited, but with a suggestion of personal investment in the labor: a sense of contributing to a shared effort, combined with a palpable pride in her own productivity.[5] For another, as household chores, these duties need not legally, culturally, or contractually be compensated at all. If familial economics are indeed exploitative, they must be so on some basis *other than pay scale*—but to appreciate this point we must first restore Jade Snow's 50 weekly cents to their historical context, as part of an American innovation of the late nineteenth and early twentieth centuries: the child's allowance as cultural norm.

In her influential *Pricing the Priceless Child*, Viviana Zelizer traces a sea change in what is deemed the child's proper economic role within the family, exposing our own present-day assumptions regarding the sanctity of childhood as a time for play and learning (*not* for laboring on behalf of the family economic unit) to have been no historical accident. "In sharp contrast to contemporary views, the birth of a child in eighteenth-century rural America was welcomed as the arrival of a future laborer and as security for parents later in life" (Zelizer, *Pricing*, 5); not only had working-class, rural, and immigrant parents of earlier eras commonly looked to the unpaid domestic labor and formal outside wages of their children to supplement meager family income, but such had been condoned as familial necessity and virtue dating back to the colonies (59). Despite the higher wages and initially increased employment of child workers in the assembly lines of the nineteenth century, however, soon a confluence of factors—including rising standards of living and "growing demand for a skilled, educated labor force" (62)—made the unskilled labor of young workers, at the expense of their education, not only superfluous but less optimal to gross national production in the long term: "By the mid-nineteenth century, the construction of the economically worthless child had been in large part accomplished among the American urban middle class. Concern shifted to children's education as the determinant of future marketplace worth" (5). Yet this shift in relations of production, Zelizer argues, would have been impossible if not powered by a pitched battle on the moral register, to construct the child as an inestimable affective asset and thus properly an indefinite financial liability: "Far from relying on his child as old-age 'insurance,' the middle-class father began insuring his own life and setting up other financial arrangements such as trusts and endowments, to protect the unproductive child" (5). That is, the good parent was now morally obligated to "invest" in his children's education—not in order to reap the greater, delayed remittances of marketable children, but for his heirs' exclusive benefit. In this new paradigm, it became outright "un-American"—a barbarous practice of immigrants—to hire out one's child for wages (71). Driven by a sweeping moral activism, "By the 1930s, lower-class children joined their middle-class counterparts in a new nonproductive world of childhood, a world in which the sanctity and emotional value of a child made child labor taboo" (6).

It is within this new ethos that the weekly "allowance" came into being—to accommodate the child who now brings into the family coffers no additional funds, yet is entitled to siphon off some portion of those coffers for discretionary spending. Tying the child's pocket money to the completion of chores was accepted as an adulterated form of the allowance, albeit a less (ideologically and parentally) virtuous version; this stipend was deemed properly "of the nature of a right rather than a wage" (108), but it was conceded that if children were to learn the moral habits of industry, this should take place in the "training" environment of the home. Given back its historical context, Jade Snow's detailed disclosure of her allowance must be read as, at least in part, an implicit case for the civilized decency of immigrants, who "value" their young via the same symbolic economies as does any good American—if not quite at the same rates of pay. Granted, Jade Snow's round of chores is likely far more extensive than that of a girl child in a white, middle-class family. Ultimately, however, in arranging to pay her, the Wongs undeniably exercise mores by which the child is recognized as a member of the family to whom funds are rightly apportioned. With allowance disbursements serving a symbolic as (explicitly) opposed to financial function, the point of said monetary exercise is not market-rate labor (or going-rate allowance), but a notion of status that derives enfranchisement from work. In *Unequal Freedom*, Evelyn Nakano Glenn traces this possessive individualist philosophy through its productions of political freedom (and bondage): "As wage work became more common, new notions arose [regarding] *independence* . . . as based on productivity and mastery of skills" to be a "necessary condition for exercising citizenship" (Glenn, 28, 21; emphasis added). It is in that "independent" status which Jade Snow exults, pleased with a sense of herself as wage earner/economically endowed agent (signaled by her description of the allowance as "income" and her keen appreciation of its purchasing power).[6] In other words, as an allowance her "income" does not make her an employee of the family, but a member-in-training of an economic democracy: "Those three dollars gave Jade Snow a wonderful feeling of freedom . . . Yes, it was worth the household chores to be able to claim independent earnings" (71).

It is vital to acknowledge the initial enthusiasm of Jade Snow's allowance disclosures, in order to account for her feelings about later contradictions in the Wong family's political-economic philosophies. By turns, Mr. Wong is said to have a more "progressive" and Western view of gender roles *in specific relation to labor* than do his "Old-World" countrymen (So, 42), and, alternately, to embody the explicitly un-American gender/labor values of a pre-modern China (JS Wong, 125). The former opinion holds that the father has embraced "New World Christian ideals" wherein "women *had a right to work* to improve the economic status of their family" (5; emphasis added)— and that these "ideals" are in some way "modern" thinking: "America," Jade Snow quotes from her father's letters, "does not require that women sway helplessly on little feet to qualify them for good matches as well-born women *who do not have to work*. Here . . . the people, and even women, have *individual* dignity and *rights* of their own" (72; emphases added). On this exuberant familial foundation, Jade Snow first builds her faith in the philosophies of classical liberalism. Yet, later in the narrative, a college sociology lecture touching on the economic philosophies of American individualism throws her familial foundations into crisis:

> "There was a period in our American history when parents had children for economic reasons, to put them to work as soon as possible . . . But now we no longer regard children in this way. Today we recognize that children are individuals, and that parents can no longer demand their unquestioning obedience. Parents should do their best to understand their children, because young people also have their rights." (JS Wong, 125)

The narrative reenacts for us, at some length, Jade Snow's epiphany as she absorbs this ideological lesson—and then the moral challenge to her family that it triggers: "Could it be," she wonders, "that Daddy and Mama, although they were living in San Francisco in the year 1938, actually had not left the Chinese world of thirty years ago?" "My parents demand unquestioning obedience. . . . By what right? I am an individual . . .I have rights too" (125). But of course, that shift in the appraisal of children so celebrated by her sociology professor is none other than the economic and moral transformation documented in *Pricing the Priceless Child*! What are we to make of the Wongs' adoption of quite culturally assimilated and contemporary parenting practices, such as the allowance, on the one hand; and Jade Snow's sense on the other that the very philosophies which these practices express are foreign to them?

Without discounting the narrator's sense of grievance, we may recognize her charges of cultural anachronism to be a symptomatic reading of the immigrant family—and with that in mind, look to her language for markers of the actual site of disconnect. "*I have worked too*," she protests, "*but* now I am an individual besides being your fifth daughter" (128; emphasis added): that is, the relationship between work and the endowed individual is not in fact a causality but a disjunction, between the terms not a "so" but a "but." Jade Snow's sense of dismay or disillusionment is, in other words, a product of bad faith already to be found within the capitalism in American practice. Possessive individualist political-economic promises persistently equivocate between work as a "right"—with the attendant, inalienable privileges of social membership—and work as a condition with which one must "earn" one's inclusion. It is thanks to this prevarication that Mr. Wong may take credit for generously "allowing" the female members of his family and community to earn money, when in actuality there is nothing particularly modern or privileged about the work-for-pay of women from poor families. These same tensions surface in the language used to codify the allowance as cultural practice: "[The child] has *earned* the privilege of recognized *membership* in the family and of this status an allowance is a symbol" (108; emphases added); even in its pure form, the allowance is riven by designs to signify at once the unearned, inalienable birthrights of democratic membership, and the earned privileges of capitalist productivity. Though she mistakes it for intercultural conflict, the paradox that powers Jade Snow's impending crisis over her disenfranchisement in the family is expressed in the very advent of possessive individualism itself: Though such individualism stakes social rights to the social "value" of labor, those unpropertied white males it first baptized as independent laborers were themselves enfranchised not by virtue of "earnings" but by expansion of social contract (Glenn, 64, 27, 20). Between the "wage slaves" they would continue selectively to be called through the Age of Industrialization, and the "free" citizens they were decreed per their "inalienable" race and gender, were differences not in wage nor labor but in legislature. Thus, the classical liberalism which seems to promise *earnable* privileges is premised on quite the opposite: categorically "independent" ownership of labor and the laboring self—within which one may produce nothing and be entitled; outside or in racial/gendered excess of which, no amount of productivity can translate into autonomous value and social legibility.[7]

As So demonstrates in *Economic Citizens*, however, where the subject is an Asian American, (and in this case, a daughter), it may become painfully apparent that she cannot by her labor earn dignity and enfranchisement; these are bestowed by other criteria—and so no amount of salary (or allowance) will buy the girl-child equality, nor the Asian subject full belonging. What breeds resentment for Jade Snow is then not the great value of the work she does, but the failure of that great value to translate into social power and standing within the family. Her financial worth does, however, transfer directly into her social status—as someone else's asset or liability. Recalling the sociology lecture at this point suggests that at the turn of the twentieth century, classical liberalism effectively expanded the scope of personhood to include the priceless child, who may now produce nothing and yet be entitled to full rights as an Individual. Subsequent to that annexation of personhood, the child has theoretically become more than the sum of her labor—so it is to her dismay, though not to her full understanding, that this allowance-earning Wong daughter finds herself still out of bounds: an economic resource and unfree.

the thing about Necessity ∾

If *Fifth Chinese Daughter* seems consumed with a crassly materialistic choice of tropes, this is because the narrator's subjectivity, relationships, and even claim to existence are measured and negotiated within the family in largely economic terms. In *Reading Asian American Literature*, Sau-ling Wong argues that the recurrence of "sacrifice" and cannibalistic imagery as motifs in *The Woman Warrior* and "several other Asian American works depicting relationships between immigrant parents and American-born children [suggests] that Necessity might have taken a peculiar and acutely distressing *form* in Asian American immigrant families" (SL Wong, *Reading*, 31; emphasis added). In a mode of existence that is "survival-driven," "conservation-minded" (13), and scored by hardships ("if not the immediate memory of privation, then the shock of permanent relocation to a white-dominated society and the daily attritions of adjustment" [20]), enormous emphasis is placed upon the productive output of all family members. The parent's experience of material hardship becomes the reasoning upon which family dynamics are structured.

The Necessity thesis thus consists of two elements critical for us here: First, that certain parenting practices are a function of financial circumstance; in the longer view, the Wong family bears this out. The Wongs had been harshest, most strict, with the older daughters, who grew up presumably at a time when the family was least financially secure (JS Wong, 88); they grew increasingly lenient in their parenting as the conditions of Necessity eased. Though her parents "claimed that they brought up all their children with the same discipline," Jade Snow notes that they "had nevertheless mellowed a great deal, and they were much more affectionate with [the youngest] child," in large part because "their economic struggles had been greatly relieved by now, since former dependents had grown into wage earners who contributed to the family budget" (207). Second, and most crucially, the Necessity thesis holds that in times of perceived adversity, children may be taken for human resources, their subject positions appraised for effectiveness and benefit. That discursive conflation we have so often observed, of the child with hired hand or productive property, comes of the immigrant family's adoption of labor relations as extended metaphors, and monetary values as social currency. These economic mechanisms then become the means through which the members' relative positions are negotiated and kept account. Placed under the microscope, Mr. Wong's early chastisement of Jade Snow and her Chinese American girlfriend duly demonstrates this, in its nearly compulsive reiteration of a single principle: the weighing of social relations in units of economic value and opportunity cost.

> Gold Spring came into the dining room where they were and right then and there Daddy gave her a lecture on *"using time."* He insisted that she came over to *waste Jade Snow's time,* and that the two *spent their moments unconstructively.* . . . The next day Daddy forbade Jade Snow ever to go with Gold Spring again, because such companionship *absorbed time from more worthwhile pursuits.* (92; emphases added)[8]

Not merely labor, then, nor explicitly monetary exchanges, but any of the child's associations and activities stand to be classified—and normalized—as matters of financial strategy. Within the immigrant mind-set dictated by conditions of material Necessity, the economic values of all resources and people take on a very literal-minded immediacy. That is to say, the *symbolic* system of the family's material relations adopts the "literal" language of economic exchange value.

When all things social can be folded into a family's tropic economy of Necessity, then we can begin to imagine the boundless exactions of its financial imperatives. Little wonder that Jade Snow responds to this situation, one of wide-open liability, with a desperation to set limits on financial claims. However illogical it may seem for her to consider money that she receives *from* her parents for her labor to be earnings "independent" (presumably) from those same parents, two things signify in this sentiment: First is the hope lurking in her logic that monetary value—and by corollary the labor that produces it, and even more audaciously the self who labors—though it may *originate in* her parents need not be *owned by* them, but may indeed be hers. Second is the untenable nature of that optimism: the "wages" that Jade Snow earns from her parents derive from different premises than those for a freely contracted employee. The waged relation her language *aspires* to may be contrasted to one in which, as the subject and product of her parents, the daughter has nothing of her "own," and so must turn over to her parents on demand what money she earns or is given. And indeed, that latter, alternate scenario is one which *also* happens in their family. At each Lunar New Year, the children are required to surrender to their parents their lucky money, even though these red envelopes are gifts ostensibly bestowed not upon the family as a unit but to the children themselves. "Some of Jade Snow's schoolmates returned to class with tales of the amount of [New Year's] gift money they had kept for themselves, but she always had to give hers back to Mama" (40). By what logic is it, then, that the same family that disburses stipends to its children with one hand may also confiscate their resources from them with the other? In her symptomatic way, our narrator would likely suppose that American models of parenting (the allowance) are being contravened by foreign practices (the red envelope); yet her equally Chinese American friends are allowed to keep their cash gifts for themselves. Likewise, she might symptomatically suppose that she carries the banner of capitalism while her parents operate by a more feudal economy, as if the second generation were trying to impose upon the first a model to which the parents are opposed; this is, however, hardly the case. Rather, it is *equally* by her parents' authority that she may collect from one hand, or must remit to the other. This leaves us to look, instead, to that dilemma *within* the classical liberalist arrangements already in effect within the family, which when activated, Jade Snow finds threatening to her sense of autonomy.

Classical liberalism emerged by setting itself against republicanist definitions of property, but managed that ascendance, as Glenn argues, by leveraging another binary: To enable the social enfranchisement of white male hired labor, the "dependence inherent in wage work was transmuted into 'independence' by being contrasted with slavery and indentured servitude" (Glenn, 28). In other words, over the course of several centuries, classical liberalism discursively isolated the "independent" wage *by way of* extracting it from such alternate forms of labor as were reserved for race and gender's subalterns. This is not to disregard the fact that white males comprised much contract labor in America's early history; indenture in the seventeenth and eighteenth centuries consisted of primarily European men. However, this is to recall that the discursive and fiscal construction of their contracts engineered the eventual assimilation of these early immigrants to American society as "free laborers": *while not necessarily paid a wage during their tenure,* they received at the end of their bonded terms "freedom dues" in the form of money or land in order to establish themselves as new, independent subjects, who at this point could call their wages their own (Bush, 29). Labor contractors in late nineteenth- and early twentieth-century America, however, recruited workers primarily from Asia, and *paid these a marginal wage* plus "return fare upon expiry of the contract"; Asian workers might be "offered incentives to sign on for a further term" of servitude, but were not welcome to settle (30). "Unfree" labor could and did take a variety of forms (often merging mechanisms from indenture, peonage, and even the free market into "hybrid system[s] of servitude" [33]), but the sociopolitical rewards which these systems were contrived (not) to yield were consistent in their racialized segregation—and the presence of a "wage" was no inherent guarantor of the laborer's autonomy. Indeed, peonage or debt bondage in particular was acknowledged as being "not all that different from some forms of free labour" (45), in the manner of its reliance on pay. Thus, the wage apparatus may—if the worker is not white and male—operate within a system that engineers a very different social outcome than autonomy.

If the mechanics of the classic wage-labor structure are such that an employer may only dispense or withhold pay from the free worker according to his or her productivity, then the operative metaphor in the Wong family is not that, but must be compared to one of the alternate forms: one in which the employer also has the option of *billing* against the worker's ledger at discretion. Under such circumstances, children may well come to understand their status in terms of market values, and relative power in terms of the balance sheet, for by dint of this alternate accounting, the child's assets—economic, social, and otherwise—may be garnished before they are so much as acquired. It can scarcely be overemphasized that the very text which first introduces Necessity as a term in the Asian American lexicon also puts the bookkeeping in question on display. Kingston's narrator expresses an anxiety to be "worthy of eating the food" (*Warrior*, 52)—to do something "big and fine" (presumably to "earn her keep") "or else [her] parents would sell [her]" (46). Remarkable here are not only the child's consent that her worth ought to outweigh the cost of her upkeep, but her *despair* that her credits may never in fact outstrip her galloping debits in the parental balance sheet. More remarkable still is the exchange in which, in quite literal dollars and cents, both Maxine and her mother equate her with the slave girl Brave Orchid purchased in China:

> How much money did you pay to buy her [the slave girl]?
> One hundred and eighty dollars.
> How much did you pay the doctor and the hospital when I was born?
> Two hundred dollars . . . American money.
> Was the one hundred and eighty dollars American money?
> No. . . . Fifty dollars [in American money]. That's because she was sixteen years old. . . . Babies were free. During the war, though, when you were born, many people gave older girls away for free. And here I was in the United States paying two hundred dollars for you. (83)

Brave Orchid's mental calculations in this currency exchange take no account of any supposed incommensurability between offspring and hireling—between the family's own daughter and the pawned daughter of another family, purchased as a servant. Rather, in this conversation the family willingly elides the bounds between contexts of supposedly quite different intimacies, in order to establish a profound and terrifying parity: that between corresponding forms of debt bondage.

Loosely defined, debt bondage is a system in which persons are contracted to redeem a debt by working, for unspecified duration, for the party who has advanced the owed sum. In its pre-modern (and pre-immigration) history, as practiced in India, Thailand, Burma, and China, peonage originated in "the pawning of relatives, usually children and often girls" to discharge a family's debts; pawned individuals worked indefinitely as servants for those who purchased them (Bush, 39–40). Brave Orchid's slave girl thus exemplifies an earlier form of this labor relation. The comparison drawn above, then, superimposes that configuration of monetary debt and material obligation onto the social relation of child to parent. In fine, rather than converting the economic into social meaning, the comparison maps the economic onto the social *without translation*, with the result that the social then functions by economic paradigms. This loaded metaphor manages, by literalizing itself in blithe disregard of symbolic nonequivalencies, to produce the child as bonded debtor, and her parent as benefactor and creditor (even if it should be the *parent's* debt that she has been pawned to discharge).

Here, the model of the debtor-creditor relation from *On the Genealogy of Morals* becomes salient to the commerce between child and parent. In a theory which places debt at the cornerstone of societal bonds, Friedrich Nietzsche reasons that the primal exchange necessarily entails the construct of promissory obligation as a corollary. Further, where one party has failed to meet her obligation to the other, that failed exchange must yield the unequal positions of debtor and creditor. Civilizations are believed in their pre-history to have developed progressively abstracted and symbolically vested concepts of the creditor, with which to anchor the power of an increasingly complex and accomplished society:

> [conceived] in increasing order of power . . . first, the individual with whom one has entered into some form of exchange of a classic debtor-creditor kind (such as trade); second, ancestors who are believed to empower the society, in return for which it owes them an increasing debt of gratitude; and third, gods, whom Nietzsche depicts as the culmination of ancestor-worship. (May, 57)

Thus, per Nietzsche's thesis, the debt which effectively binds the subject "need not have been explicitly agreed with a creditor," but may be retro-actively derived—as are "most debts to ancestors and gods" (58)—from the benefits presently enjoyed. Set in this framework, the analogy forged between slave girl and daughter may be described as exploiting the continuum between cultural forms: collapsing the exchange value and individual creditor of the first phase into their counterparts in the second, which latter inflate to such dimensions that "the question arises for the debtor whether their credits can ever be repaid" (58). Inside the layers of this discourse, the parent may at once embody the vastness of ancestral munificence and act as collector of a material debt come due. What we commonly know as "filial obligation," then, hews in its deep logic to the metaphor of debt bondage, along with the power-to-subject relation that such peonage implies. Jade Snow "[a]cknowledg[es] that," within the discourse of her upbringing, "she *owed her very being* . . . to [her] ancestors and their tradition" (JS Wong, 110; emphasis added). It is this splicing of debt to family that brings altruism and accounting, martyrdom and profit, into collaboration.

As Nietzsche elaborates, at the heart of the debtor-creditor paradigm lies an operative paradox—one on which the relation's perpetuation depends and which, by no coincidence, can also be found structuring the familial terms of Necessity. Already at inception a thing of immeasurable value, ancestral debt grows by a mechanism bound to outstrip all attempts to pay it down:

> The conviction reigns that it is only through the sacrifices and accomplishments of the ancestors that the tribe *exists*—and that one has to *pay them back* with sacrifices and accomplishments: one thus recognizes a *debt* that constantly grows greater, since these forebears . . . accord the tribe new advantages and new strength. (Nietzsche, 88; emphasis in original)

The debt mechanism dictates, in other words, that whatsoever the descendant may produce accrues to the benefits for which she is beholden, and thereby binds her further rather than earning her independence. Likewise, the mechanics of Necessity in the immediate family deliver quite the reverse of what one might anticipate. As conventionally presented, the Asian immigrant "parents' labors [are] meant to break the cycle of Necessity, to make possible the luxury of choice for the next generation" (SL Wong, 33). As a goal, "luxury of choice" implies a freedom from lifestyle constraints, and certainly indicates a freedom from financial pressures. Ideally, then, parental sacrifices enable the next generation to live lives unfettered by the practices and psychology of close bookkeeping. In actuality, however, as Sau-ling Wong points out, "the code of Necessity creates its own enslavement: one sacrifice calls for another" (33). Whereas in theory, Necessity works itself out of existence—immigrants work hard so that with success they and theirs will no longer have to work hard—in practice, Necessity reproduces itself, perpetuating its mind-set and demands onto the next generation, even after the conditions of material adversity have come to an end:[9] "Parental self-sacrifice [often] generates expectations of filial self-sacrifice, and the entire family is trapped in endless cycles of pain" (32). We have in Jade Snow's case the contradictory state of affairs wherein her parents do seem to become more lenient with their children as their financial circumstances become more stable (in keeping with Nietzsche's remark that "The 'creditor' always becomes more humane to the extent that he has grown richer" [Nietzsche, 72]); yet the language of debt and obligation does not dissipate. Rather, as the child grows into her own achievements and attains the means for financial autonomy and prosperity, the advent of this, Necessity's ostensible "endpoint," may instead occasion the *increase* of her indebtedness. For if her parents' labors and sacrifices are assumed to be the pre-condition of the child's achievements, her success simply demonstrates the immeasurable value of her debt to them:

> The fear of the ancestor and his power, the consciousness of indebtedness to him, increases, according to this logic, in exactly the same measure as the power of the tribe itself increases, as the tribe itself grows ever more victorious, independent, honored, and feared. By no means the other way around! (Nietzsche, 89)

If her success she owes to her parents, then paradoxically whatever she makes or achieves *compounds* her debt—adding interest onto interest, rather than paying against the principle. Thus, rather than attaining an endpoint at which its objective has materialized and the economics of Necessity may drop away from the immigrant family's structure, the system is more likely to move past its putative destination, and continue to exact payment for a debt that folds all subsequent "yield" into itself.

The familial economy that pays the child with one hand and collects with the other now makes its logic plain: though her wages may acknowledge the descendant's productive achievements, these achievements derive from her ancestors—and thus regardless of whether it is her parents or her employers who pay her, those benefits make her not more autonomous from but rather more beholden to her family. The feeling of freedom young Jade Snow experiences from her allowance, sanguine in its possessive individualist expectations, does not last; it is canceled out by debt. When the sociology-inspired narrator challenges her father's dictates, he demands, "Who brought you up? Who clothed you, fed you, sheltered you, nursed you? Do you think you were born aged sixteen? You *owe* honor to us before you satisfy your personal whims" (128; emphasis added). In the face of insubordination to his authority, "Daddy's" response takes the direct form of calling in his daughter's obligations—and in terms that are not only openly financial in association ("owe"), but logically derived from support of a material nature (clothing, food, shelter, etc.). As Jade Snow herself earlier remarked, her parents indeed supplied all her major, material needs (71); no child's red envelope can hold its own against a deficit so large it makes even her earnings moot.

What's more, however, while it may be financial in language, the filial debt is certainly not merely financial in nature. In *Beyond Contract*, Alan Fox delineates as two categories of exchange what he calls the "social" and the "economic," the "'basic and most crucial distinction'" between them being that "'social exchange entails unspecified obligations,'" while the prototypical economic exchange "is a transaction resting on a 'formal contract which stipulates the exact quantities to be exchanged'" (Fox, 71).

> Social exchange "involves the principle that one person does another a favour, and while there is a general expectation of some future return, its exact nature is not definitely stipulated in advance." It involves "favours that create diffuse future obligations, not precisely defined ones." (71)

He later elaborates that "family relations [are] hardly contractual; no detailed listing of rights and duties" obtain between members, and there prevails an "assumption that any member of the family will go far beyond normal responsibilities in case of need" (154). While the present argument may take issue with Fox's terminology—the social "exchange," as we have seen it, being very much economic in nature—the essence of his distinction holds true: The symbolic system of familial relations, while perhaps literal-minded in its materiality, is not actually arithmetic in its methods, because of the expansiveness with which it construes the terms of the exchange. Fox explains that, in an "economic" exchange, "'since the favours are being specifically defined in advance, the way is open for bargaining over the terms, whereas in social exchange, . . . the nature of the return cannot be bargained about'" (71). A social debt of this nature expects payment not in monetary remunerations (alone), but in illimitable subjective resources—and it is non-negotiable: "What can one give [the ancestors] in return? Sacrifices . . . *above all, obedience*" (Nietzsche, 89; emphasis added).[10] Given that obedience is the first term of repayment, there can be no such thing as an economic transaction in the family conducted "only with money" (So, 44); children are paid, and may be held to repayment, in denominations of selfhood.

In the dim view it takes of the family, the present argument may seem to replicate the dominant, sentimentalist view of childhood which Zelizer cites as condemning immigrant avarice—a bedfellow troubling to contemplate. We have in actuality, however, long passed the point either of enforcing the popular faith in the altruism of parenthood, or of defending its imagined opposite. That contemporary, mainstream ethos of American parenting which holds the child sacred from the commercial world (Zelizer, *Pricing*, 9) eschews the language of cost and benefit—and demands of the family the fiction that in raising a child "money is no object," whether in the sense of goal or obstacle, objective or objection: all is done for the sake of the child. Yet, as Lee Edelman suggests, such dogma works less for the child's sake than in her name (Edelman, 11), and as such is surprisingly compatible with its very expedient, logical opposite. That opposite is the dictate that the child be ceaselessly productive: a "credit" to her parents (JS Wong, 108) in every sense, and in every sense convertible to the material, such that the dollar becomes a functional general equivalent for familial relations. By one standard, the child is a priceless individual; by the other, her worth is relentlessly calculable. It is our position here, however, that they are both ideological fabrications—and within the Asian immigrant family, *complementary* rather than antagonistic. If the former model is one of rhetorical altruism and even martyrdom, and the latter model is that of cost and benefit, then each is equally integral to the inexhaustible directive to repay ancestors for their sacrifice. Indeed, those mechanisms represented by Jade Snow's allowance and her red envelope—though they may seem at first to enact two competing philosophies of subjectivity, relationality, family, and economics—are in actuality interconnected components within a single apparatus of capitalistic endeavor: one in which the subject, answerable to her own pricelessness, may incur neither cost nor benefit without increasing the absolute value of her obligation.

costs of passage: filial obligation ❧

Of course, within greater Asian American experience, systems in which debt usurps payment have included not just filial but formal labor. Formal systems of debt bondage constituted the preeminent mode of labor relations for a significant phase of Asian American immigration history. Far from being an economic throwback to feudal barbarism, peonage was long (and especially for undocumented Asian immigrants, continues to be in the present day)[11] a key player in the international movement of modern labor and capital (Bush, xi). In the years after the Thirteenth Amendment abolished other forms of unfree labor, peonage systems were the primary labor importation mechanisms for "large-scale capitalist enterprises such as plantations and mines" until the Immigration Act of 1924, and they brought a massive influx of Chinese and Japanese to Hawaii and the West Coast (45).[12] Indeed the irony alluded to earlier, in which the child may be produced as debtor and her parent as benefactor *even if it should be the parent's debt that she has been bonded to discharge*, describes to uncanny accuracy the long-standing labor arrangements in Hawaii in particular, as obtained on the plantations amongst the immigrant families who worked their fields. As a form of contract labor, peonage was distinguished by service as tethered not to a defined length of employ, but to the balance of a loan—the initial sum of which was typically incurred to pay the laborer's cost of passage to the United States, but the balance of which often rose rather than fell over time, with the worker's paltry wages more than offset by extortionist "maintenance" costs charged against the worker's account.[13] Thus, although in theory peonage was discrete and "could be quickly terminated" "upon the discharge of a debt," in exploitative practice "it might well last a lifetime—even longer in societies where indebtedness was inheritable" (39). Such exploitations of debt prevailed on the plantations of Hawaii, where workers were charged exorbitant sums for "housing, food, and supplies purchased at the company stores," as well as other non-optional dues (Glenn, 201), such that what began as a simple cash advance "easily degenerated into an inextricable debt that could tip the bonded person into slavery" (Bush, 44). The longer the laborer toiled under such a system, then, the greater grew his debt—and where that laborer established a family, as in the case of Japanese plantation workers especially, the labor of his descendants was enlisted into repayment of that monumental liability. For the boys of the Oyama family in Milton Murayama's *All I asking for is my body,* for instance, debt is the controlling term of their lives: in the first order, the insurmountable $6,000 sum the family owes to the plantation's stores and services for their living expenses, accrued from the very first day of their arrival in Hawaii; and in the second, the obligation of a son, to repay his parents for his upbringing by working off the family's debts. David Palumbo-Liu expresses the Oyama boys' situation as a "devastating double *contradiction* between the political and labor economy of American capitalism and an ethical Japanese tradition made absolutely exploitative in its displaced context in America" (408; emphasis added). Thus articulated, the above suggests a *pair* of systems of obligation, derived from varying and even opposing values, exacting different fees (money versus devotion), but *between* which a son is caught fast. Yet the primary text calls repeated attention to the likeness of these systems— to the insight that their propaganda and their practices are not at odds but rather one and the same. Speaking of the parents of the Japanese community,

Toshio (the narrator Kiyoshi's older brother) seethes, "they like it for their sons to be dumb. They like them to obey. They consider you a better man if you said yes all the time." To this Kiyoshi directly replies, "The plantation the same way" (Murayama, 68). Through the brothers' conversations, we are led to understand that between "American capitalism" and "Japanese family ethics," the conduct prescribed and values espoused for the "model" subject are of a kind: "The best [virtues] are *filial piety*, patience, knowing your place, loyalty, knowing your duty, *hard work*" (35; emphases added). In their obedience, the model capitalist worker and the model Japanese son merge into a single figure.[14] Their unity is spelled out plainly when Murayama likens plantation owner to patriarch: "He acted like a father, and he looked after you and cared for you provided you didn't disobey. Union talk was disobedience and treason, and if you were caught talking it or organizing, you were fired and your family and your belongings dumped on the 'government' road" (96). This capitalist institution provides guardianship, expects loyalty as gratitude, and banishes the insubordinate from the province of its law with the sovereignty which we will recognize shortly from disownment. Finally, the manner in which monetary obligation on the plantation is structured—unavoidably incurred upon arrival, and helplessly accrued by the necessities of daily life—aligns flush with that of the filial debt: incurred by birth and binding the subject, by virtue of living, to an ever-increasing principle.

The extended parallel in debt structures between a historical form of peonage and a discursive construct of filial obligation implies no necessary cause-effect relation from one to the other; certainly, as the historical form in question was most particular to Japanese immigrant families, while the major texts from which we have been busily deriving the construct are both Chinese American, that can scarcely be the case. Rather, what we describe here is a powerful homology, one that will do a great deal of heavy lifting for us in the analytical work ahead. While not necessarily of common provenance, these respective systems of obligation in the national and familial economy share structure and function: recruiting labor into wages that advertise but cannot "earn" autonomy or its privileges. Correlations between filial obligation and peonage allow those discourses, in combination, to amplify the depth and reach of their power; such are the physics, after all, of resonance. Even among those Asian Americans for whom debt bondage is and has always been more metaphor than term of employment, the structural relation it expresses has explanatory power for the private and public productions of Asian American subjects within capital—tethered to the moment of immigration. Among immigrant communities, Asian Americans in particular count themselves compulsively back: third-generation, second-generation, first—to that generation which first bestowed America upon its descendants, and is hence perhaps the last and most awesome ancestral creditor. The debts of filiality and peonage present themselves equally as the *costs of becoming an American*—that is, the unredeemable fares of immigration come due. Such are certainly the implications of the parental rhetoric of having *sacrificed to come to this country* for the *sake of their children*: a martyrdom for which they are entitled repayment.

It should come as no surprise, in such a context, that what Jade Snow herself dubs her "declaration of independence" (JS Wong, 129) takes place less through speech acts than through financial report:

> You expect me to work my way through college . . . You expect me to exercise judgment in choosing my employers and my jobs and in spending my own money in the American world. Then why can't I choose my own friends? . . .You must give me the freedom to find some answers for myself. (129)

The immigrants' daughter signals her defiance in the language of bookkeeping: "She had shown her father and mother that without a penny from them, she could balance her own budget and graduate from college" (181). She recognizes, in other words, that in order to assert any measure of freedom from her parents, she must reduce or put an end to her financial dependence upon them, for she is beholden for each sum or item in a symbolic if not truly arithmetical economy. However, in attempting to claim her childhood allowance as independent earnings, and in taking credit for having put herself through college, the narrator asserts something of an optimistic and untenable departure from the logic of filial indebtedness. After all, the language of property- and labor-ownership on which she premises her argument is inapplicable to her status as bonded labor; she does not have the autonomy with which to earn autonomy—as admitted by the request to be *granted* freedom which concludes her supposed declaration thereof. Her line of reasoning suggests that Jade Snow partly misapprehends the nature of her position: While astute in its recognition that the family has trained her to be a viable worker in a market economy, her logic is too fixated on the rhetorical glitter of the wage to see that its promises do not apply to her—that its presence does not make her a free and endowed individual in either family or nation. She is, in effect, on the *wrong side* of classical liberalism's wage binary in both contexts—though she feels her disadvantage impinge far more keenly in the close confines of the home than in the larger economy, so it is within the family that she feels comparatively silenced and exploited, and to her white employers that she gladly flees.

If Jade Snow can neither lay claim to her productivity nor buy her freedom with earnings, then minimizing the costs of her upkeep becomes an important activity—perhaps the only intelligible option in slowing a mounting debt. Choosing at age 16 to live as a domestic in a white household, she shifts the costs of her room and board outside of the family as soon as possible. Like her Mills College fees, which are paid for partly by grant and partly by work exchange, these arrangements literally enable her to reallocate part of her maintenance to external accounts (held by her white employers, to whom she is now more beholden instead), and mitigate the claims of her ancestors. We will encounter this cost-cutting impulse again in Wong's literary successors, who will take the logic to much greater extremes. Meantime, however, it is worthwhile to note that, having chosen to defy her parents by single-mindedly striving to close the gap, Jade Snow best assures her own continued failure, and obedience.

∾ disciplinary technologies

Structured by paradox, the economics of filial obligation were our first introduction to the function of *designated failure* in the parent-child relation. We shift now to a Foucauldian examination of technologies of power within immigrant family dynamics, with the expectation that disciplinary practices, too, will prove to have their engineered impossibilities. Indications that Jade Snow's daily life operates in compliance with disciplinary principles as well as economic imperatives, surface in such mundanities as time management. The Wongs not only task their daughters with formidable lists of things to do, but micromanage their productivity with the close use of schedules: Between piano lessons and practice, Chinese school and homework, grocery shopping and housework, "[a]t eleven" years of age, Jade Snow complains, "this daughter could hardly find a moment of her life which was not accounted for, and accounted for properly, by Mama or Daddy" (65). Thanks to rigid temporal structuring, her minutes are calculated to the task, and trimmed of leisure: "When she was old enough to go alone [on errands, she] . . . was allowed exactly enough time to accomplish her purpose and return without any margin for loitering on the streets" (65). Such a jealous fixation with time resonates with our earlier discussion of the Gold Spring incident, in which Necessity proved to manage not only the subject's social interactions, but indeed her pool of *minutes* as if they are bankable resources:

Daddy gave her a lecture on "using time." He insisted that [Gold Spring] came over to waste Jade Snow's time, and that the two spent their moments unconstructively. . . . such companionship absorbed time from more worthwhile pursuits. (92)

The economic moralism invoked in this scene fits hand-in-glove with Foucault's description of the time-table:

The principle that underlay the time-table in its traditional form was essentially negative; it was the principle of non-idleness: it was forbidden to waste time, which was counted by God and paid for by men; the time-table was to eliminate the danger of wasting it—a moral offence and economic dishonesty. (Foucault, *Discipline*, 154)

But as Foucault continues, of course, such rudimentary measures are only the gateway to more comprehensive disciplinary principles such as "exhaustive use":

Discipline, on the other hand, arranges a positive economy; it poses the principle of a theoretically ever-growing use of time: exhaustion rather than use; it is a question of extracting, from time, ever more available moments and, from each moment, ever more useful forces. This means that one must seek to intensify the use of the slightest moment, as if time, in its very fragmentation, were *inexhaustible* or as if, at least by an ever more detailed internal arrangement, one could *tend towards an ideal point* at which one maintained maximum speed and efficiency. (154; emphases added)

Though less directly expressed in the narrator's accounts of work-to-time ratio per se, exhaustive use animates the general principles of her upbringing, as is apparent in her parents' response to Jade Snow's eager announcement that she had been skipped a grade: "Daddy quietly stopped the child's rush of excited words, 'That is as it should be.' That was all he said, with finality" (JS Wong, 19). This dialogue establishes an achievement that is objectively extra-ordinary as merely standard. And if the standard is not to be celebrated, this implies that it is the exceptional which is expected. Yet paradoxically, no achievement warrants exultation, because no performance surpasses expectations. The implications for Jade Snow, as a subject of disciplinary formation, are that in her usage of time and application to tasks, it is not possible for her ever to be productive "enough." For, in a philosophy of inexhaustible usage toward an ideal point, there is no such thing as "enough"; there is only "more."

The subject who is not structurally enabled to achieve success within a disciplinary apparatus of time is, however, certainly structurally enabled to fail. When Jade Snow spends an evening rolling bandages for the war effort at the neighborhood YWCA under her oldest sister's supervision, and is whipped for returning home seven minutes late, her punishment instances what Foucault cites as discipline's "micro-penality of time" (Foucault, *Discipline*, 178). Effecting a disciplinary system is "a question of . . . making the *slightest departures from correct behavior subject to punishment*," such that "each subject find himself caught in *a punishable, punishing universality*" (178; emphases added). So vigilant is punishment that Jade Snow can hardly avoid infraction through the most minor of "latenesses, absences, interruptions of task" (178). So ubiquitous is punishment that Jade Snow may find herself at any moment guilty, failed, criminal—and, perhaps most notably, *in ways she cannot anticipate*. Until confronted by their father, neither Jade Snow nor her oldest sister had suspected that—having obtained his permission for the evening's activities, as well as his subsequent consent for an extension of the time frame—their actions would incur their father's wrath. The element of surprise in their punishment is significant in that it indicates the unfeasibility of full obedience. For Jade Snow's complaint is not merely that the "daughters of the Wong family were born to" exceptionally exacting "requirements"—but that they "were born to requirements exacting *beyond their understanding*" (JS Wong, 67; emphasis added). The issue is not merely that the standards for her behavior are exorbitant, but that the bar to which the daughters must rise is set at a height not disclosed to them: "*These requirements were not always made clear*, until a step out of bounds brought the parents' swift and drastic correction" (67; emphasis added). Thus, it is in *The Woman Warrior* that the narrator relates,

> The adults get mad, evasive, and shut you up if you ask. You get no warning you shouldn't wear a white ribbon in your hair until they hit you and give you the sideways glare for the rest of the day. They hit you if you wave brooms around or drop chopsticks or drum them. They hit you if you wash your hair on certain days, or tap somebody with a ruler, or step over a brother whether it's during your menses or not. You figure out what you got hit for and don't do it again if you figured correctly. (Kingston, *Warriors*, 185)

Given the stringency and scope of disciplinary requirements—closely regulating not only time and productivity, but "behavior (impoliteness, disobedience), . . . speech (idle chatter, insolence), . . . the body ('incorrect' attitudes, irregular gestures, lack of cleanliness), [and] sexuality (impurity, indecency)" (Foucault, *Discipline*, 178)—the fact that infractions are typically identified as such only *after the fact* makes obedience less a question of walking a line than of picking one's way through a field of land mines. "[L]ife was a constant puzzle," she tells us. "No one ever troubled to explain. Only through punishment did she learn that what was proper was right and what was improper was wrong" (JS Wong, 3). Much as she may try to behave, Jade Snow is impeded by a training principle which, as she notes again and again, declines to lay out the parameters of good behavior in advance, and proceeds to punish all deviance as if ignorance were fully synonymous with deliberate insubordination.

The prerogatives of power exercised in the father's verdict point to a law that is answerable to no higher authority than itself. Giorgio Agamben identifies such a structure of law as "sovereign power," and his description of the form of guilt which underlies it bears striking analogy to the descendant's position in relation to the ancestral debt. Indeed, Agamben defines such guilt (guilt "not in the technical sense that this concept has in penal law, but in the originary sense") as "indicat[ing] a *being-in-debt*" which is precisely the condition of being subject to the law (Agamben, 26; emphasis added). Like filial obligation, filial guilt is structural: not actively incurred to start, but product of a social relation which the subject has power neither to initiate nor to check. It is the sovereign who traces a threshold between that which is inside and that which is outside of the law (15), "producing" his subjects as such, as well as deciding from among the activities of living what may fall under governance. Thus, an item that, at some given moment, may rate none of the sovereign's notice, may at the next be deemed to express or imperil the full essence of his law. For instance, both Wong's and Kingston's narrative families clash, interestingly enough, over the affair of indoor footwear. As Jade Snow relates,

One of the household procedures on which [her father] had always insisted was that all members should be completely dressed before they emerged from their bedrooms, even before they washed up in the bathroom. Everyone dressed immediately upon rising, and retired immediately after they undressed. Therefore, nobody needed slippers in his house. *However, slippers had never been specifically forbidden.* (JS Wong, 83; emphasis added)

Having blithely obtained for herself some "coveted red mules," Jade Snow runs afoul of her father when he condemns the slippers as "bedroom attire" and devises a punishment designed to mortify her publicly "[s]o that you may never forget this lesson" (83). Decades later, Brave Orchid broods that her children "would be sorry when they had to walk barefoot through snow and rocks because they didn't take what shoes they could, even if the wrong size. She would put the slippers next to the bathtub on the linoleum floors in winter and trick her lazy children into wearing them" (Kingston, *Warrior,* 120). While the episode is made deliberately absurd, it nonetheless proves a point: In forcing her children to wear shoes they do not want, need, or fit properly, Brave Orchid disregards criteria for the Necessity of footwear, but does effect her will upon her children's bodies. Both Wong's and Kingston's texts instance a sovereign power which is disciplinary in its establishment over and/or intention to form "docile bodies," and is in each case appropriately focused on the smallest of details.

Given that it is the sovereign who determines when and how the order of law applies, this position is decisively occupied, in Jade Snow's narrative, by her father. In Daddy's universe,

> Guilt refers not to transgression, that is, to the determination of the licit and the illicit, but to the pure force of the law, to the law's simple reference to something. This is the ultimate ground of the juridical maxim, which is *foreign to all morality,* according to which *ignorance of the rule does not eliminate guilt.* (Agamben, 26; original italics removed, emphases added)

Thus, while he may affect every air of offended morality—citing his subject's "responsibilities," her broken "word," her "sins," and characterizing his response as a pedagogical enforcement of the law—that which the sovereign exacts is not necessarily a penalty for transgression (i.e., the mere enforcement of law). Rather, it is often (as in the clash of the slippers or the case of the broken curfew) the enactment of sovereign law itself: the exercise of his prerogative to shift the threshold of penalty at will. Jade Snow's response to her father's anger speaks indeed to this latter dynamic, conveying the sense that it is her responsibility to extrapolate and anticipate what the sovereign's judgments and commands in a given situation will be: "Jade Snow was dumb with surprise. Such an interpretation should have occurred to her, but it had not. She could only remain silent" (JS Wong, 82). It is her obligation to foresee the placement of the threshold of law at any given point, regardless of the unfeasibility of knowing a law before it in fact exists. No less unfeasible, unfortunately, are the narrator's attempts, in relating incidents of this nature to us, to expose the injustices of he who is empowered to define justice. As one who is subject to the force of sovereign law, she bears guilt in its pure form, and the morality or immorality of her actions is not an argument, in the face of that authority who effectively invents the moral code.

The system we may understand as "designated failure" is thus composed by a concatenation of structural contradictions—powerful in paradox, yet mutually reinforcing. In a universe that regulates the child-subject's every turn, the sovereign power—whose desires she must anticipate, whose judgments she cannot challenge or negotiate when she has guessed wrong—is also hostile to discovery: Decisively, it shuts out such requests for information as might allow the child to determine the parameters of her behavior "before" an infraction may arise. As Kingston's Maxine complains, her parents "never explained anything that was really important," and therefore the children "no longer asked" (Kingston, *Warrior*, 121). Jade Snow relates her own experience in arrestingly similar terms: "At first she asked questions, being curious. But her father did not like questions. He said that one was not supposed to talk when one was either eating or thinking, and when one was not eating, one should be thinking" (JS Wong, 4). Her father's dislike of questions implies that, apparently, one should be able to discover all necessary things for oneself merely by "thinking"—and therefore not knowing is itself already a failure. Such a method of training is not only defined by the impossible—the child is punished if she does not know before she learns, and only learns piecemeal by failure and punishment—but can be said in fact to manufacture failure, by building it into the very (underlying, unacknowledged) expectations of the system. Agamben describes the structure of sovereign power as being "a law that is *in force without signifying*, and that thus *neither prescribes nor forbids any determinate end*" (Agamben, 52; emphases added). The disciplinary processes of a subject formation premised on sovereign power, are predicated on the production of the unfilial child.

As Sandra Lee Bartky notes of the disciplinary formation of the Western "feminine," the Foucauldian subject must first and perpetually be constructed as deficient, defective, and therefore as requiring corrective measures, in order to be subjected (in order that she may subject herself) to a disciplinary regime.[15] As with cultural norms of femininity, familial norms of filial obedience are devised in such a way as not to be attainable—and are, something like the proverbial carrot on a stick, effective precisely *because* they cannot be attained. These classic features of disciplinary technology, which Bartky calls its "setup," are among the more reliable devices of designated failure: "The ideal point of penality today would be an indefinite discipline: . . . a procedure that would be at the same time the permanent measure of a gap in relation to an inaccessible norm and the asymptotic movement that strives to meet in infinity" (Foucault, *Discipline*, 227). Thus it is that *The Woman Warrior's* Maxine dreams not of "sufficient" filiality, but "perfect filiality" (Kingston, 45). Several of the daughter-narrators in *The Joy Luck Club* echo Maxine's language of failure and perfection: "In all of my imaginings, I was filled with a sense that I would soon become *perfect*. My mother and father would adore me. I would be beyond reproach" (Tan, 133, emphasis in original; 37). As for Jade Snow, however earnestly she may attempt or intend to abide by her father's parameters, any deviation (practically, and by sovereign disposition, inevitable) will be construed as willful disobedience—because it is a *necessary condition* of her disciplinary formation that she be discursively produced as the *intractable body and will* which ever require the diligence of power, and ever fail to achieve the ideal.

While the function of its given "norm" is therefore central to any disciplinary technology, that which operates in Jade Snow's case may be particularly noteworthy. For the normative concept that recurs in her text is not specifically cleanliness, nor frugality, nor temperance, nor industry, nor any combination of these or other quintessentially disciplinary qualities, but simply "propriety" itself. The term "proper" punctuates her descriptions of her upbringing: "[T]he few problems she had were entirely concerned with what was proper or improper in the behavior of a little Chinese girl" (JS Wong, 2). "[O]ne did not dispute one's father if one were a dutiful little girl taught to act with propriety" (4). And "propriety" as it is meant in this context is a norm *par excellence*, for it is purely self-referential, even tautological: "Only through punishment did she learn that *what was proper was right and what was improper was wrong*" (3; emphasis added). Here one defines rightness by propriety, not propriety by moral rightness. The notions "right" and "wrong" abandon any attempt to signify ethical absolutes, and are cast instead in the die of pure parental prescription; "right" and "proper" come to refer only to each other. Propriety is therefore the norm most appropriate to sovereign power, for what remains is simply that that which her parents deem acceptable is acceptable (proper), and that which they deem unacceptable is unacceptable (improper). Such a norm does not offer even the pretense of an outside referent, an objective measure. It is the prime number of norms: divisible only by obedience.

✍ filial forms

Despite Jade Snow's implicit recognition of the paradoxes in her upbringing, however, the book she writes is neither protest novel nor polemic. Though she compiles meticulous reports of the circular logic or studied unreason that organize many of her parents' choices and actions, it is important to realize that she nevertheless composes a scrupulously genteel account of their family life. As others have noted, Jade Snow's "admission of rebellion is more often repressed than expressed" (Lim, 257); this identifies a tension generated by two competing narrative impulses: On the one hand, the text's design is clearly intended to give vent to what the narrator perceives as the injustices of her youth, in demonstrating all that she has overcome in order to occupy her current position of relative recognition and cultural prominence. In her introduction the author states that in childhood she had "suffered from repression, . . . [and] been cruelly—and sometimes inexplicably—punished" (JS Wong, x). Recalling her thoughts from her teenage years, Jade Snow reveals that she considered her family's treatment of her to have been characterized by "neglect and prejudice" (93), usage for which she felt she deserved atonement ("To make up for . . ." [93]). Hence, what Elaine Kim characterizes as the "enraged" tone of the autobiography may certainly be located in the text. On the other hand, however, the text maintains a certain protective reticence around the narrator's thoughts and feelings about her family, affecting the distance of an auto-ethnographer and shunning the intensity or intimacy of a personal diatribe; no Sylvia Plath, she. Indeed, Wong claims an intended neutrality of representation in the following (also introductory) statement: "There is no attempt here to judge individuals, only an attempt to evaluate personal experiences . . . I have not been concerned to discover whether they were good or bad, but rather to what extent they affected one individual's thinking, purpose, and action" (xiii). This statement is belied by actual narrative moments, in which Jade Snow does "judge," and her "evaluations" of her family's parenting practices chart very much on the axes of "good or bad," sound or unfair. But it is the duality of Wong's narrative impulses that explains Kim's observation—otherwise puzzling, in light of her preceding acknowledgment of the narrator's rage—that "the emotional life that Jade Snow Wong might have expressed in her autobiography never fully emerges" (E. Kim, Defining, 71). The emotional and narrative reserve Wong maintains around her subject matter is foremost effected through her idiosyncratic uses of the third person and the subsequent choices she makes in developing the narrative point of view.

Wong's decision to write her autobiography in the third person has garnered much critical commentary. She claims its use out of a "Chinese habit" of "modesty" or humility, a "submergence of the individual" (JS Wong, xiii) encoded within the written language, but for various reasons that authorial choice seems a "textual fiction" (Bow, *Betrayal*, 88) with ends other than cultural authenticity. As both Shirley Lim and Leslie Bow argue, "Wong's choice of voice" has a distancing effect (88), dissociating her both from the "constant puzzle" of her family life, which can then be "presented at a distance, as an object" (Lim, 257), and from "Jade Snow's unfilial behavior" (Bow, *Betrayal*, 88). However, while the distancing third person attenuates Wong's identification with her own subject position, perhaps "splitting" her self into a removed figure of the "bad daughter," the voice signifies above all her discomfort with her disclosures; it is *not*, in other words, an enabling narrative strategy which permits the author then to expose her family's doings and her own opinions at will, but instead marks the boundaries of what she is not willing to say. After all, a third person narration does not categorically or by definition prevent the narrative identification with or imagination of a character's subjectivity or point of view. It is specifically in Wong's case that the third person is so far from omniscient, and instead regulates a euphemistic glossing of her protagonist's thinking:

> [S]he was now conscious that "foreign" American ways were not only generally and vaguely different from their Chinese ways, but that they were specifically different . . . Jade Snow had begun to compare American ways with those of her mother and father, and the comparison made her uncomfortable. (JS Wong, 21)

Here and elsewhere, Jade Snow limits the accounts of her sentiments to generalizations, abstains from explicit accusations, and gestures toward a critique but does not actually perform it. Lim points out, in reference to this moment of glaring understatement, that

> Ironically, the passage treats "specificity," the "specific differences" [between American and Chinese ways], in the most general terms. The objective author/narrator, describing the (auto)-biographical subject, represses the very subjectivity of the subject . . . Thus, the new "consciousness" of specific splittings, so crucial to the story of Jade Snow's early life, is muted and distanced in Wong's memoir; the reader is merely informed, "the comparison made her uncomfortable." (Lim, 258)

Such muting is a curious tactic for one whose creative motivation is to *"prove to [her] family that they have been unjust"* (JS Wong, 108; emphasis added), for proof does not function without indictment backed by the substantiatingly explicit. She leaves her views of each incident and her analysis of her childhood either expansively announced, or mildly implied, but neither charged nor "proven."

In another reticence of at least equal significance, Wong eschews any effort to imagine the subjective realities of her parental figures. She attributes to them spoken dialogue, ventures to describe (in only the briefest of terms) externally manifested reactions such as surprise or temper, but does not hazard even the smallest speculation on psychological content; "Mama" and "Daddy" are given no interiority beyond what surfaces to empirical observation. They are authorities opaque to insight; as such, they are also impervious to interpretation. Restricting her characterizations of her parents to the words and deeds available to a strictly external third-person point of view, Jade Snow not only approximates objectivity by refraining from overt judgment, but denies her narrative the possibilities of judgment embedded in the rendering of character. It is instructive to contrast Wong's technique to the representations of parental figures in *The Woman Warrior*, and Kingston's use of first- and third-person narrative voices. Lim points out that a "first-person narrator who is able to move through all the personal pronouns (I, they, everyone, we) permits no distance between herself and her cultural materials" (Lim, 257), and indeed we find in *The Woman Warrior* a pervasive sense of intimacy and familiarity quite absent from *Fifth Chinese Daughter*. Kingston's "I" is at times Maxine, and at others (namely in "White Tigers," when the narrator speaks as Fa Mu Lan), has morphed into another consciousness. What's more, the narrative voice in "Shaman" makes use of the first and third person *at once*—an effort of imaginative projection which insists on the relation of self to other, speaks of the other in the third person, and yet takes ownership of that subjectivity: "My mother." "My mother relished these scare orgies" (Kingston, *Warrior*, 65). "My mother may have been afraid, but she would be a dragoness" (67). Dialogue Maxine attributes to her mother from the years in China is speech she could not have observed, but spins out of her own conception of what she believes her mother to have been like and would have said. The (heroic) rendering of the mother in "Shaman" is thus unabashedly interpretive; whatever value judgments lie therein are in the very weave of the authorial construct. A novel's villains are villainous, its heroines heroic, very much because the author has chosen to make them so; characterization has an authority which is, in a sense, absolute.

It is thus with all the authority and credibility of authorship that Kingston enters Brave Orchid's subjectivity in "At the Western Palace." Lim maintains that with Kingston's use of "plural and shifting pronouns," the various subjectivities and voices of the novel are "transformed, 'digested' by an omnivorous and multiple subject," processed in the end into a single if heterogeneous consciousness (Lim, 257). I believe this to be true of all sections but "At the Western Palace," in which Kingston regulates a fastidious separation between the subject (m/Other) of the chapter, and the composite narrative self of the book. For in this chapter, and this alone, the "I" (and acknowledged eye) of the narrator disappears. It is as if (in deliberate effect, even if not in fact), Maxine the narrator has stepped away, removed herself from her function, and we are enabled to see the mother without her daughter's intercession. And seen thus directly, in this ostensibly objective light, Brave Orchid is an irrational, self-righteous woman with little sense of American realities, who yet imposes her will upon those within the scope of her power, often to their injury. Unlike Wong, who refuses to point fingers or name names, declining to interpret or to specify what she believes the temperament of her parental figures to be, Kingston "exposes" the maternal figure by devoting an entire chapter to the indirect discourse of Brave Orchid's mind.[16] In other words, this singular chapter breaks with the "first person other" which sutures the other chapters' personas together via identification, relation, and influence; isolated by the harsh lights of the third person omniscient, the immigrant figure appears without benefit of ancestral stature. It is not incidental that "At the Western Palace" identifies Brave Orchid not as "Mama" or "my mother" but by first name—and in alienating, Anglicized translation such as would not be customarily used by *anyone* to address or refer to this person, in English or Chinese; this choice signals the most emotionally distant and yet narratively enabling form possible of the third person. In stark contrast, while Wong refers to herself as the impersonal Jade Snow, she calls her father not Mr. Wong, but Daddy. As Daddy, he looms large in the story as a figure of insistent familiality, of inescapable proximity—of ancestry personified. Whereas Wong's third person narration marks, as we have seen, what she will not say (indeed, what fear of her father will not allow her to say), Kingston's third person narration does the opposite, facilitating the articulation of an uncomfortable moral judgment on the mother's character.

"At the Western Palace" demonstrates that to enter the subjectivity of a parental figure can be an act of aggression, one which, in performing an implicit critique, requires a breach of propriety—constitutes an act of unfiliality. When imagining Brave Orchid as a young woman (i.e., *prior to* the birth of her American children), Maxine is able to intimate a subjective proximity, an identification with a woman she views in glowing terms. Specifically in the period of her life when she lived without family, Brave Orchid is a figure with no relation to Maxine; yet it is to this stranger that the narrator can extend acceptance as both predecessor and kin. In turning to describe Brave Orchid *as her mother*, however—as the woman whose authority Maxine has navigated daily and for years—she condemns her as ineffectual but oppressive, not wise but unreasonable. Alongside choosing to do this, Maxine also erases her relation to the character; she does not distinguish herself among Brave Orchid's children, preferring not to identify herself in the chapter— thereby hiding, not only from her mother, as all the siblings seem to do,[17] but from her own narrative. This unflattering portrait of Brave Orchid becomes at once an act of disobedience and an act of disownment: in this narrative moment, Maxine will not own her mother. Thus, blatantly unfilial behavior requires a cutting of ties (even if only in the figurative) for which Wong's narrative, apparently, has no stomach. In the blackout she maintains around her parents' subjectivities, Wong effectively denies her narrative the latitude to undermine, redefine, or even accuse. Ever her father's daughter, she intercedes for him throughout—and increasingly as her troubles allegedly come to a happy close.

The last paragraphs of *Fifth Chinese Daughter* make a concerted push to resolve the Wong family's tensions into an exuberant ending, but it is one which critics have found unconvincing, "forced" in its tidiness (Bow, *Betrayal*, 89). In the book's final words, Jade Snow informs us of a newly idyllic state of parental acceptance and a new "attitude of respect" (JS Wong, 245) which she claims that her parents now extend to their 24-year-old daughter. Such transformation is redolent with the mythology of a marching evolution of immigrant behavior, especially as a function of upward mobility;[18] it is, as we have seen, a particularly American mythology to which Wong is particularly partial. And yet, the description of her narrative emancipation recites devoutly from the discourses of filial obligation and debt bondage—narratives in which emancipation, as we have shown, is unintelligible:

For Jade Snow the moment of triumph had come. She had *proved that Mama could raise her children to be a credit to the Wongs*. She had shown her father and mother that *without a penny from them, she could balance her own budget* and graduate from college, *not in debt*, but with one hundred of the original hundred and seventy-four dollars still in the bank. (181; emphases added)

Furthermore, Jade Snow's choice of survival tactics, (tactics presumably vital to bringing about the book's happy ending), have required no reworking of the familial relations she previously found so oppressive. The narrator professes to the strategic compartmentalization of her life, selectively pursuing her own priorities while leaving her parents' principles and requirements, wherever possible, intact. Yet, we as readers are to believe that, within a disciplinary and economic logic which recognizes no limits on obedience or debt, the daughter may set aside whole realms of her life and activity as not subject to the rule or law of parental authority, and enjoy approval rather than face censure:

> Jade Snow no longer attempted to bring the new Western learning into her Oriental home. When she entered the Wong household, she slipped into her old pattern of withdrawal, and she performed her usual daughterly duties . . . in the role of an obedient Chinese girl. But now she no longer felt stifled or dissatisfied, for she could return to another life in which she fitted as an individual. (168; see also 202)

Finally, even the vindicating speech she presents as evidence of her "family's change of heart" (245) reflects quite the opposite: a deft corroboration of ancestral greatness and filial indebtedness, instead. When, on the very final page, Daddy turns to her with long-awaited praise for her achievements, it is in the context of recalling how vast indeed was the value of the American immigration costs *he advanced* for her:

> When I first came to America, my cousin wrote me from China and asked me to return. . . . I still have the carbon copy of the letter I wrote him in reply. I said, "You do not realize the shameful and degraded position into which the Chinese culture has pushed its women. Here in America, the Christian concept allows women their freedom and individuality. I wish my daughters to have this Christian opportunity. I am hoping that some day I may be able to claim that by [coming to and remaining in America,] I have washed away the former disgraces suffered by the women of our family." (246)

The conclusion of *Fifth Chinese Daughter* is all but suffocating in the language of obligation, bounded by discourses with no exit.

Not that in so concluding, its narrator acknowledges these ongoing confines in the least. Rather, she proves herself in the final pages of the book as ardent a booster and apologist for her sovereign as for her state, representing the latter as a race- and sex-blind meritocracy (194–96),[19] and the former as having been a stealth feminist. Leslie Bow's reading of the ending's "conversion" of the patriarch into "the primary agent against [gendered] injustice" provides an indispensable account of the emotional manipulativeness and conservatism of the conclusion—and invokes a comparison well worth extending here: "Like the dissonant emergence of a lost letter in *conventional melodrama*, the letter sets right a mistaken identity: the figure who resisted change is revealed to have advocated change all along" (Bow, *Betrayal*, 88; emphasis added). Were the melodramatic narrative in question a gothic romance—with its heroine trapped inside a labyrinthian home, atmosphere ominous with indefinable traps and ancient threats—then the lost letter would reveal the villainous captor by plot's end to have been the heroine's secret benefactor, and thereby reconcile the heroine to a revisionist dismissal of her oppression.

If such conservative cultural forms are known for their attempts to submerge and deny the anxieties that they raise, however, they are also known for doing so ineffectually, and the critical consensus on the hollow ring of Wong's resolution seems to bear out this generic failure. As Michelle Massé notes of the marital gothic—in which melodramatic narrative, too, heroines trapped by their traditional domestic obligations come to be assured of the baselessness of their anger and distress—"[t]he ending's reassurances have specious weight when balanced against the body's mass of suffering: there is a surplus of anxiety still unaccounted for by the [conclusion's alleged] 'reality'" (Massé, 19).[20] It seems reasonable to infer, then, that the slim content of the recalled letter is simply inadequate to the revisionist transmogrification it is tasked with performing; the ending provides too slight a lever to move so much ideological mass. Let me suggest, however, one more possibility: We need not marshal evidence that Jade Snow was unsuccessful in resolving the paradoxes and power struggles of her youth—though certainly there is that in plenty—if we grant that to undo those paradoxes and unlock the power struggles was never her objective. As critics have agreed, "Jade Snow does not question the necessity of the [family] hierarchy as much as she does her place within it" (Bow, *Betrayal*, 80). Her manner of dealing with iniquities of power within the household, then, can be paralleled to her beliefs in dealing with the greater white American society: acceptance of its essential values and arrangements, paired with an ambition to advance along the prescribed pathways toward individual recognition and relative success. Thus, if it is indeed as Bow remarks and "in spite of textual assurances to the contrary, Jade Snow's position in the world at the end of the narrative is neither secure nor settled" (78), the problem with the ending may be not only that it is too slight—but that it is too early. If *Fifth Chinese Daughter* may be productively compared to a gothic romance, it is one in which the heroine is still intent upon denying her own suspicions of the horrors of the home—because she has not yet opened any of its forbidden doors. Her slightly hysterical insistence upon the straightforward progression of her narrative may be our most telling emotional index that our heroine has not allowed herself to venture, even in authorial imagination, beyond its hallways. The story Jade Snow tells, in other words, has only just begun; the paradoxes it has yet even to confront in daylight will recur to haunt the dreams of its young narrator, and of many narrators after her, for decades of Asian American literature to come.

2

Refractions of Harm

Maxine Hong Kingston

> Dreams and expressionist texts are both structured by a representational economy that disdains the rules of realism . . . as well as those of rational logic, and both ignore the imperative to represent "objective reality," favoring, instead, an emphasis on subjective emotions, and relying on the "distortion," "exaggeration," "fantasy," "violence," "graphicness," "repetition," etc., produced by a dynamic and functional deployment of various formal elements. . . . [A]s in a dream, the dramatis personae are characterized by fluid, interchangeable identities that very often operate collectively in pursuit of a singular goal.
>
> Abdul JanMohamed, *The Death-Bound Subject*

Maxine Hong Kingston's *The Woman Warrior* opens with the most famous of her chapters: the story of the No Name Woman. This family fable, in which Maxine's aunt drowns herself and her newborn in the family well on the night of the villagers' masked raid, contains violence, judgment, illicit sexuality, and retribution—the elemental high drama of fairy tales, folk legends, and nightmares.[2] It is said by the narrator to exemplify the manner of story her mother would tell, and, like the more broadly circulated versions of childhood's oral traditions, it serves to mark out the parameters of gender, morality, family duty, and societal membership. The mother concludes her telling with an unequivocally stated lesson, and an equally manifest threat: "Now that you have started to menstruate, what happened to her could happen to you. Don't humiliate us. You wouldn't like to be forgotten as if you had never been born. The villagers are watchful" (Kingston, *Warrior*, 5). Maxine tells us that with such stories, her mother "tested [the children's] strength to establish realities" (5), but the above passage makes clear that the fable is more than a means of merely testing coping skills; it is a vehicle first and foremost for composing belief systems, setting life's conditions and criteria—indeed, for establishing the realities themselves. Such narratives are, as Maxine realizes, "stor[ies] to grow up on" (5).

Forced to strike a compromise between the proprieties of feminism and Asian American cultural nationalism, early literary criticism of *The Woman Warrior* negotiated a no-man's land of interpretation which bounds readings to this day. Among this foundational scholarship, that of Elaine Kim and King-Kok Cheung argued to the effect that the locus and true measure of the immigrant Chinese family's attitude toward its daughters, as depicted in Kingston's work, is not to be found in the miasma of such narratives, but located in the details of an alternate "real life":

> While anti-female adages about the necessity of wifely servitude and obedience and about the uselessness of girls abound in the Chinese immigrant culture, *actual subjugation of women exists only in the stories*, in Chinese operas, in jokes and aphorisms, and in the imaginings of the narrator, *not in real life among the immigrants*. (Kim, *AAL*, 203; emphases added)

This compromise is reached, however, by imposing an unfortunate hierarchy and false dichotomy between discursive production and an apparently non-discursive "real": privileging the "actions" of immigrant life over (and even to the exclusion of) its words. The implications of this model are dangerously such that any text of cultural discourse, if found to be dissonant with apparently "factual conditions," may legitimately be evacuated of meaning: declared extraneous to material realities to which they arbitrarily give the lie. Later scholarship has revised the assumptions of that value structure, to insist upon what Leslie Bow terms the "discursivity of the material" (Bow, *Betrayal*, 24): the position that the discursive is inextricable from any "real life," as it is produced or experienced. As she cites of Foucault, "in any society, there are manifold relations of power which permeate, characterise and constitute the social body, and these relations of power cannot themselves be established, consolidated nor implemented without the production, accumulation, circulation and functioning of a discourse" (Bow, *Betrayal*, 23).

This corrective allows us to recover a thesis essential to the text itself, manifest within its pages but lost in the balance of the great compromise. In explaining the misogynistic discourse of the following passage, Cheung takes a position similar to Kim's:

From afar I can believe that my family loves me fundamentally. *They only say*, "When fishing for treasures in the flood, be careful not to pull in girls" . . . But I watched such words come out of my own mother's and father's mouths . . . And I had to get out of hating range. (Kingston as quoted in Cheung, *Silences*, 97; ellipses in original citation, emphasis added)

The apparent connotations of "They only say" readily steer us toward an interpretation that divorces what the family "merely says" about its girls from what it "actually means." And indeed, by Cheung's account, "The narrator has come to realize that her family's apparent disparagement of girls (often by the folk sayings they mouth) does not reflect the feelings they do have for their own daughters" (97). I would maintain, however, that Kingston's text does not support so clean an opposition. Both the immediate and greater contexts of this clause indicate an ongoing tension in, rather than a definitive resolution of, what the family "actually means." The full sentence from which this quote is taken is specific in its reference: "They only say, 'When fishing for treasures in the flood, be careful not to pull in girls,' *because that is what one says about daughters*" (Kingston, *Warrior*, 52; emphasis added). There is a distinction of nuances between "only saying a thing and not meaning it," versus "only saying a thing because that is what everyone says." The latter sense makes reference to a scaffolding of cultural norms, values, and assumptions, upon which the speaker relies *and which the speaker does not question*. The latter sense, then, is more akin to the sense that the speaker "only believes" a thing because it is "what one believes" than to the interpretation that the speaker says what he says but does not believe it at all.

Thus, while the definitive critical impulse has been strong, to tone down or explain away the narrator's felt harm, textual evidence is not ultimately so obliging. Cheung argues that the daughter "has come to realize" the feelings her parents "do have" for her: that is, Maxine has concluded that her parents do love her, proverbs notwithstanding. Yet the statement "I can believe that my family loves me fundamentally" comes not at the conclusion—the destination—of this narrative moment, but rather at its forefront. The narrator *proceeds* from that acknowledgment to puzzle through the incongruities of parental feeling. From where Cheung's excerpt leaves off, Maxine continues, "I read in an anthology book that Chinese say, 'Girls are necessary too'; I have never heard the Chinese I know make this concession" (52); despite scholarship's best efforts to read closure into the daughter's grievances, then, Maxine is still very much in the midst of sorting through the strands of her parents' affections.[3] For to be in the company of her parents is to "watch . . . [hateful] words come out of [their] mouths," and to "[look] at their ink drawing of poor people . . . pushing the girl babies on down the river" (52). This passage demonstrates in brief the narrator's struggle to "read" her parents, as she turns even the act of hearing into a textual process: She *watches* words being spoken, looks at illustrations, pores over the printed page, then juggles and compares these pieces, but cannot derive a coherent interpretation. Compounded by inconsistencies within and across the cultural texts themselves ("When we Chinese girls listened to the adults talk-story, we learned that we failed if we grew up to be but wives or slaves" [19]), Maxine's difficulty in reading these messages against any certainty that her parents love her is an object lesson to her readership. That fundamental contradictions order the daughter's experience is one of the book's principal insights; if, as Kim notes in a separate essay, "One of the main points of *The Woman Warrior* is that a marginal person . . . derives power and vision from living with paradoxes" (Kim, Defining, 152), then the ambivalent home cannot be so neatly absolved by sentimental resolutions. Significantly, it is only "From afar"—a distance sufficiently "out of hating range"—that Maxine can feel confident in her family's love. To be a daughter in this context is to be subjected to a low buzz of discursive violences in that very space which is home, and to be so afflicted by what one hears and sees that one cannot discern the image or tone of love through the storm of static. The position that the misogyny spoken in the family "does not matter," that only the "reality" of parental love does, can no longer serve us. Maxine's remark that "When [she] visit[s] the family now, [she] wrap[s her] American successes around [her] like a private shawl" (52) attests, among other things, to a sense that she needs psychological protection in order to go home, that she feels profoundly unsafe there.

If chapter 1 of *Ingratitude* was particularly concerned with parental power's mechanisms for quantifying its claims on the child-subject, this second chapter is preoccupied instead with perhaps the least quantifiable aspects of its systems: the discursive workings of sovereign power, and the phenomenology of harm. Kingston's memoir remains both the most seminal text of second-generation Asian American women's literature, and the most aesthetically distinctive for its refusal to tell the difference between "what's real and what [is] ma[d]e up" (202). This chapter argues that the latter achievement has everything to do with the former; in its equivocations with fact and form, *The Woman Warrior* gives indelible first expression to an implacable truth of the Asian immigrants' daughter's experience: that of being conditioned by violences visceral but not visible. At the outset of her narrative, Maxine enlists her readers by direct address, in what the text presents as one item in a list of puzzles and hurts it presumes we share: "how do you separate what is peculiar to childhood, to poverty, insanities, one family, *your mother who marked your growing with stories?*" (5; emphasis added). With this last, the text sets our sights on precisely those violences that leave no marks, and engenders as a result a critical language of hypochondria, of insidious trauma, of discursive violences and dubiously valid suffering. As the earlier Kim and Cheung readings illustrate, measured by conventional standards of history and medicine, the events of Maxine's childhood are, like those of Jade Snow's young life, not recognizable as violences nor, indeed, as events at all.

This banality of second-generation experience is a structural constant and, in fact, an anxiety shared across the present body of literature. In *The Joy Luck Club*, Amy Tan dwells upon and, somewhat problematically, exaggerates that inherent, generational disparity in historical scale. As Patricia Chu notes, Tan chooses to make "the Chinese mothers a generation older than they logistically need to be," representing their "daughters [as] the children of *second* marriages" (Chu, 156) or otherwise aging them such that their life experiences include the more spectacularly traumatic possibilities of a pre-revolutionary, archaic China, or the war traumas of the Communist Revolution itself. In even more decided contrast, then, are the daughters' middle-class material comforts: A long-suffering mother will remark, "[M]y daughter does not hear me. She sits by her fancy swimming pool and hears only her Sony Walkman, her cordless phone, and her big, important husband asking her why they have charcoal but no lighter fluid" (Tan, 67). Likewise in Jhumpa Lahiri's "Only Goodness," the Bengali American daughter observes, "In [her immigrant parents'] opinion their children were immune from the hardships and injustices they had left behind in India, as if the inoculations the pediatrician had given [them] when they were babies guaranteed them an existence free of suffering" (Lahiri, 144), and that, as a result, "Her parents had always been blind to the things that plagued their children: being teased at school for the color of their skin or for the funny things their mother occasionally put into their lunch boxes" (143). It is in the same vein that Maxine remarks repeatedly upon the disparity between the drama of her imaginary life (set in China), and the unsatisfactory proportions of her American realities: "My American life has been such a disappointment" (Kingston, *Warrior*, 45); "What fighting and killing I have seen have not been glorious but slum grubby" (51). Where her parents are haunted by war planes dropping bombs from above, American-born Maxine and her siblings learn to huddle at the sound of commercial jets whirring harmlessly overhead (93). The second-generation daughters across these texts exist in a particularly mediated relationship to "History," if "'History' [is] imagined as a set of objective and agreed-upon facts, dates, and political events" (So, 128), upheavals of national or international dimension.[4] If they seem to respond to their cushioned circumstances with strange frustration, it is because that mediation conditions their life-narrating possibilities and, as we shall see, the formal construction of their narratives.

∿ relative harm

This study is not the first to recognize that Maxine's experience comprises a painful alienation from recognizable pain; it may be the first, however, to apply that critical insight to familial relations. Anne Cheng's *The Melancholy of Race* examines the pivotal role that suffering—both the externally verifiable variety and the "invisibly" psychical—has been given to play in the workings of racial law and advocacy. Cheng finds that the alchemy of American political representation turns, not unproblematically, on the "conversion of the disenfranchised person from being subjected to grief to being a subject speaking grievance" (Cheng, 7); in other words, within this "symbolic, cultural economy," there lies in certain signifiers of victimization a kind of inverted cultural capital, from which political agency can be manufactured. For all that the racial formation of Asian and black Americans are "related processes" (21), however, we know the discourse of Asian racialization to be distinctive in its duality: undecided between Yellow Peril and Model Minority, between inflicting racial injury and according racial privilege. This discursive ambivalence hobbles a rhetoric of political oppression, restitution, and legitimacy—by compromising the claims of injury and injustice on which an agency of resistance would be based. If the voluntary immigrants who make up this model minority cannot convert their material contributions into social representation (So), neither, it seems, can they "translate" the intangible tolls of Asian American racialization into politicized material deficits. Indeed, it is very telling that for the touchstone of a thesis on the political economy of psychic pain, Cheng chooses no episode of Asian American history, but instead the *Brown v. Board of Education* ruling informed by the Clarks' famous doll test;[5] to speak intelligibly of even the presumably more subtle, "'intangible' effects of racism," Cheng's model must refer (and defer) assiduously to the paradigms of African American racial injury. Even the "invisible . . . aspect[s] of racism" (4) which are her focus, then, are more easily viewed in black racial formation than in Asian. This suggests that, on an order still greater than that of their black compatriots, Asian American "racial grief . . . cannot definitively speak in the language of material grievance." This failure of articulation stems for Asian Americans not from the mere mechanics of translation, but from paucity of perceived content; considered by many (including, among more conservative factions, themselves) to be pretty-much-white (22), Asian Americans are accorded little or no racial grief at all. By any metrics derived via racial comparison, they rate nothing to say.

Cheng's work offers an elegant recalibration of suffering to Asian American proportions—arguing that by historical and discursive production, this category of racial subjects is prone to meandering in melancholia instead of proper mourning, for losses it is not entirely clear it has suffered, and to which suffering the subject is perversely attached. Yet in positioning the (uncontested history of) material tribulations and (consequently, considerably greater accredited) psychic injuries of African American experience as the gold standard of racial suffering, Cheng's model further commits Asian Americans to playing catch-up in an awkward bid for political capital. In working from this unfavorable comparison, Cheng has plenty and venerable company, as for instance in the very literary origins of Asian American identity politics. The *Aiiieeeee!* anthology of the 1970s is not only founded on a compare-and-contrast exercise with black racialization; it is powered by a curious envy for the violent oppression and "racist hate" historically directed against African Americans.[6] Such is the legacy of this politics of comparative grief that the field is compelled to generate political value from its hate crimes, auditing with solicitous care its bodily or spectacular losses; or that scholarship has taken to reflexively trotting out its sub-par Southeast Asians, whose material deprivation is only too-scant argument for the falseness of the model minority myth, and on whose continued failure must rest the hopes of entire academic and political platforms. All of these rhetorical moves expose the nerve-wracking lack of "lack" that haunts Asian American political advocacy, which is thereby made incurably susceptible to being accused of whining. Of this legacy, Cheng's work is at once symptomatic *and* a corrective. To describe the blight of Asian racial subjectification, Cheng borrows scale and intensity from such African American contexts as historical slavery and social obliteration (20–21). Even as this comparison penalizes Asian American claims, however, its contrast also serves the book's larger purpose of lending expression to the less "quantifiable" (6) racial violences which are its primary concern. Indeed, in these formal choices, Cheng and Kingston seem to be of a mind: that there are aspects of especially "Asian American" experience which find speech only in the borrowed language of misrepresentation.

Maxine recounts in *The Woman Warrior* having a decidedly peculiar affliction, one that involved spending "eighteen months sick in bed with a mysterious illness," during which time she experienced "no pain and no symptoms" (Kingston, 182). Insofar as that illness can arguably somatize social injuries, its (missing) symptoms are overdetermined; like fever or nausea, they may index multiple maladies in a compressed response.[7] For one, the affliction may certainly figure a racialization peculiar to Asian Americans: A condition without recognized pain or symptoms, sufferers of which may rather enjoy the privileges of special treatment, is a dubious oppression. Implicit in the illness's departure from form, then, is a contrast in paradigms of suffering: Asian American rather than black—but also second-generation rather than first. Maxine's illness literalizes the "existence free from suffering" that Lahiri's immigrant characters imagine to have bestowed upon their children, via first-world "inoculations" which make the next generation "immune from hardship" (Lahiri, 144)—psychical pain being spurious when the body is so hale.

Likewise, the proliferation of Ghosts in earlier chapters expresses simultaneously a racial formation and a generational comparison—indeed, they figure generationally differentiated relationships to historical oppression. Consider that the narrator tells with great envy and admiration the story of her mother's life-and-death struggles in China, in which Brave Orchid defeats, for one, a grisly Sitting Ghost (Kingston, *Warrior*, 69). In the immigrant's past, in other words, oppression manifests in literal and physical form: The literally phantasmic *materializes*, becoming solid enough to engage in pitched battle, by hand, as it threatens to (op)press the life out of her.[8] Consider on the other hand the phantoms of Maxine's experience: Milk Ghosts, Mail Ghosts, Meter Reader Ghosts, and Garbage Ghosts (98). The mundanities of American life for this Asian immigrant family are terrifying, and yet "objectively" without harm. In feeble comparison, then, are the second-generation narrator's hauntings, in which material infrastructures and physical realities turn insubstantial and phantasmic. Maxine's Ghosts figure, if anything, her struggles with a coded, changeable, institutional racism: anticlimactic chimeras of enemies whom she does not know how to fight, nor even whether she ought rightly to fight them at all. Together, these metaphors of illness and phantasm suggest hypochondria as a structural aspect of the second-generation subject's position. In its colloquial sense, wherein the extent or reality of the subject's phenomenologically experienced suffering are met with skepticism,[9] hypochondria speaks to that bias by which the daughter's "real life" racial *and* familial oppressions are given no credence, because terror for her is inflicted "only in the stories" (Kim, *AAL*, 203).

the harm of threat   ໑

In a sense, this chapter takes up where *The Melancholy of Race* leaves off, confronting intangible injury in the familial-ethnic spaces and relations of the immigrant home. We begin by expanding the taxonomy of psychic injury. Cheng's reading of Kingston takes the not uncommon perspective that Maxine's suffering is a vertically transmitted trauma, wherein the original material and cultural losses Brave Orchid endures devolve into what is sometimes called "secondary" or "intergenerational" traumatization:[10] "the immigrant trauma of the mother (surely not even fully registered by the mother herself) has been passed down to the daughter *as* inherited trauma, trauma without an origin" (Cheng, 88). While certainly this paradigm speaks at length to the diminished scale and hypochondriacal quality of Maxine's struggles, it also has the problematic effect of implying that the daughter's troubles are fundamentally *not her own*. Indeed, Cheng asserts by this logic that the daughter's account of selfhood may be read as "an ongoing ventriloquy of the mother" (88), of whom she is a "telescoped" extension, and over whose pain-*qua*-subject-matter she has no direct claim. In casting the narrator's pain as *a function* of the inability (first her mother's, then her own) to come to terms with *the mother's* experiences, that analytical account precludes itself from being able to parse pain which Brave Orchid passes on to her daughter, from pain which she inflicts upon her. Hope of discerning the power relations obtaining between two parties is greatly foreclosed when the thrust of a reading is, somewhat symptomatically, to collapse them into one: "The daughter is a melancholic echo of the mother. To speak against the mother is also to be the mother" (88).[11] By itself, then, the model of inherited trauma stops us short.

In order to conceive for Kingston's narrator the possibility of a pain that is not on loan, I add to these etiologies of suffering a concept of violence taken from feminist psychoanalysis, described by Laura Brown as follows:

"insidious trauma" . . . refers to the traumatogenic effects of oppression that are not necessarily overtly violent or threatening to bodily well-being at the given moment but that do violence to the soul and spirit. [Maria Root's] model suggests, for instance, that for all women living in a culture where there is a high base rate of sexual assault and where such behavior is considered normal and erotic by men, . . . [this constitutes] an exposure to insidious trauma. Most women in North America today are aware that they may be raped at any time and by anyone. . . . How then, do we understand the woman whose symptoms of psychic trauma have occurred entirely at secondhand, as it were, through the mechanism of insidious trauma? (Brown, 107)

Brown and Root offer the perpetual prospect of rape as classic example of a condition which engenders insidious trauma, and that archetypical instance can be readily mapped to Maxine's response to her No Name aunt's story.[12] I locate within this structural paradigm the conditions of an unrelieved potential disownment. It is true that Maxine herself is never offered up for sale, nor abandoned to her death, nor expunged from family annals for sexual transgression—but these possibilities make up the formative logic of her upbringing. The "threat" of such punishments or prospects is both indirect, in terms of her interpellation into (and thus perceived subject-position vulnerability as part of) a population to whom such things have been known to happen; and explicit in the forewarnings of her mother.[13] Her status as a daughter, as her mother makes plain, is conditional. Though she has never been and may well never be disowned, her affiliation to her parents is alive with the threat of disownment, much as a woman's existence may be shaped by the threat of rape though she herself is never raped. While I would like to suspend judgment on the question of how and whether the concept of clinical trauma is fully applicable in this context,[14] I believe the point of damage done is clear enough, and useful. As psychotherapist Maria Root herself asserts, "Validating distress is possible without assigning a psychiatric label" (Root, 258).

Of course, the fact that the harshest possibilities of Maxine's daughterhood are restricted to a discursive rather than an empirically lived reality is not without its import. It bears remark in Maxine's case, however, that despite their absence and unlikelihood in her life, grave possibilities are vivid and ever-present to her imagination—made so by her mother's efforts. "Now that you have started to menstruate, what happened to her could happen to you. . . . The villagers are watchful" (Kingston, *Warrior*, 5). Brave Orchid's statement here is at best exaggerated, but realistically evaluated, misleading, untrue. Should Maxine become pregnant with an illegitimate child in Stockton, California, of the

1960s, no chickens will be grotesquely slaughtered. No one will don masks to raid the Hong family home. In this context, Brave Orchid's desire to "warn [her children] about life" takes on multiple and more ominous meanings: Her cautionary tale holds less a defensive impulse—that which seeks to safeguard her girls from someone else's agenda—than an offensive one, which advances terms of her own by preemptive ultimatum. Should Maxine or her sisters perceptibly stray from chastity, whatever punishment befalls them will not arrive in the form of a community's vengeance upon the entire household, will not in this time and place spell destruction to the lives or livelihood of the family. It would be naïve to think Brave Orchid oblivious to this difference in context and implications—not only Orientalizing, but unfounded to imagine that the mother is trapped in "old-world" delusions, or unable to adjust her mind-set to a "new-world" reality. Rather, the injunction Brave Orchid delivers between the last sensational parts of her story is a moral distilled into the modest proportions of an immigrant family life: "Don't humiliate us." And the threat that follows is an entirely practicable one, entailing no grassroots-organizing of villagers, as it promises consequences consisting simply of parental prerogative: expulsion from the family, "to be forgotten as if you had never been born." The mother's warning is an ultimatum in the sense that living under the threat of disownment is always already an ultimatum: behave or be disowned. Yet through the aunt's story, a rhetorical act of parental control is recast as a preventative measure. Couched in these terms, disownment becomes an aggrieved family's response to a wayward child's wrongdoing, and Maxine's sexual conduct is entered into an equation whereby, in wreaking destruction upon herself, she will also bring harm to her family and oblige the family to injure her in order to preserve itself. The bare expression of power is thereby avoided: Disownment is but the regrettable end product of such an equation, and the child's responsibility to avert. Thus, the fact that "nothing happens" in what Kim terms "real life among the immigrants" *is* meaningful—but not in the sense that it cancels out or negates the discursive content of the culture. Rather, the "nothing" that seems to happen exists in a particular relation to power, power which prefers precisely the discursive, the disciplinary, rather than the directly dominating.[15]

the state of disownment ⁊

We have previously encountered the language of sovereign power in relation to the singular parental prerogative to determine, and not to determine, the boundaries of law. In tracing the threshold between the lawful and that which is outside the law, however, it is also the province of sovereign law to decree banishment, to disown. For the ruling made by sovereign power does not merely distinguish allowable from "unlawful" or "illegal" acts; rather, it decides between "the normal situation" (that which can be and is ruled by law), and "chaos" (to which law ceases to apply) (Agamben, 16). The "very space in which the . . . order [of law] can have validity" must be created and defined (19), and this task the sovereign accomplishes through the act of deciding the "state of exception." As the moment in which law chooses to suspend itself, the exception reveals the elemental mechanism of law: "the decision" of the sovereign, "in absolute purity" (15); the exception constitutes that threshold which bounds norm from chaos and *enables* the jurisdiction of the sovereign. A corollary of the prerogative to dictate the province of law is then the authority to assign citizenship or exile, selecting those who will or will not be considered subject to (within the province of), that power. Indeed, Agamben argues that the "*originary relation of law to life is not application but Abandonment*" (29; emphasis in original). It is the sovereign's prerogative to ban his subject which constitutes and upholds his power. Brave Orchid's preemptive ultimatum must be understood in these terms. Maxine, and her narrative, are haunted by the threat of abandonment: the ghost of the aunt expunged from the family, the narrator's oft-repeated fear of being "sold," "unloaded," as a daughter unworthy to keep (Kingston, *Warrior*, 190). "I would not have sold a daughter such as that one" (80), Brave Orchid remarks of her slave girl; but to Maxine's horror, this is very much *not* the same as saying, "I would not have sold a daughter."

Daughterhood is conditional in a universe of sovereign parental power, and the ever-present ultimatum is a function of this conditionality. Disownment underlies each behavioral directive and every expectation that goes unspoken or unarticulated, even those that have not yet been imagined. Each transgression, small or large, violates not a single rule, but the very contract[16] of filiality: behave or be disowned. This "condition of impending 'exile'" (Bow, *Betrayal*, 32) underpins the sovereign state per Agamben's characterization, "in which the most innocent gesture of the smallest forgetfulness can have most extreme consequences" (Agamben, 52); it also explains the frequent seeming disproportion of penalty to transgression in Jade Snow Wong's narrative, which she describes as "[h]aving been cruelly—and sometimes inexplicably—punished" (JS Wong, x). Her father inflicts punishment on her, not for being seven minutes late, but for "disregard[ing her] word to [him]" (66); not for wearing slippers around the house, but for "turn[ing] the organization of [his] household into chaos" (83)—in other words, for failing her conditions as a daughter, and violating the order of his sovereign law. Evincing a similar logic in *The Joy Luck Club*, Jing-mei's mother declares "Only two kinds of daughters . . . Those who are obedient and those who follow their own mind! Only one kind of daughter can live in this house. Obedient daughter!" (Tan, 142). Because obedience encompasses everything, the conditionality of daughterhood and order of law are manifest in even the minutiae of family life: whether "you wave brooms around or drop chopsticks or drum them" (Kingston, *Warrior*, 185). And thus it is the whole unwieldy mechanism of the ultimatum which is brought to bear in each transgression, large or small. There is no such thing as transgression in fractions, because there is no such thing as disownment to scale. Filiality, like the very structure of an ultimatum, is either/or: all or nothing.

∾ the form of suffering

In a universe so ruled by sovereign power, it is improbable that the subject have spent 13 good years of conditioning without having been once (or regularly) exposed to the threat of Abandonment. The story with which the memoir opens is thus unlikely to have been Maxine's first initiation into the contract of disownment, but it *is* the one with which she chooses to initiate her readers. In attempting to imagine her aunt's history, Maxine expresses a preference for those versions of conduct, courses of action, with which she herself can "relate"—in the very distinctive sense that these are versions which can help her explain something about herself. She calls the unknown woman "my aunt, my forerunner" (Kingston, 8), and thus claims likenesses of lineage with this figure from whom she is not directly descended. Indeed, it is with transfusions of her own subjectivity which the narrator fills that cipher of filial failure, in order to imply a vaguely causal logic between them: "Unless I can see her life *branching into mine*, she gives me no ancestral help" (8; emphasis added). In that version she savors most elaborately, Maxine ascribes a purposeful agency to this forerunner, including both intent to stray and methodical implementation:

> She wanted him to look back (9)
> her hair lured her imminent lover (10). She brushed her hair back from her forehead, tucking the flaps behind her ears. She looped a piece of thread, knotted into a circle between her index fingers and thumbs, and ran the double strand across her forehead. . . . Then she pulled the thread away from her skin, ripping the hairs out neatly. (9)

In other words, if across all the possible versions of this forbidden story the ending is the same (destruction, death, disownment), it is only the beginnings that can differ—and of those possible beginnings, Maxine prefers the versions which both flirt the most with disaster and wind most closely to her. It is as if the wistful re-teller of this tale, herself, deliberately courts that end half of the if/then ultimatum. The willful disobedience she ascribes to her aunt reflects back on the self-styled successor, as she toys with the thought of coming to a similar end, drowning and all. As one whose psyche is abuzz with threats that never materialize, injuries that do not bear telling, the niece displays a mixture of fear and envy for the undeniable brutality and narrative impact of the aunt's demise: Maxine claims that "[her] aunt haunts [her]— . . . waits silently by the water to pull down a substitute" (16).

Casting the "No Name Woman" into such prominence as the first of five chapters of her memoir (and by implication a veritable cornerstone of her own subjectivity) permits the writer to infuse the language, imagery, and proportions of her aunt's story into her own narrative. As a narrative tactic, this one gains her by proxy the borrowed dimensions of a violent breach, a traumatic ending—indirection being the fitting means through which to generate the echo of anger, the refraction of violence. To make sense of her own sexual anxieties, for instance, Maxine begins by speculating that her aunt's lover may have been a villager or kinsman, and conjures from that perspective a situation in which the anxiety of incest is projected onto every potential union:

> Any man within visiting distance would have been neutralized as a lover—
> "brother," "younger brother," "older brother"—one hundred and fifteen
> relationship titles. Parents researched birth charts *probably* not so much
> to assure good fortune as to circumvent incest in a population that has
> but one hundred surnames. Everybody has eight million relatives. How
> useless then sexual mannerisms, how dangerous. (Kingston, *Warrior*, 12;
> emphasis added)

From here Maxine segues immediately to her own present-day anxieties, relating them to this conjectural cultural and familial past: "As if it came from an atavism deeper than fear, I used to add 'brother' silently to boys' names. It hexed the boys, who would or would not ask me to dance, and made them less scary" (12). It having been her mother's practice to employ morality tales of this order in shaping Maxine's expectations, convictions, and fears, the young narrator's compulsion to desexualize the boys of her acquaintance, and to "hex" herself thereby so that she has "no dates" (12), is not an unreasonable manner of abiding by Brave Orchid's charge that Maxine not allow "what happened to [the aunt to] . . . happen to [her]" (5). The language she chooses alludes to the specter of rape, and to an unsettling sense of culpability for one's own violation—having invited the gaze and thus the assault: "I had no idea . . . how to make attraction selective, how to control its direction and magnitude" (12). Such indiscriminate fear is a common expression of sexualized (insidious) trauma, and as Maxine proceeds to elaborate on her own feelings of endangerment in connection with female sexual agency and kinship, these themes catch the flashpoints of the aunt's speculated history: desire, rape, guilt, victimization.[17] These are the very ingredients which the narrator handles, combining them in different ratios to imagine alternate histories for the No Name Woman.

However "imaginary" the genetics of atavism here, the trope of lineage has its uses, making Maxine very much heir to her aunt's legacy, if not via genetic coding so much as by way of its consistent deployment in her socialization—and via the narrator's own assertion of an extended comparison between them. Collapsing the disparities between these far-flung episodes of Chinese-village past and Stockton-California present enables the narrator to imply a certain intergenerationally iterated "plot" under way, one which may culminate in a predetermined outcome: However dissimilar the aunt's story and her own may seem, all versions of conduct, all courses of action, all beginnings are likely to yield the same failure and punishing ending. In thus linking the No Name Woman's story to her own, Maxine employs not only an associative logic which leaks the tone and atmosphere of traumatic events into her mundane history, but also the architecture of analogy, which opens her "American-normal" (87) story to the possibility of dire consequences. A narrative of Maxine's "real life" as apart from "the invisible world the emigrants built around [their children's] childhoods" (5)—a narrative limited to demonstrable events and devoid of a cultural and familial imaginary of penality, disownment, and rape—would be incorrect to the conditions of her upbringing. Choosing to represent her aunt's history as a portentous reflection of her own thus enables the narrator to map out the paradoxical: threats which are present in their absence, insidious in their violence, real in their suspended actuality. Like Cheng, then, Kingston opens her book with the story of someone else's pain, and proceeds with what is a kind of reversed mirror-stage, in which the reflection adopted is both truly the self and a fiction; in this case, however, the subject assumes as herself an image more shattered than her own, because it articulates a sense of fragmentation that no mirror can extrapolate from her own, smooth surface.[18] How difficult otherwise to express an imaginary inflected by disasters which have not yet, but yet may happen.

Let us be mindful, however, that diligent though the comparison with her aunt may be, Maxine is no stranger to the fundamentally fictional nature of this identification, and to the irreducible differences between them. Even in the midst of drawing analogies, the narrator cultivates a constant misalignment between their stories, of which we are made implicitly aware. Conceivably, she might have chosen to draw a parallel between those anxieties surrounding potential sexual encounters she imagines for her aunt, and the anxieties with which she herself has come to struggle in negotiating an adult sexual life and identity. Instead, however, she juxtaposes her aunt's full-grown fears, actions, and consequences with the ineffectual angst of a grade-school girl—even though it has been "twenty years since [she] heard [the] story" (16) and an older perspective is certainly a viable authorial option. We downshift from discussing women and men, "inseminators" (11) and "lovers," to considering "boys" in "class"; and the operative questions are no longer the identity of one's inseminator, but "who would or would not ask [a girl] to dance" (12). This lopsided pairing produces a sense of diminishment which mocks the very equivalence it proposes; by thus amplifying it the narrator draws attention to (and acknowledges) a contextual dis-parity. Like her mother, Maxine is aware that factually and literally speaking, her aunt's fate is highly unlikely to befall her: no villagers, no chickens. And like her mother, Maxine proceeds to translate the moral of this tale into terms more in keeping with her own life: "The real punishment was not the raid swiftly inflicted by the villagers, but the family's deliberate forgetting her" (16). Like Brave Orchid, the narrator recognizes that punishment, and power, within their immigrant family are less the flashy violence, more the silent enactment. Yet Maxine reveals the bias of her position when she says that a daughter's "real punishment" is disownment. In weighing more lightly the raid and the pigsty, and more gravely the forgetting perpetuated by her own parents in the present, the narrator continues to cultivate the difference between herself and her aunt, but reevaluates the misalignment such that the dramatic afflictions undergone by the aunt no longer stand as the measure of true suffering. Rather, one knows a daughter by the suffering they share: her sheer vulnerability—active even in the seemingly mildest of circumstances—to that structural relation which is banishment, that discursive exercise which is erasure from discourse.

If the examination above hints at some measure of defensiveness in the narrator's stance, such is arguably the case. Much lies at stake for her in the definition and quantification of "true suffering," for suffering is a variable in the calculus of debt. Between her own life-story and those of the first generation, Maxine perceives a gulf of disparity in narratable misery: In *China Men*, in the midst of relating a conversation with her mother's youngest sister, Maxine confesses to us that, "I would never be able to talk with [women of my aunt's age]; I have *no stories of equal pain*" (*Men*, 207; emphasis added). This statement attests to a sentiment that suffering yields returns in legitimacy, or authority to speak, as if status in a dialogue (the ability to "talk *with*," not "talk to") must be earned through tears, sweat, or blood. The second-generation narrator is at a distinct disadvantage in this respect, given that her sufferings amount neither to legends of folk history nor to epics of nation-building, no great toil nor trouble. As we have seen, even her bodily suffering makes for no decent story at all, as its most noteworthy instance is that in which "Nothing happened" (*Warrior*, 182). What she has instead are strange one-liners in a "laundry" list:

I had grown inside me a list of over two hundred things that I had to tell my mother so that she would know the true things about me and to stop the pain in my throat. When I first started counting, I had only thirty-six items: how I had prayed for a white horse of my own—white, the bad, mournful color . . . How I had picked on a girl and made her cry. How I had stolen from the cash register and bought candy for everybody I knew . . . How I had jumped head-first off the dresser, not accidentally, but so I could fly. Then there were my fights at Chinese school. . . . And the obscene caller that phoned us at home when the adults were at the laundry. (197)

Given voice, her experiences "sound . . . like nothing" even to her own ears (198); and to her mother, whose life is replete with stories of human and paranormal drama, climax and denouement, Maxine's stored-up confessions sound like "[s]enseless gabbings," a "[w]hispering, whispering, making no sense" (200). Her attempts to communicate and process her distress are disabled by its triviality and incoherence. The fragments that make up Maxine's experience have no narrative order, no discernable story line, and therefore no claim to pathos. As we see it here, the list is a form bereft of linkages, unmindful of all but the loosest of contexts, and made to contain those things which one might otherwise forget, because they are consummately forgettable. Sheer accumulation of the small and seemingly unrelated gains in absurdity rather than consequence; personal testimony rests, it seems, on its ability to produce narrative for its claims on readerly identification and sympathy. In the second novel, the narrator mentions the tug-of-war between another aunt in China and her son in the States, in which the mother alternates between pleading that he return and admonishing that he stop spending money on his American children (especially the daughters), to remit the funds to her.[19] She reasons, "If you don't have stories that are equally heart-rending, you have nothing better to do with your money than send it to me" (*Men*, 175). The alchemy which converts suffering into story, pathos into dues, applies itself directly to intergenerational comparisons and the resulting economics of the family.[20]

In her account of Mad Sao, Maxine quotes from a procession of letters written by the mother to her son, detailing her hardships; excerpts from the mother's letters follow one after another without a word interjected from the son. The narrator indicates that her cousin does *respond* to his mother's correspondences: He sends photographs of his life in America, and one would surmise that along with these pictures come written messages of his own. Yet the narrator omits altogether the son's verbal replies, as if they are irrelevant or immaterial—whatever he may write, the essence of his response is in the wordless, narrative-less snapshot; whatever he may say, his is not to talk *with* his mother in an exchange of words, and to talk *to* is equivalent to saying nothing at all. Moreover, the narrative bars readers not only from the content of the cousin's letters, but from knowing the nature or direction of his reaction to his mother's requests. American children— -born, -raised, or apparently in this case, -identified ("Sao firmly established his American citizenship by serving in the U.S. Army in World War II" [171])—who cannot counter narrative with narrative may opt to disregard the suffering of older generations as it accrues indebtedness to them, or they may opt alternatively to acquiesce to its demands. "He did nothing for her, *or* he did plenty, and it was not enough" (173; emphasis added). But neither of these options is desirable, and the narrator suggests that in effect they are neither very different.[21] The two options seem interchangeable, and equally insufficient; the end in either case is the same: a slighted mother, a mad son.

Several moments in the narrative suggest that Maxine may have chosen the first course of action: In living away from the family, she refuses compliance with what her aged mother claims is the "only one thing that I really want anymore. I want you here . . . I want every one of you living here together" (*Warrior*, 107). Like her cousin, she resists a mother's pleas to come home. In her late-night conversation with Brave Orchid, Maxine exhibits an intense resistance to hearing her mother's stories of pain, for they wind implicitly, inevitably, toward intimations of debt.

> [Brave Orchid] leaned forward, eyes brimming with what she was about to say: "I work so hard," she said. She was doing her stare—at what? My feet began rubbing together as if to tear each other's skin off. She started talking again, "The tomato vines prickle my hands; I can feel their little stubble hairs right through my gloves. . . . Oh, but it's the potatoes that will ruin my hands. I'll get rheumatism washing potatoes, squatting over potatoes." (103)

The narrator's response is first severe discomfort, a sense—suspicion or paranoia—of incrimination. The words "I work so hard" signal, much as "Once upon a time" signals, the beginning of a genre of narrative, and the listener braces for the story and unvarying homily to come.[22] Her response is next to suggest, "'Mama, why don't you stop working? You don't have to work anymore'" (103)—plausibly an attempt to abort the developing recital, or perhaps to prevent the addition of future iterations (and slow the accumulation of future debt). The attempt, however, proves unsuccessful, as her mother continues storytelling. "'I have not stopped working since the day the ship landed [in the U.S.]. I was on my feet the moment the babies were out. In China I never even had to hang up my own clothes. I shouldn't have left, but your father couldn't have supported you without me'" (104). And within moments we have arrived at the naming of parental sacrifice: ancestral sacrifice for the sake of the descendant/listener. At this, Maxine moves quickly not only to shut down the narrative, but to dismantle its claims by disclosing the contradictions, the illogic of a story which holds the child to account for parental decision-making: "'If you hadn't left, there wouldn't have been a me for you two to support. Mama, I'm really sleepy. Do you mind letting me sleep?'" (104). The narrative faintly reflects upon and signals her callousness in this instant ("I do not believe in old age. I do not believe in getting tired"), much as it will later censure her brisk dismissal of her mother's labor, exhaustion, and complaints about the unrelenting American pressure to work:

> I have worked too much. Human beings don't work like this in China. Time goes slower there. Here we have to hurry, feed the hungry children before we're too old to work. . . . I would still be young if we lived in China.
> Time is the same from place to place," I said unfeelingly. (105)

Nevertheless, the moment is one of filial rejection, a fending-off of the impending request for her return, to live as a child in the family home.

In a move more subversive still, the narrator continues by comparing her disobedience to her parents' own "unfiliality," and thus positions her parents, like Mad Sao, as failed American children: "The gods pay her and my father back for leaving their parents. My grandmother wrote letters pleading for them to come home, and they ignored her. Now they know how she felt" (108). In this way it is implied that, with the very fact of immigration, the first generation has unwittingly established an altered order of debt and payment; the very decision which Brave Orchid would have represent her selfless sacrifice for her daughter ("I shouldn't have left, but your father couldn't have supported you without me"), is re-narrated as a selfish act of unfiliality, and the point of origin for a new intergenerational pattern. Rather than reigning as the last and greatest ancestor, the immigrant generation is rewritten as the first and worst descendant, after which the accounting system flips: accruing to them penalties rather than interest. Maxine's refusal to return home is then not a refusal to repay her parents, but instead the proper and poetic payment, by decree of the gods.

the structure of ambivalence ∾

With such an argument the narrator seems firmly entrenched in her stance of refusal—her indifference to parental claims—but in fact while she resists those claims Maxine is much affected by them. "To be the objects of . . . ambivalence," as Cheng notes, "means having ambivalent responses of one's own" (Cheng, 70). Much as the beginning of her mother's story induces in her the impulse to chafe the skin off her own feet, the narrator who "shut her teeth together, vocal cords cut, they hurt so," because she "would not speak words to give her [mother] pain" (Kingston, *Warrior*, 101) does not show the true disregard in her resistance which, for instance, her aunt's teenage boys do. Brave Orchid's youngest sister reports, in the previously mentioned conversation with Maxine, that her boys "shout at [her] and tell [her she's] too stupid to understand. They hardly come home, and when [she] ask[s] them what they're doing, they say [she's] dumb. . . . [A]nd after all [she has] suffered for them" (*Men*, 206). Maxine's boy cousins model the wholesale rejection of parental need, and such seems to require not only a keen personal indifference, but an offensive (even if perhaps as a form of the defensive) willingness to cause injury.[23] In contrast, the narrator perceives, and experiences, Brave Orchid's verbalized request for her return as an acute infliction, of pain and of duty, upon herself: "A spider headache spreads out in fine branches over my skull. She is etching spider legs into the icy bone. She pries open my head and my fists and crams into them responsibility for time, responsibility for intervening oceans" (*Warrior*, 108). Despite her various attempts to overturn and undo the logic of her indebtedness, the narrator continues to feel deeply implicated, the bearer of these responsibilities even if against her will.

It is not entirely surprising, then, that Maxine seems alternately, in other moments, to acquiesce to her mother's wishes, accepting the terms which manufacture debt ("I would never be able to talk with them; I have no stories of equal pain"), and thus her beholden position. "I did not want to hear how [my mother] suffered, and then I did. I did have a duty to hear it and remember it" (*Men*, 207). The very notion of duty entails a sense of moral obligation, and of course some manner of dues. What's more, the narrator's very swordswoman fantasies, another of the first novel's imaginative axes and principal discursive realities, turn upon a wish for "perfect filiality": to provide for her parents such that her efforts leave nothing wanting, and the ever-watchful villagers would finally approve.

> My mother and father and the entire clan would be living happily on the money I had sent them. My parents had bought their coffins. They would sacrifice a pig to the gods that I had returned. From the words on my back, and how they were fulfilled, the villagers would make a legend about my perfect filiality. (*Warrior*, 45)

Obligation takes familiar shapes in Maxine's dreams: the sending of (enough) money, and the child's return to the home. The words etched onto her swordswoman's back list not only grievances (35), but accounts to be settled—settled upon the family's oppressors, to be sure, but also settled by the daughter herself: "'Wherever you go, whatever happens to you, people will know our *sacrifice*,' my mother said. 'And you'll never forget either'" (34; emphasis added);[24] her flesh bears a promise, a contract, which in the persona of Fa Mu Lan she is able to "fulfill." In her daily life as Maxine, however, the narrator faces the dilemma she confers on Mad Sao: "[she] did plenty, and it was not enough." In their late-night conversation, the narrator assures her mother that, "'I'll be back again soon. . . . You know that I come back,'" to which Brave Orchid responds, "'You have never come back. 'I'll be back on Turkeyday,' you said. Huh'" (101), negating her daughter's assertion outright. Yet Brave Orchid's accusation is factually false—it belies Maxine's physical presence in her childhood bed in the very moment that the statement is uttered—and signifies the erasure of not only this return but all others. If the narrator's incremental acts of compliance do not "count" then, as we have seen in *Fifth Chinese Daughter*, no "plenty" can build up to an "enough" of filial obedience. Obedience is again an all or a nothing; "perfect filiality" is legend precisely in that it is myth, fantasy, fairy tale.

Given the heartlessness of one and the hopelessness of the other, the two options presented to Maxine (to try to please her parents and fail, or not to try at all) leave her little option but to invent a third. Rather than turn a deaf ear to her mother's sufferings, and rather than verbalize an existence which itself goes unheard, the narrator attempts through a new configuration of memoir to secure a validity for her realities, and a place for herself in dialogue. The complex and experimental formal structure of Kingston's memoir has been acknowledged as a dynamic and even interactive construction: the mixtures of genres and discourses "execute[ ] disarrangements and defamiliarization," Wendy Ho observes, which convey that "writing is not transparent but something to be decoded and reconstructed through the reader's or listener's collaborative efforts" (Ho, Writing, 236). Shirley Lim characterizes the book's structure as "fragments, of stories, ideas, thoughts, images, asides, which *circle around* and *accumulate* to form the expression of the idea of Chinese American female subjectivity" (Lim, 263; emphasis added). The consensus would be that the text actively generates meaning through juxtaposition and disjunction, ambiguity and irresolution—through the open-ended connection between seemingly disparate parts. We will spend some time building on such observations here, for in the particulars of Kingston's formal inventiveness are articulated the terms of Maxine's third option.

The five sections of the book, and the movements within them, are joined by no clear logic of chronology or convergence; these are chapters in a particular order, and yet not linear in development; they are not numbered. In fact, the format of the title page suggests not progression, but a list. Unnumbered, the items do not reflect an ordered hierarchy, but instead a looseness as if gathered by their implicit association: they are all equally the "Contents" of the text, the "contents" of the memoir's subjectivity. The table of contents thus offers a visual representation of Maxine's new narrative form: she has made a story out of her list, and a list out of her story. Each "item: in the table, like each of the "over two hundred things that [she] had to tell [her] mother" (Kingston, *Warrior*, 197), has countless stories "behind" it. But when a young Maxine attempts to "narrate" her list she relates it via her actions, relying on chronological sequence and realist setting, and casting about for "the end": "'I killed a spider . . . I returned every day to look at its smear on the side of the house . . . It was our old house, the one we lived in until I was five. I went to the wall every day to look. I studied the stain'" (198). Her utter inability to communicate the meaning of this item, as evidenced by its reception as "nothing" and "senseless," reveals that the plotted narrative of incident is grossly inappropriate to her experiences as a Chinese American daughter of immigrant parents. A gap in representation such as we noted in *Fifth Chinese Daughter* shows itself plainly here, for no strand of occasions, however finely strung, suitably amounts to an account of Maxine's qualitatively uneventful life. As an older and wiser narrating persona, Maxine thus makes a crucial adjustment: The chapters of *The Woman Warrior* do not stand for "the time that" such and such "happened"; their titles refer to things that never actually "happened" in her life at all. Like the title of the book itself, they name, instead, components of the discourses that form her, the stories she grows up on: "No Name Woman," "White Tigers," "Shaman," "At the Western Palace," "A Song for a Barbarian Reed Pipe." (Wong's chapters, in contrast, are named "Girl Meets Boy," or "A Life Plan is Cast.") Drawing upon the various figures of her subjective cosmology enables the narrator, as Gayle Sato observes and we have seen, "to reconstruct the context of her own disappointing American life" (Sato, 203)—and, moreover, to foreground that psychical and discursive "context" as the very substance of her life worth narrating. The events of Maxine's life may be negligible, but in the economy of heart-rending stories, redefining the content of narrative also redefines the forms of suffering upon which it is based. One might say that shifting the threshold, the province, of story is the prerogative of authorial power, and that if Kingston deems Maxine's suffering worth telling, then Maxine has stories to tell. Unlike Wong, who focuses on the mundanities of her factual history and chronicles exemplary incidents, Kingston dedicates almost no paper to these, composing her story instead out of the elements of her imaginary. And strategically so, because the realities of the imaginary need not be proven; its realities are true by virtue of being imagined.

Earlier in this chapter we traced the narrator's convoluted use of the fable of the unfilial daughter; weaving back and forth between differences and similarities, Maxine speaks at times with a voice distinct from her aunt's, at others with a subjectivity folded into hers. If her intricate identification with the No Name Woman integrates into Maxine's narrative the reverberations of violence, her assumption of Fa Mu Lan's subject position gains her access to a reflected filiality. The voice and authority of the mythic, *exemplary* daughter offer themselves to her disposal, and enable the narrator to articulate *within the first person* an achievement of the unattainable daughterhood, fulfillment of the impossible task: "My mother and father and the entire clan would be living happily on the money I had sent them" (Kingston, 45).[25] The ethos of this legend, furthermore, neatly echoes the terms of Brave Orchid's disciplinary horror story, and reverses it: rather than carrying out the mother's punishment, "the villagers would make a legend about my perfect filiality." Within the realm of the imaginary, Maxine can demonstrate that she has heard her parents' wishes as well as assert her sincere desire to meet them; these sentiments have no need of material proof when spoken like needs in a dream. Her filiality is real by virtue of her stating that it is so. Within the imaginary, Maxine is even able to work out a step-by-step program of deeds and actions which will lead her to the desired endpoint of becoming a "good daughter." Ironically, the superhuman feats of Fa Mu Lan's education seem far more reasonable and attainable than the quotidian requirements of Jade Snow or Maxine's girlhoods, because of the respective pedagogical systems in which they operate: "The two old people led me in exercises that began at dawn and ended at sunset," Maxine-*qua*-woman warrior tells us, and "I learned" (23). Arguably, then, the imaginary enables for Maxine a discursive intervention into, commentary upon, and answer to the discourses of her formation: She models in this alternate reality an alternative set of training principles, a structure which is not built around designated failure, and which therefore allows for actualization—pending the appearance of fairy godparents.

And on that condition rests a great deal of what we are to make of Kingston's contribution to the political unconscious, as that collective effort to resolve in art that which defies resolution aside of it (Jameson, 64). While Kingston is able to access within her memoir a filial persona in that of the woman warrior, she is forever mindful of the gap between them, and the two identities do not become one. The narrator is selective in her identification, and vigilant about letting the seams show. Reminders of disparity between herself and this fabled persona are even more dramatic and unequivocal than her strategies for signaling difference from the No Name Woman. The fantasy of "perfect filiality" breaks off into a series of direct contrasts, as abrupt as starting from a dream:

My American life has been such a disappointment.
"I got straight A's, Mama."
"Let me tell you a story about a girl who saved her village." (Kingston, 45)

The narrative is thus a dream *about* dreaming, its structure of resolution a fairy tale once-removed. Even more than it wishes for the fulfillment of filiality, Kingston's memoir is about the successes and failures of borrowing, the power and shortcomings of discursive intervention. Sato terms Maxine's layering of identities a "superimposing" of realities, and I would second this argument by adding that the variegated elements of the narrative are not subjected to a homogenizing synthesis or convergence, but remain deliberately multiple. Patricia Blinde recognizes in *The Woman Warrior* a "tension generated by the work . . . which arises [not only] from the content but . . . from the struggle of forms" (Blinde, 61). However, she also claims that an autobiography such as Jade Snow Wong's "imposes a pattern of life and constructs out of it a coherent story" (59), while Kingston's narrative does not. Blinde praises Kingston's form as "report[ing] 'reality' at its most real—namely the unstructured flow of events, thoughts, places, and people without the constraints of time, place, or other predetermined concepts" (61)—but disjunction, multiplicity, and paradox are not the same as unstructured formlessness. Rather, Kingston's text has a very distinct form and pattern, making story of list and list of story. The list which "forms" this story does not synthesize its assorted items, but it nevertheless creates a larger unity: the logic of the list itself, which not only contains its elements but implies and enables linkages between them which it does not fix or specify. Such a form is in practice the most elaborate of structures: one balanced on ambivalence and defined by irresolution. Such a form makes apparent not only the events, thoughts, places, and people of its narratives, but the "tensions" that bind them together. Kingston's work is therefore not a narrative of incident, but of the forces of resistance which act between two bodies, even when they are at a standstill; it is a narrative of *friction*, embodied in the narrative form itself. That which eludes Wong's autobiography, and/or that which she seeks to suppress or rebury, becomes the "subject matter" and focus of Kingston's: the dissonance between dueling discourses, the inability to match up, which constitutes the true content of her reality.

The Woman Warrior's experimental structure implies a certain incommensurability to Maxine's subjectivity. Its many stories, each a fable of origin, each an explanation of self, insist that no solitary structure can subsume the diverse fragments into a single logic. The narrative structure is resistant, rebellious, hostile to reconciliation. The longing for a resolution its structural integrity cannot achieve, however, is the note on which it begins and ends. Maxine's near-end epiphany that, as far as the list of her life is concerned, there is "No higher listener. No listener but myself"[26] (Kingston, 203) is belied by the book's dedication: "To Mother and Father." That dedication page, followed immediately by the table of contents, suggests that all in all, the bent of Maxine's third option is still very much to tell her list to her mother, "so that she would know the true things about me and to stop the pain in my throat" (197). And the book's last fable is distinctly redemptive in tone, unironic in a way that Cheng, ironically, finds out of character, "staged" and unconvincing (Cheng, 90).[27] The tale of the artist in exile whose work Maxine pronounces to have "translated well" (209) symbolizes both Brave Orchid and her daughter, melding their identities much as the story itself forms a single continuity of their work: "Here is a story my mother told me, not when I was young, but recently, when I told her I also talk-story. The beginning is hers, the ending, mine" (206). There are no markers of difference or reminders of disparity in this last fable, not between any two of the three identities in play. The result is the implication of a smoothly continuous familial line, heredity without a hint of intergenerational conflict—which lies against the grain of the overall narrative. Yet if, again, "no text is entirely compromised by its narrative resolution" (Bow, 110), this text is even less so than most. For the concluding talk-story, with its decisive "happily ever after, "is not so incongruous with its predecessors as might first appear. If what we have witnessed, in "At the Western Palace" for instance, has been Maxine's figurative disownment of her parents, then the last movement of the memoir is but a figurative reconciliation. It is a myth, an imaginative conjecture, of what redemption might be. It is voiced in neither Maxine's terms nor her mother's, but in a third option. It is an ending finally different, regardless of what its recurring beginnings may have been. It is imaginatively, discursively real, and yet importantly distinct from waking life: The text does not claim that the Hong generations have made familial peace, does not force that ending. It tells a story, of what has not yet, but yet may happen.

3 §

The Caring of Jailers

Evelyn Lau, Catherine Liu

This journal covers the two years of my life after I ran away from home. . . . Although it may sound hard to believe, all the events that took place during these two years were easier on me emotionally than living at home, which is why I have never gone back there to live.

Evelyn Lau, *Runaway*

Although expecting one's daughter to become a doctor or law-yer may not be an outrageous demand by parents in any cul-ture, . . . Lau paints her mother as a dictator . . . Paradoxically, her parents are also presented as failing to support her career development even though she was on the honour roll every year and won some junior literary competitions. They forbade her any playtime and disapproved of her interest in writing and her involvement in the peace movement.

Lien Chao, "From Testimony to Erotica"

I want somebody to slap me around and hurl abuse at me. I can't hurt myself enough—why?

Evelyn Lau, *Runaway*

Though it catapulted her to mainstream fame, and notoriety, the publication of Evelyn Lau's *Runaway: Diary of a Street Kid* (1989)[1] was not well received by the Chinese Canadian community. An abridged journal of the teenager's two years on the sidewalks of Canadian cities, in and out of social services and strangers' homes, the book devotes the bulk of its pages to her harrowing accounts of homelessness, hunger, beatings, drug use, prostitution, and to her ongoing dialogue with her psychiatrist. Framing and underlying these accounts, however, are the writer's condemnation of her parents and bitter rejection of the immigrant home. Deploring what she believes to be Lau's political (and financial) opportunism, Canadian critic Lien Chao reported that the bestseller's "nationwide promotion . . . offended the Chinese Canadian community collectively" (Chao, 171). Whether this collectivity takes into account all (subject) positions is open to question, but the book and its popularity do seem to have drawn the ire of prominent community figures:

> In an article reprinted in *Chinese Canadian Women's Forum* from an earlier publication in *The Newsletter of Chinese Canadian National Council*, Beryl Tsang, board member of the CCNC Toronto Chapter, points out that *Runaway* presents "the Chinese Canadian community in a negative light" . . . "It presents Chinese families as authoritarian, overly strict and unidimensional." (171)

Chao's careful tracking of the authorial and print sources of the statements above is intended to convey the cultural legitimacy of the view expressed therein. For our purposes, however, it also reveals the investments of the speaker, the origins of its bias: If to speak ill of the family is tantamount to portraying the community in general in a "negative light," then the community is considered coextensive with the family unit itself, and Tsang speaks from his position at the *head of* an imagined family or extended (collective of) families. It is from this place in the familial and communal hierarchy that Tsang pronounces the author a bad daughter and subject, redoubling the actions of her own nuclear family. Moreover, Tsang's language in effect disowns her, defining Lau *out* of both the Chinese Canadian community and Chinese family by referring to her "portrayal" of these institutions as if the daughter/writer herself were an abjection—perhaps in the body, but not of it. Tsang demonstrates that the community, like the family itself, is defined by its heads, not by its products, who are policed for their loyalty to a collective whose "good" may not take them into account. This official community statement recalls the retaliation of villagers for Kingston's No Name aunt's indiscretion, at the same time that it represents the family-community's indignance at having "lost face" to the other "villagers" of the nation. Thus, the community's excommunication of Lau is, in essence, a penalty for perceived disloyalty. The act of disownment, like the "language of betrayal," "signals the artifice of naturalized racial, ethnic, or national belonging" (Bow,

Betrayal, 11); both deployments of power lay bare the means by which "affiliations are formed and then consolidated," by revealing the identifications of those whose interests they move to defend. And if so, it is useful to consider, as Leslie Bow proposes, "reconceptualizing 'disloyalty' as resistance to repressive authority. If women have a reason to be . . . 'disloyal to civilization,' then this betrayal of racism, patriarchy, . . . a repressive state"—or the family or community—"constitutes a form of creative activism for Asian American women" (11).

Catherine Liu's *Oriental Girls Desire Romance* (1997) has not met with the kind of contentious response (or widespread publicity) that greeted Lau's first book; billed as a novel, it forgoes the sensationalistic cachet of a 14-year-old's nonfiction diary. Set in New York in the 1980s, the book compiles a fragmented portrait of a second-generation Chinese American woman, a graduate student in philosophy, via accounts of "her uncompromising Communist father and depressive mother, her teachers and lovers, drag queens, . . . her experimentation with drugs, a series of temporary office jobs, and a stint as a stripper"—aspects regarded as "essential components of her identity" (Strecker), at least for the time being. Described by the author as a "fictional autobiography," however, it is written in the first person from the perspective of a narrator whose name is never revealed,[2] and is structured loosely as a series of vignettes rather than by a continuous story arc. In these ways, the book recalls some of the narrative challenges and formal strategies of *The Woman Warrior*—and reads more like a journal than most novels are wont. Whatever critical slings and arrows their predecessors' work may have suffered for disappointing expectations of communal loyalty, however, it would not be surprising if Lau and Liu's texts have suffered worse. The critical and rebellious sentiments that drove Wong's storytelling in *Fifth Chinese Daughter* were laboriously offset by equal and opposite measures toward suppression and containment, and Kingston's representation of familial dynamics in *The Woman Warrior* was often more figurative than frank.[3] Whether through narrative discretion or narrative extravagance, in other words, these earlier narrators relied on strategies of distancing, so as not to commit themselves unequivocally to the uncomfortable position of exposing and indicting their own parents. By contrast, those parental prerogatives which Jade Snow described and Maxine stylized as frustrating and inexplicable events, the narrators of *Runaway* and *Oriental Girls* lay bare as modes of surveillance, as patterns of discursive domination, and as parental investments less in the well-being and more in the submission of the child. Harsh to the ears though their indictments of familial power may be, however, I suggest that the critical indignation these texts have drawn for breaking rank is ill-placed. As Barbara Christian reminds us, for marginalized subjects, "literature is . . . one way by which they come to understand their lives better"; here "in narrative forms, in the stories [they] create," such subjects seek to "unmask [. . .] the power relations of their world" (Christian, 38). It is hardly our place to stop them.

This chapter will trace the evolution in economic relations within the immigrant family over the latter half of the twentieth century, in response to changing opportunities for the model minority. Lau and Liu's narratives suggest that, as second-generation children become viable capital investments, raised to enter the lucrative math- and science-based professional fields now open to them, the unprofitable pursuit of literature can become an overdetermined act of self-preservation and disobedience, and an interesting precursor to other forms of masochistic rebellion. While *Runaway* and *Oriental Girls* are, in many thematic respects, remarkably similar, it should prove informative rather than redundant to examine them in conjunction. Juxtaposed, they demonstrate, as neither alone could, the degree to which conventions of the Asian American model minority have been codified and have pervaded familial culture. In other words, it is precisely the unpremeditated consensus of these two texts that deserves attention, the very degree and detail to which they echo one another that beg understanding:

> I would be in my room minding my own business when I'd hear [my mother's] footsteps on the stairs. I'd put away my book [a novel] and start staring at my math notebook, which would be lying open to yesterday's math homework. She'd stand in the doorway, arms akimbo, and say with a frown, what are you doing over there. (Liu, 269)

> I went submissively to my bedroom and stayed there, descending into months of depression alleviated only by the fact that I would continue to write secretly under a math textbook. My mother would sneak into the room very quietly to check if I were doing my homework; I would hold my textbook tilted upwards with one hand and write with the other, slamming the book down when I heard her footsteps. (Lau, 11)

Whatever differences distinguish one book from the other must be read in light of the sheer interchangeability of the passages above, which are more than plausibly iterations of a scene in a single household, played out with but incidental variations from one week to the next. Captured in this, the same moment, are glimpses of the patterns which will preoccupy both narratives: in the fetishization of math, the direction of parental expectations; in the fetishization of literature, the direction of filial resistance; within the walls of the bedroom, the convergence of captivity and escape.

∿ doing the math

The math textbook stands, with metonymic succinctness, for the present educational and future professional development desired of the child. While she may be expected to excel in all scholastic subjects, it is "math" to which the child is required to direct her dedication, for as Catherine explains, mathematical proficiency is imagined to be the road to deliverance: "Math fit into [my mother's] fantasy of who I was going to be one day. I was going to be successful *because of my expertise in math*, and I was going to get a lucrative job that would pay me enough to support her" (Liu, 270; emphasis added). The circuit that moves from math to money to filial obligation in a continuous loop derives in part from the logic of Necessity. In *Fifth Chinese Daughter*, the code of Necessity defines children as resources (or liabilities) in the household economy, and thus saturates familial relations with monetary terms through which debt and personhood are negotiated. Fifty years hence, Lau's and Liu's texts echo the disciplinary, exhaustive use of limited resources reported by Jade Snow—"My mother couldn't deal with the possibility that for just one minute, one minute of my existence, I might have no more homework, nothing to study, no more chores to do—a minute of my own" (Lau, 163)—but to that structure, premised on survival and repayment, add a dimension of capital investment. For the impetus in the scene described above is not only to regulate the productivity of the child's day-to-day labor and activities (i.e., to generate a steady flow of revenue), but to manage her development in view of future payoff (an anticipated return on investment).

> Math was the beginning of all of this. Math was practical, math would guarantee this future. She only wanted what was good for me. It was a well-known fact that Chinese students excelled at math. The Chinese believed in the power of math. With it, I could be a doctor, lawyer, engineer, chemist, physicist, M.B.A. (Liu, 271)

The narrator refers to a cultural common sense which she understands, not as an essential racial or "Chinese" superiority in mathematics, but to be a pragmatic reverence for a skill of professional value. These rationales express a reverence for or faith in mathematics, yet make no mention of qualities inherent to the discipline or its practice; its value, it would seem, is contextual rather than intrinsic. Indeed, grouped within the short list of the child's occupational options (from which "math teacher" is conspicuously absent), is one not discernibly based on math at all—but law enjoys a parity with the other professions enumerated because they are all, well, lucrative. Thus, while rhetorically efficient, math is ultimately non-essential to the enterprise it represents: a provisional means, not an end. It is the financial yield of a child's occupation that becomes the definitive measure of its value, and validity. Catherine reports being told that, "If what I did involved a lot of money, [my parents] might have understood better. They could have tolerated my becoming an MTV vee-jay, for example, but being broke and studying literature was a kind of black hole to them" (302).

Though meant hyperbolically, Catherine's flippant example of an alternate career path is in fact a rather astute expression of a society and economics in which engineers and MTV personalities represent a common sensibility—an ethos which conditions the possibilities for becoming a model minority in the present day. In *Cultural Capital*, John Guillory confronts the newest permutation of class structure in the United States: "the emergence of a technically trained 'New Class,'" "a 'professional-managerial class'" (Guillory, x) which has "been fully integrated into mass culture, [that] media culture mediating the desires of every class and group" (263). Within this emergent structure, the social machinery produces and the free market rewards a techno-bureaucratic work force bred on the consumer culture of the mass media, and proficient at running its operations: "In the current context . . ., universities and the institutions of higher learning are called upon to create skills" in order "to supply the system with players capable of acceptably fulfilling their roles at the pragmatic posts required by its institutions" (82). The foregoing is (not coincidentally) an equally plausible account of the model minority—indeed, Guillory's thesis posits that, in contrast to the bourgeoisie of old, the New Class is by definition "culturally heterogeneous" (263); the new order is permissive and even welcoming of a postmodern racial and ethnic diversity so long as all participants are unified under the ideals of capital. For those students who "select the chutes labeled 'pre-professional'—pre-med, pre-law, and so forth" (44), the "technical knowledge" that "mathematics" loosely denotes is a valuable commodity—because it is on the strength of such technical expertise that they themselves are valued. Neither innate nor "culturally" Chinese, Catherine's mother's fixation on math is in actuality opportunistic, shrewd, and specific to an American marketplace which conspires "to produce a new class of technical/managerial specialists possessed of purely technical/managerial knowledge" (261). Accordingly, parents interested in cultivating such members of the professional-managerial class concern themselves single-mindedly with (their children's) "acquisition of technical knowledge in order to maintain [the family's recently attained middle- or upper middle-class status], or to become upwardly mobile" (46).

The parental anxiety to direct and/or determine a child's career toward these professional-managerial paths represents itself easily as survival ("practical," "guarantee this future") or even altruism ("She only wanted what was good for me"), but its expectations are layered by more self-serving motivations: "They told me that . . . I was a great disappointment to them"; "They said that . . . their friends' children [now grown] . . . gave their parents money every month. I asked them why they did that—the parents certainly didn't need any money—and they would get angry" (Liu, 301). Above and beyond the calls of subsistence or recuperation, the ideal of successful child rearing looks for monetary return in excess of need or costs. *Couched in the language of Necessity is the ideology of profit.* Evelyn recounts, in clear reminder of designated failure, that despite having become "what could be considered a model daughter—I never went out, helped with the housework, had no boyfriend and few friends, brought home good grades, never experimented with alcohol or drugs," she was subjected to her mother's "constantly telling me that I wasn't worthy and wasn't good enough" (Lau, 12). On the one hand, such disciplinary mechanisms preordain that one can never reach an ever-receding point of completion; on the other, for a schema of investment, a point of completion simply need not exist—as the "point" of profit is excess, and by definition there is no limit to excess. In practice, the logic of impossibility which characterizes designated failure is indistinguishable from the logic of profit-making: in both cases, the "enough" of attainment is hostile to their project. Profit-driven ideology merges readily with the formative technologies of discipline, and reveals itself indeed as the latter's proper concern.

of geese and girls   ୭

The model of child-as-capital-investment is not categorically new in the literary history of Asian American parental discourse, having made appearances in family chronicles of Jade Snow Wong and Maxine Hong Kingston's generations—but it was then prominent and direct only in accounts written and narrated by men. Milton Murayama's *All I asking for is my body* is one such account, referenced earlier in the first chapter's discussion of a homology between public and private institutions of capitalism: As the Hawaiian plantation owner in Murayama's story acts in capitalist paternalism toward each of the working families, from their indebtedness drawing labor and from their labor drawing profit, so the Oyama family in its turn acts in capitalist paternalism toward each of its working sons. Their eldest, Toshio, recognizes his own economic exploitation in the family, and rejects the ethics which would condition his acquiescence to the hierarchy: "[Papa] got all the good cards. All he need to do is sit tight . . . and act like a nice guy. I'm the guy who's losing. They skinning me alive and I supposed to act *samurai* and take it. . . . The more you shut up, the better they look" (Murayama, 47). He grasps that though its ostensible mechanism may be debt, the motive of a capitalist order is profit, as exemplified for him by his "thief" of a grandfather who, invoking filial piety, relocated his family to Hawai'i, worked Toshio's mother and father and two uncles for 12 years, and then left for Japan with all the money (30). For Toshio, the institutions of family and plantation are neither opposed nor in contradiction, but indeed differently scaled components of a *single* capitalist system, interested in producing subjects who "pay and pay and pay and . . . never pay enough" (47).[4] Discourses of honor, family, or nationhood—these collude to convince him that this arrangement is right. As children raised for the purpose of bringing revenue to the family, Toshio and his brother Kiyoshi have but one operative quality: they are filial or unfilial, a successful return on investment or not.

> "[Tosh]'s not bad," I said [to mother]. "He's not a drunk or a gambler like some of the others. . . . He's not a braggart or bully or liar like many filial sons" . . .
> "Kiyoshi, what are you saying? . . . How can you be unfilial and not be all bad?" (43)[5]

Mother's salient interest in Toshio is that he not leave and take his earning power with him (44), and this narrow profit-use is the crux of his anger and critique: "I'd have been happier as an orphan than having you as parents! You raise us like we were pigs!!" (92).

Murayama's comparison of children to livestock interestingly recalls Sauling Wong's reading of a "quasi-cannibalistic" motif in Fae Myenne Ng, Maxine Hong Kingston, and Frank Chin's varied versions of immigrant family life. In this Necessity-based model, offspring are handled as if "also a food source, valued only for what they can give, to be slaughtered, cashed in on, when the time for repaying previous feeding comes" (SL Wong, *Reading*, 33). Quasi-cannibalism applies the "ruthless standard" of "usefulness" (i.e., of resource or liability) to all members of the family; children are accordingly forced to be "'good for something,' namely, able to bring money and 'face' to the family, or else they are 'rotten, no-good, dead [things]'" (32). Such a logic does emerge from the form of filiality which the Oyamas practice—(it is in fact Toshio's mother who first makes the analogy between raising children and raising pigs [Murayama, 92])—but as a metaphor, cannibalism does not fully encapsulate the paradigm of child as investment, so much as it is symptomatic of it. As coined by second-generation narrators, the tropes of slaughter and cannibalism, though critical in their intent, derive from and accept as true an implied economy of hardship. To kill and eat that which one has raised is characteristic of subsistence farming rather than commercial agriculture, and as an act of subsistence constitutes an indisputable need. Whatever sacrifice is demanded of the child, therefore, is premised on such need: selective forfeiture as a condition of survival. If the offspring "feel themselves sacrificed," it is to be "made into a food source . . . for the parents" (SL Wong, 37), ostensibly a source *without which they cannot live*. It is this link between Necessity and sacrifice to which a child is asked to relinquish his or her own interests and, even, well-being. In actuality, however, the governing design for raising a son in plantation life is not so much cannibalism but capitalism: "The intergenerational conflict here is inscribed within a cultural and political economy that negotiates parent/child relations in terms of bodies and their capacity for labor, which is seen to produce wages that are in turn seen *not as sustenance*, but as money that will go to pay off the [parental] debt" (Palumbo-Liu, 408; emphasis added). Palumbo-Liu's alimentary choice of terms neatly distinguishes between parental *need* and parental interests. The expectation that a child submit, as Toshio expresses it, "to throw away our lives" (Murayama, 30), to be "buried" or "skinned" alive (47), so that a parent may eat and live, is human sacrifice even by the standards of survival; implemented so that a parent may prosper, it is the redeeming of investments, and a kind of deceit. In aspiring for excess—for profit—investment blurs the distinction between Necessity and Extravagance. Sau-ling Wong identifies these paired constructs as "function[ing] mainly rhetorically" (SL Wong, 13); this includes the use of Necessity to justify and impose certain preferences, directives, modes of behavior; Extravagance to invalidate or prohibit undesirable elements. If, however, the parental demand for a lifetime of their son's earnings (Murayama, 27), or indeed for "straight As that would lead eventually to medical school" (Lau, 95), maneuvers for Extravagance in the name of Necessity, then at the heart of this future-looking investment is not only a paradox, but a lie.

If the daughters of the Oyama family do not feel the brunt of a "slaughter" mentality, it is because they are not appraised to be valuable investments. As the girl children are only nominal presences in the narrative, *All I asking is my body* offers limited insight on the particulars into which a common system may be differently articulated by gender, but the guiding principles of that differentiation are outlined by Toshio: "Don't educate the girls. They're no good. They'll get married and won't be any help to the family. Educate the boys!"; "You're going to depend on the boys later!" (Murayama, 55, 92).[6] Capital investment may adopt various forms, specific to the opportunities permitted by historical contingency; in the time and place of Murayama's narrative it is specific to sons because, in the greater economic configuration of plantation life, it is men who are formally employed. To educate daughters, who marry and won't contribute financially, is a waste of resources— but *not* due to a die-hard cultural resolve to cut girls and their income "out" of the family upon marriage; such cherished customs can be astonishingly disposable when it is economically expedient.[7] Economic (mis)use is determined by economic means, and girls on the plantation have little expectation of an independent, money-making livelihood: barring prostitution, their chief occupational prospect is financial dependency. In the following passage, purportedly a meditation on his sister's education and its implications for her future, the narrator runs through what immediately becomes a list of job options for the men she might marry: "High school graduates married other high school graduates, 'Canetop College' people married their own kind, and you couldn't get anywhere on the plantation without a high school education, unless you were an athlete and even then the highest a *nisei* could be was a *luna*" (75). In this context, daughters represent primarily domestic labor, and with negligible earning power, are ultimately pegged as negative returns on investment.

Accordingly, a girl may be greeted—as in the Oyama, Wong, or Hong families—with comparative "disappointment" from birth (Murayama, 27; JS Wong, 27) and (as a spinster would remain a dependent in the parental household), would be groomed to marry appropriately, but with no particular pressure to cultivate occupational advantages—given a foregone conclusion of loss. Unsurprisingly, then, the logic of profit is only a thwarted and secondary presence in Wong's and Kingston's texts—relevant in how it *does not*, rather than how it does, apply to the female narrators. The aspect of her upbringing which Jade Snow alleges most angers her is her father's decision to finance higher education only for her brothers, despite her own strong qualifications and desire for college. To the end of producing "creditable daughters and illustrious sons" (60), her father judges that for Jade Snow a high school—mandatory, public, and therefore free—education is sufficient, whereas he "must still provide with all [his] powers for [her] Older Brother's advanced medical training" (109). Thus, it is precisely the gender differentiation whereby she is *not* cultivated as a future payoff, *not* apportioned a share of venture capital, that outrages Jade Snow. Much of Maxine's anger, likewise, derives from her sense of the differing expectations reserved for the sons and daughters of her family: "'There's no profit in raising girls. Better to raise geese than girls'" (Kingston, *Warrior*, 46). Her family takes no particular interest in managing the "appreciation" of Maxine's financial value, and look to her educational or professional development with no pronounced emphasis. Rather, the "straight A's" we will subsequently see fetishized in Lau and Liu's texts are here continually disregarded, dismissed as worthless:

> "I got straight A's, Mama."
> "Let me tell you a true story about a girl who saved her village" (45).
> In China there were solutions for what to do with little girls who ate up food and threw tantrums. You can't eat straight A's. (46)

Without the long view of producing upward mobility, the daughter's academic achievements have no meaning for daily, family balances of liability and labor, expenditure and return—no material value: "You can't eat straight A's." Such references to the buying, raising, and selling of girls as are abundant in Kingston's narrative can be instructively reread in this light as the subject's anxieties around her displacement; the capitalist system that has little use for her resents senseless expenditures on her behalf, whether in the form of start-up capital (hospital delivery expenses [83]) or of ongoing operating costs ("eating the food" [52]).[8]

This gendered schema of investment does undergo conspicuous reconstruction in later texts, becoming both more equal-opportunity and more lucrative with the reorganization of the American work force in the 1960s on: as that work force permits the professionalization of racial minorities, and as it admits women into the professions. Equal access to the familial investment venture doubtless corrects something of the galling devaluation of girls but, as their brothers might rail, becoming the vehicle of a project to turn (or raise) a profit is also a costly advantage to gain. On Murayama's plantation of the 1930s and '40s, high school education is a rarified privilege for second-generation boys as well as girls, and college or graduate work is unheard of. Given the limited opportunities to be bought with a diploma—a nisei boy who graduates high school may well return to the cane fields just the same (91)—education holds little value for Toshio and Kiyoshi's parents, who take their sons out of school early to put them to work in the fields. Beginning in the postwar years, however, pricked by the hypocrisies of fighting white supremacy abroad, the United States began to implement "civil rights statutes [which] outlawed racial discrimination in employment" (Le Espiritu, *Panethnicity*, 28), thus "mark[ing] the first time that well-trained Chinese and Japanese Americans could find suitable employment with relative ease" (31). According to census data, rates of education for Asian Pacific Americans changed dramatically between 1960 and 2000: Whereas in the early part of this span, the greatest number of Asian Americans had less than a high school education, by the turn of the millennium nearly half of the Asian American population held a college or graduate degree (Lai and Arguelles, 9). Among these advanced degrees, Asian Americans showed a heavy bias toward professional schools and "math-related" professions, taking almost two-thirds of their PhD's in the hard sciences, for instance, and almost a third of their Masters' degrees in Business Administration alone (205).[9] By the 1970s, as reflected in the San Francisco Chinatown of Frank Chin's "Year of the Dragon," the pressure is on to turn boys into "doctors, lawyers, engineers" (Chin, 86). The model minority/filiality paradigm has taken its turn toward professionalization, such that "even though Fred has given up college [and his writing aspirations] to take over his ailing father's travel business and support Mattie (Sis) through college" (SL Wong, 176), because he has "no college graduation" (Chin, 108), is "no dockah no lawyah" (109), his father still considers him a failure. All of the above behaviors may be equally "Necessary'" to the patriarch in rhetoric, but in practice—for Fred as for Toshio—all other good conduct is rendered moot if the child does not deliver on the desired capital investment (that component which is, in actuality, Extravagance). In Fred's experience, a son is still measured by his filiality alone, and filiality is still measured by return on investment; where his predicament departs from Toshio's is that the measures of investment and return are now specific and explicit to professional achievement.

Written in the seventies, Chin's play still makes no mention of comparable career pressure for girls, as the Eng daughter seems to have married and left home to become a cook,[10] with no apparent expectation that she do or be anything in particular. That decade will begin to see, however, a new phase in career prospects for women—opportunities opened up by the passage of the Civil Rights Act in 1964, and incorporating women of color by corollary. Through its provision to forbid "discrimination in employment on the grounds of race, creed, color, or national origin *as well as sex*" (Kessler-Harris, *Pursuit*, 239; emphasis added), this act ushered in a "new generation of young women [which] began to emerge from colleges and universities" (Kessler-Harris, *Out*, 311), and increasingly entered "professional schools of law, medicine, architecture, and business" as admissions quotas in those institutions were challenged and dropped (*Pursuit*, 274).[11] College, medical, and business school educations are costly, however, and an immigrant family is likely hard-pressed to finance such expenditures, even as investments, for more than a few children. It makes fiscal sense, then, to reduce family sizes, since "extraneous" children, who could not be groomed as investments, still must be raised and still sap resources. Moreover, if daughters have become as viable as career-professionals as their brothers, then girls need not be "extraneous," and it is not necessary to keep trying for a boy: a family can afford to have fewer children, and invest in those few they do have, regardless of gender. Following the passage of the Civil Rights Act, the "number of female lawyers, doctors, and dentists" in the United States doubled "in the space of a decade" (*Out*, 311), with sufficient cultural impact that by Catherine and Evelyn's childhoods in the early eighties—each of them a daughter in a two-child household—it has become the requirement that these girls grow up to be well-salaried professionals. "By kindergarten, I was already expected to excel in class, as the first step in my pre-planned career as a doctor or lawyer" (Lau, *Runaway*, 9).[12]

∿ the wages of writing

That both girls grow up instead to be writers, then, is conceivably contrary enough to expectation to be deliberately so. Conventionally perceived as the polar opposite of mathematics in the pure disciplines, literature is also its inverse to the market-driven family. As Guillory argues, the New Class of techno-bureaucrats certainly esteems *capital* and, along with that, its own organically emergent forms of *cultural capital*; the latter, in this case, is distilled down to the set of skills required to succeed professionally: whatever "competence [is] necessary for the performance of its specialized functions" (Guillory, 263). As previously remarked, math serves as notational shorthand for areas of technical knowledge deemed most desirable. However, neither the professional-managerial class, nor the model minority encompassed within it, recognizes historical *symbolic capital*: cultural capital in the form of "a kind of knowledge-capital whose possession can be displayed upon request and which thereby entitles its possessor to the cultural and material rewards of the well-educated person" (ix). Traditionally identified with literature and the humanities, such symbolic capital is the marker of older forms of privilege, province of the old "culturally homogeneous" bourgeoisie. As that class fades from socioeconomic currency, its values also are rendered obsolete. Given the new order, those who would compose the model minority "professional-managerial class [have] made the correct assessment that, so far as [their] future profit is concerned, the reading [or writing] of great works is not worth the investment of very much time or money" (46). Therefore, where in the eyes of the immigrant parent math is practical and career-oriented, the reading and writing of literature are useless, wasteful activities, stolen time. Appraised by this world view, to dedicate one's resources to an enterprise of no market value is not only perverse but finally unintelligible: "beyond . . . comprehension" (Liu, 302).

As the antithesis of a filial ideal, the pursuit of literature holds a privileged place for Catherine and Evelyn: it is the equal-and-opposite reaction; it is the form of disobedience. That the practice of writing should enjoy an elevated status in any given literary production verges on tautology, but in fact the spirit and basis of its elevation are not the same for these contemporary Asian American narrators as for their predecessors. Where Maxine makes only rare and figurative references to writing or the written, and Jade Snow's esteem for the written word is based on its contextual value and external rewards,[13] Lau and Liu's personas record at length their feelings about and processes of writing, and cherish it at least in part because of its devalued status, its exclusion from their parents' scope of interest: [14]

> I would win writing awards, but my parents would become angry rather than proud, rebuking me for not doing my homework instead. (Lau, *Runaway*, 12)

> I considered my writing to be the part of me that was beyond anyone's control, that could not be owned, the way I felt every other part of my body and my life belonged to my parents. (Lau, *Inside*, 138)

Such statements are foreign to both Maxine and Jade Snow, for whom, while certainly there is a measure of taboo in the telling of secrets or exposure of family life to public scrutiny, whatever their transgression may be lies in the content and not the *act* of composition. The point of anxiety and focus for Maxine is oral—the talk-story, constraints on her voice and tongue; it is not writing per se but *speaking* which is held from her, and which she must do. Writing for Jade Snow is the stuff of essay contests, a means (not functionally distinct from pottery) for access to recognition and advancement; and while she seems to relish infiltrating the male province of letters (and enterprise), she does so with a defiance that seeks approval, not one that tempts punishment.

Both Catherine and Evelyn, on the other hand, seem repeatedly compelled when referring to their writing to bring up the ways that they have disappointed their parents' wishes, as if that act and those wishes move in lock-step opposition in their minds. Evelyn insists that, "Outwardly, I was not rebellious. I never displayed anger, since that invited punishment" (*Runaway*, 10), and recalls striving in demeanor and achievement alike to meet her parents' requirements (12). However, in "The Observing Ego," the chapter of Lau's memoir dedicated to thinking through her "obsession" with writing, Evelyn relates having taken up that career path in direct rejection of model filiality. She remembers a childhood conversation with her family doctor, an older Chinese woman, in which the woman generously offers to act as Evelyn's mentor and role model, so that she might become a physician herself. "'No. I'm going to be a writer,'" she replies, and recalls that her parents "were furious on the ride home" (*Inside*, 106). She realizes that she "could have just kept quiet, nodded politely in the doctor's office," and her parents would have been proud of their model daughter (107)—but in stating her commitment to writing, she declares a commitment to dissent, the evidence of which she vigilantly expunges from all other aspects of her behavior. Liu's narrator expresses an analogous, youthful yearning to satisfy parental demands (Liu, 279, 281), and arrives despite that at a comparable investment in writing. In a chapter titled "M.B.A.," a grown Catherine carefully juxtaposes her own position in the corporate world—as a poorly paid and temporary "word processor"—against the positions held by "the children of my parents' friends," who "were working . . . as analysts and associates" (284). She describes these rival figures as "acting in good, middle-class immigrant ways, remaining upwardly mobile and accumulating good credit and stock portfolios" (285), and then ponders her process of (academic) writing—not as an alternate form of success, but as a contrasting failure to which she has pledged herself: "When I got home from a day of temping, I often had papers to write, but I didn't know how to begin because I had been word processing all day.... [I]f nothing came to me during the time I set aside for writing, I became angry and unhappy. I railed against what I thought of as my fate" (284). Judging from these associations, the quality that would appear to define Catherine's writing, word processing, and temping alike is not productivity so much as immobility. As *inactivities* that enable her to "[avoid] the thought of being or doing something" else (283), they are less directed acts than a resistance against action, a passive defiance by which eventually she "[falls] quietly out of the middle class into which [her] parents had elevated themselves" (285). In *The Joy Luck Club*, Amy Tan composes a similar moment for her own writer-persona, who also grew up in the era of equal-opportunity professionalization. In reaction to feeling that her mother wanted her to be "someone that [she was] not," June proceeded doggedly to disappoint: "I failed [my mother] so many times, each time asserting my own will, my right to fall short of expectations. I didn't get straight As. I didn't become class president. I didn't get into Stanford. I dropped out of college" (Tan, 142). In June's case as in Catherine's, the writer's rebellion is couched as a disobedient passivity: the "determin[ation] *not to try*" (138; emphasis added).

civil disobedience ❧

Certainly, such persistent inaction is antithetical to the hard-working model minority, but it is the notion that an unruly subject might, via such non-action, "fall quietly" out of favor which merits particular attention, for it speaks to the contradictory impulses that bring Lau's and Liu's narrators to literature. Why would otherwise dutiful children—anxious to be "model daughter[s]" and willing in all other respects to fulfill what is asked of them[15]—choose to persist in this single disobedient act? One early, easy motive has to do with the potential for classic escapism literature offers. Not unlike consumers of romance fiction, homebound women who chafe at the binds of their restrictive family lives, these girls turn to their far-fetched stories because "reading was like living in a fantasy world; it had become my form of escape" (Lau, *Runaway*, 9).[16] The readers of Janice Radway's study, comparable to our narrators in their ambivalent compliance as well as in their selective use of literature, consistently express a need to "get away" from their daily existences, but rather than leave their families for "exotic places" and distant locations, or alter their realities through drugs or alcohol, their escapes of preference take the more "innocuous" form of reading: In this momentary and circumscribed release, these women remove themselves "from . . . duties that they otherwise willingly accept as their own" (Radway,

93); engrossed in a story, they feel *"my body is in the room but the rest of me is not"* (87–89; emphasis added). This yearning for imaginary departure to remote settings stands in even more poignant, painful contrast to Evelyn's and Catherine's captive state within the four walls of their bedrooms. Through the reading (and writing) of "romances and mysteries and science fiction" (Lau, *Inside*, 90), Lau's and Liu's narrators remove themselves from the "sad, gray home planet of real life" (Liu, 272). Acutely aware of their parents' hovering threat and relentless monitoring within the physical confines of the family home, both narrators periodically refer to themselves as prisoners (Lau, 56; Liu, 273), implying that their parents behave like wardens; Catherine bluntly calls this being subjected to "surveillance" (107)—giving the condition its proper Foucauldian name. Not unlike inmates in Jeremy Benthams' *Panopticon*, the girls in their rooms are suspended in a searing state of isolation without privacy: "[The cells] are like so many cages, so many small theatres, in which each actor is alone, perfectly individualized and constantly visible" (Foucault, *Discipline*, 200). In conditions of such heightened exposure, acts of disobedience best look like nothing to see.

Escapism is a limited and double-edged contrivance, however, insofar as it functions as a safety valve: channeling rebellious energy away from "destructive" or material dispute, onto paper; and making confinement more tolerable. Radway finds that for her subjects, "The Act of Reading the Romance" (as the title of the chapter goes) "enabled them to deal with the particular pressures and tensions encountered in their daily round of activities" (Radway, 86), and worked to deflect and re-contain their "dissatisfaction with the status quo in the family" (100). Ironically, then, the pursuit of literature is also very much an escape into imprisonment. For such young girls as Evelyn and Catherine, getting as far as possible from the direction of exacting parents also means entering their holding cells.[17] They cannot leave; as children they have no resources for survival outside the home. But to withdraw thus into their rooms to read or write is one part escape from and one part acceptance of captivity, equal parts resistance and acquiescence to power, and a paradox especially insomuch as their dependence upon literature is a *product* of their confinement:

I wasn't allowed to spend much time with the neighborhood children; consequently, I always had my nose in a book. (Lau, *Runaway*, 9)

She kept me in my bedroom, studying between one school day and the next, and it was in there that my writing developed in the form of short stories, poetry and even two book-length manuscripts. (11)

Evelyn's language in the passages above reflects neither desire nor agency; it is her mother who decides her movements and placement, and "her writing" that develops. She portrays herself reading in the most passive possible of terms ("had my nose in a book"), as if it is a position rather than an activity, and she herself posed there, puppet-like, as the "consequence" of external causes. While the comparison between bedroom and panopticon naturally has its limits, it is valid to the extent that disciplinary and surveillance mechanisms are implemented in the family, as in any other institution, with the aim of controlling their subjects, of producing docile bodies—and children quietly arranged with nose to book (regardless of whether math text or fantasy novel) do suggestively embody that. It would seem, then, that literature is not entirely what these narrators *choose to do* but also what *happens to* them, an unwished-for effect of incarceration. It is the passive dimension of this single, selective disobedience that makes it possible for the girls to seem, even while performing an act which is expressly discouraged and even forbidden to them, to be "doing nothing." Literature is already a "nothing" in the sense of investment waste and loss; to "do" literature is also to "do nothing" in the sense of inactivity, avoidance, resistance rather than action—even compliance without struggle. Thus, to do "nothing" is not a fearful challenge to power but an inoffensive coping mechanism, a subdued refusal, a quiet falling.

To recoil into reading and writing is in one sense, then, an act of the helpless: born of both insubordination and subterfuge, as the needs of self-preservation hedge defiance. Liu's narrator indicates that she chooses her occupational limbo, preferring it to "adult life" or responsibilities, but offers upon her chosen life this complicating commentary: "I believed that only the paralyzed and powerless, like myself, didn't do the things they longed to do" (Liu, 3). Even after years of living outside the rooms of her parents' house, for Catherine writing continues to oscillate in the tension between agency and subjection, between labor of love and lack of alternative. Indeed, her very choice to begin studying literature in college is bisected by conflicting needs, to appease and to survive: "I took English literature courses because I thought that perhaps I would major in English and go on to law school. My mother assured me that I could always write on the side" (155).

At some point for both young women, however, writing comes to exceed its original purpose of enduring containment. At some point, Evelyn tells us, "a shift happened" (Lau, *Inside*, 90), and she began to write not about imaginary places from inside her room, but about her life—as if from a place outside, removed. Whereas the escapism of Evelyn's and Catherine's early reading and writing permit their sustained non-confrontation, their choices to invoke, without cover, terms of domination and subjection in *Runaway* and *Oriental Girls Desire Romance* allow the writers scant retreat. Within their first three pages, both Lau's and Liu's texts generate the expectation that they will take power to account; they also make themselves frighteningly accountable to that expectation: "[My mother] felt powerless over [my father's inadequate] employment, but she wasn't powerless over me, and that was where she poured all her energy" (*Runaway*, 10). In this statement, the speaker recognizes her familial relations to be neither natural nor divine law, but behavior conditioned by material circumstances and governed by the motivations and agendas of human subjects. To make such statements entails, however, such profoundly exposed disobedience that the speaker seeks refuge in a subject position alienated from the very self and family she lays bare: Evelyn describes her writing as a kind of "reporting," which "enabled [her] to detach so completely from [herself] that [she] became two people, one who lived and one who stood next to [herself], recording the other's motions with pen and notepad" (91). The journalistic objectivity she assumes or imagines for herself permits her to "look at my own parents *as if I were a stranger . . .* instead of seeing them as . . . the hallowed mother and father, to be obeyed and respected" (93; emphasis added). Through this narrative or authorial persona, Evelyn creates distance from the home, dissolves her affiliation to her parents; she must treat *herself* as a stranger in order to critique the familiar.[18] It is writing, in this loaded function, that she elevates to the status of being "the necessary thing," her "one tie to the earth":

There was nothing else of comparable value. Not even my family, not the woman who had given birth to me nor the man whom I loved more than anyone else in the world . . . If they did not understand my commitment to my writing, if they stood in its way, then I would have to leave them. I would have to write about them, which meant seeing them as they were, not through a filter of love and obligation. (92)

So constructed, writing is a duty to which she owes greater allegiance than her parents—it is an *obligation higher* than filiality. And having thus superceded them in her mind, writing becomes a latent condition for her departure from the family, even a potential excuse to leave. Again, here through the rhetoric of a "calling," the narrator occludes her agency with a screen of compliance and winds up exposing her discomfort with her own disobedience. Nevertheless, because her belief in Art as a kind of higher authority serves to sanction, as discharges of duty, whatever unfavorable representations of her parents she may put to paper, with this device Evelyn grants herself in writing a freedom, justification, and even responsibility to articulate grievances which her allegiances as a daughter demand that she suppress, and which have no other reason or court in which to be heard.

Such constructs of moral authorization are critical, if these diligent young women are to allow themselves acts they feel only too keenly to be insubordinate. Lau's and Liu's narrators catalogue a painstaking critique of the circumstances of their upbringings—often in their recollections reprising grievances aired in Wong and Kingston: Structures of designated failure, principles of paradox and impossibility . . . these make themselves felt as sharply in Catherine's and Evelyn's memories of their childhoods as in their predecessors', forming a common basis of complaint across the four sets of experiences.

Prohibitions from speech and expression:

- "always being unable to talk back, always silently screaming . . .. never [being] allowed a mouth." (Lau, *Runaway*, 24)
- "I tried to tailor my opinions and my desires to fit [my father's] idea of what I wanted. If they didn't, then I was in big trouble." (Liu, 128)

Unresolvable and unending debt:

- "I hadn't ever been able to satisfy my parents" (Lau, 215), "To them it's my fault that I was fucking born." (134)
- (reported with irony) "He provided the money for the food . . . He paid for the house we lived in. . . . He rarely missed an opportunity to remind me that I was his dependent. In fact, I owed him so much that there was nothing I could ever do that would have been an adequate expression of my appreciation." (Liu, 131)

Disciplinary regulation and punishment:

- "My mother couldn't deal with the possibility that for just one minute, one minute of my existence, I might have no more homework , nothing to study, no more chores to do." (Lau, 163)
- "He didn't want to punish me; he was obliged to. I accepted this reasoning and kept trying to be the perfect child. It all seemed very simple. I always tried to do the right thing, but sometimes I slipped up. I needed to improve, to have more self-discipline—then everything would be alright." (Liu, 149)

Sovereign power:

- "[M]y mother would stalk in, . . . saying she would leave me and then who would look after me? . . . It is that moment I remember more than any other, how dangerous and frightening her face had looked, the terrible power she had of taking everything away." (Lau, *Inside*, 190)
- "They were the ones who never let me forget that they were the ones who loved me. They were the ones who provided for me. . . . They said they knew me best. They told me what my weaknesses were, and then they punished me for them." (Liu, 127)

It is a particularly acute sense of injustice, however, that prompts each of the later women to refer to aspects of their upbringings as (*monetary*) crimes—financially motivated, moral offenses punishable by law: "My parents stole my childhood and most of my adolescence" (Lau, *Runaway*, 218); "The Fat Man and his Wife [her father and mother] were the king and queen of emotional blackmail" (Liu, 131).[19] Discerning not only parental power but parental *investment* in power, Lau's and Liu's texts attribute to the parents a critical component of *intentionality*: that damage to the girls is not merely the unwitting side effect of good intentions, but that in the course of maintaining sovereign power, the parents are willing to see and bring about some measure of harm to their children, in order that their will be done. When Evelyn leaves home, she receives a letter from her father in which he prophesies, "You will be suffering for the rest of your life for your actions" (Lau, *Runaway*, 35), a pronouncement that she recognizes to be a "stab"—an attempt to inflict upon or wish her harm—in response to her disobedience. When Catherine takes up a drug habit—on "principle," she says, "in a silent debate with [her parents] about the real causes of [her] so-called problems"—her parents try to stop her but, unable to manage their wayward daughter, respond with a sense of spite: "It was their fantasy to find me overdosed one day, lips blue from oxygen deprivation, stone-cold on the floor of some sleazy motel room. They seemed to get some morbid satisfaction from the idea that I was becoming a depraved human being" (Liu, 69).[20] Rather that the child suffer abjectly than that she defy them and prove right.

∿ conditional life

The manner of parental rhetoric that pegs a child's security to her obedience is not merely wishful but, as we saw in chapter 2, operational. It is core to the larger discourse of disownment, which hinges ultimately on the linking of transgression and annihilation. In the examples of sovereign power listed in the section above, both sets of parents are shown to allude, with varying levels of obliqueness, to threats of banishment or abandonment. Such language shows sovereign power to *depend*, in its indispensable uses of disownment, on a certain violence to the subject's well-being. In these moments disownment is represented not only in theory, as a forbidding abstract, but as a practice which acts upon a particular relation: When called into play, the threat of disownment may take different apparent directions—banishment, in which the child is forced to leave the family, or abandonment, in which the parent willfully leaves the child—but the material issue in either of these forms is the threat's exploitation of dependence and attachment. Whether Catherine is ordered "to get out of the house" and "not to think of her [mother] as [her] mother anymore" (265), or Evelyn is frightened with the specter that her mother "would leave [her] and then who would look after [her]?" (*Inside*, 190), what these threats leverage is the child's need, emotional and material, for her parent. Like Judith Butler in her formulation of passionate attachments, Lau's and Liu's narrators postulate that "a child tended and nourished in a 'good enough' way will love, and only later stand a chance of discriminating between those he or she loves" (Butler, *Psychic*, 8): As "small, watchful, easily damaged creatures" (*Inside*, 44), Evelyn muses, "you loved these people, helplessly," because "you were given no choice in the matter of loving them" (205). "[A]ttachment becomes a threat" (*Runaway*, 196), where need and devotion are regular instruments of control—because power is no respecter of 'love,' but predicated upon it instead.[21]

But furthermore if, as Butler argues, love is a kind of helpless effect (affect) directed toward those who enable one's material existence, and passionate attachment is thus a function of physical survival, then at bottom what disownment threatens is the child's life. As we have seen in previous chapters, power is sovereign by virtue of its prerogative to banish—indeed, the "originary relation of law to life," and the very premise of power, is understood to be Abandonment (Agamben, 43). Within the parent-child relation, Abandonment means the potential withdrawal not only of recognition or "love," but of the material functions of parenting. Sovereign power as a whole plays, therefore, not only on the child's fear of loss, but just as keenly or more so on her fear (however inchoate) of death. The more regulatory or prohibitive manifestations of sovereign power are, then, but overlays on a threat of disownment which makes the child's most basic well-being conditional to her submission to parental directives, however large, or however small: to come home at the stated time, to get straight As, to stop crying, to shut up.[22] The difference when power makes disownment overt, is that survival becomes the conscious rather than the subterranean content of the power struggle: "I had nowhere [else] to go" (Liu, 266); "Sniffling, I try very hard to stop [crying] because the vision of being alone and helpless is terrifying" (Lau, *Runaway*, 88). In light of power's hold over livelihood and existence, it is increasingly unsurprising that so many of Jade Snow's, Maxine's, Evelyn's, and Catherine's disputes with their parents should begin with, and never leave, accounts of food provided and eaten, reports of shelter and clothing proffered and accepted. In these tokens of physical dependence, it is life itself which has been given, which is now due in repayment, and which power would claim the prerogative to take back.

Marcel Mauss's work on "the gift" speaks directly to this social configuration of contract and exchange. Far from being "free," free-flowing, or voluntary in nature, the gift is shown in Mauss's work to be a regimented means of establishing relationships—bonds not of camaraderie so much as of dominance over other parties. Mauss postulates not only that the "first gift," the "opening gift" between individuals or parties, is a "starting point, one that irrevocably commits the recipient to make a reciprocating gift" (Mauss, 26), but that in this exchange the recipient is as if "sold" to the gift-giver (52), and "puts himself in a position of dependence *vis-à-vis*" the giver (59) until such time as he is able to return from his "own property . . . the equivalent" of the original gift "or something of even greater value" (6). Furthermore, it appears that "[n]obody is free to refuse the present that is offered" (19); thus, not only does the initiator of an exchange automatically put the recipient in his obligation, but he can by "giving more than can be reciprocated," humiliate and gain power over the other (Rubin, 172), as "punishment for failure to reciprocate is slavery for debt" (Mauss, 42). Maurice Godelier suggests that "By its very nature, the gift is an ambivalent practice," for in entailing the creation of obligations, it "can be, simultaneously or successively, an act of generosity or of violence" (Godelier, 12, 14). For the child, life and its continuance are "gifts" that she was never in any position to refuse, and they place her irreversibly under obligation to creditors whose gifts she categorically cannot match or surpass. When life is framed as a gift, then, the child's relation to her existence is necessarily ambivalent. However, disownment places the child in an interesting position. For in the context of the gift, the threat of disownment acts on the full expectation that the child cannot afford to reciprocate—and will be subjugated by this further failure to pay. What are we to make of those instances, then, when the child chooses not to submit, but to be disowned? Mauss argues that "to refuse to accept [a gift] is tantamount to declaring war; it is to reject the bond of alliance and commonality" (Mauss, 13), and it is reasonable to deduce that when 14-year-old Evelyn runs away from home, she has rejected her parents' gift as an act of aggression. The truth, however, goes deeper than that. When the "gift" in question is life itself or at least its means, to reject the gift is to accept abandonment, and the possibility of one's own demise. During her time on the streets, Evelyn is exposed constantly to the risk of violent death, but even more fundamental a condition of her life once beyond her parents' home is that clothing, shelter, food, and all other requirements of survival become unpredictable and scarce. If to love the gift of life is to love those who give it, then to reject those who give it, is necessarily to reject the gift of life.

Such suicidally informed relations appeal because they are checkmate in a game that allows the child few moves of advantage. If Evelyn believes she can prove that "my life was my own to destroy" (Lau, *Inside*, 17), this is because destruction is the ultimate prerogative of ownership, the utmost show of power and possession. Mauss speaks of instances within the circuit of gifts exchanged wherein one party may, in order to gain dominance over the other, choose *not* to deliver his gift to the opposing party but instead ritualistically to burn it down; so destroyed, the sacrificed goods still count as a "reciprocation" to the opposing party, but one from which that party loses rather than gains. Such action may be taken by either party, whether originally giver or recipient, and he who takes it expresses his great disdain for an exchange for which he has no use, need, or desire.[23] When the child immolates herself as gift, her act becomes one of aggression in that it deprives the parent of the benefit of the child's life. Though often threatened, disownment is not to the parents' advantage, then, in its realization. When the father of Murayama's story orders his son to "Get out and stay out!" and Toshio, in fact, gets up to leave, the mother quickly intervenes: "Father, you can't let him go yet!" Turning to Toshio, she repeats, "You can't go yet . . . Every child must repay his parents" (Murayama, 44).[24] But it is not without reason that the threat of disownment is oft-repeated. As that specter is wielded over and again, to punish and manipulate the child, it becomes apparent that words of banishment are a speech-act of a particularly revealing variety: a declarative designed precisely *not* to effect the new reality it declares, but to remain suspended—a calculated verbal gamble, a bluff. The threat of disownment works most effectually when there is no danger of its actualization—when directed at a subject so helpless, she is powerless even to obey: "I could not leave the house as she had ordered—I was too young and had nowhere to go" (Liu, 266). Such a subject will remain securely under the hold of power, regardless of how carelessly the horror of banishment is brandished, or how often its sentence is pronounced. To take disownment at its word, then, to leave the house, to run away—notably, an act of subterfuge, against the will of power—is to call its bluff, and test the limits and investments of familial authority. It is this paradox, that banishment is its own reciprocation and disownment its own revenge, which Catherine knowingly exploits when she responds to her mother's order to leave the house by resolving at first opportunity to do just that: "I promised myself that when I could leave, I would leave forever and never look back" (266). Thus, self-forfeit as potlatch is an act of ascendance insofar as it rhetorically devalues the gift, and one of strategy in that it is well-nigh impossible to answer. Ironically, however, it is also intrinsically one of reciprocation, in that existence/subsistence is the only meaningfully commensurate form of payment.

subjection begins in the home ‿

In the wake of Freud and Foucault, Butler's formulation makes clear that passionate attachment is by definition an attachment to power, and inescapable: There is "no formation of the subject without a passionate attachment to those by whom she or he is subordinated" (Butler, *Psychic*, 7); hence, "[t]o desire the conditions of one's own subordination is thus required to persist as oneself." In this deeply paradoxical fix, one must "embrace the very form of power—regulation, prohibition, suppression—that threatens one with dissolution in an effort, precisely, to persist in one's own existence" (9).[25] This defection or betrayal by the affective self comes to bear upon the greater context for the Asian American subject in that, while not political "in any usual sense," the formative "situation of primary dependency" within the family "conditions the political formation and regulation of subjects and becomes the means of their subjection" (7). Quite simply stated, "This is the beginning of all hatred, all desire and love" (Lau, *Inside*, 197). The family that meets discontent with "he's your father, you have to love him" (Liu, 131) capitalizes on primary dependency to inspire "unquestioning obedience and reverence" (128) to authority, and may even extend this model of devotion explicitly to the social or national setting:

> [When Jade Snow entered] an American public grade school [, . . .] Daddy and Mother both took her aside and gave her solemn instructions: " . . . at school a teacher will be in charge, who is as your mother or your father at home. She is supreme, and her position in all matters pertaining to your education is as indisputable as the decisions of your mother or father at home."
> Thus, Jade Snow accepted another authority in her life (JS Wong, 12).

Compliance then follows from attachment in a structure of feeling. Such a model may well be supposed to condition political subjects who continually and manifestly love, honor, and obey the forms of power. Model minority accommodationism is disparaged, when critiqued, for just such embrace of the systems of domination: "Amazing. . . . I always thought everybody low on the pecking order hated it. Not so. Not you. You *love* getting pecked from above, you enjoy pecking those below" (Murayama, 33; emphasis added).

To the extent that second-generation Asian American children do enter the medical, legal, and other approved professions, their disproportionate numbers validate the leveraging of passionate attachment to compel life choices. In other words, the disciplinary and discursive measures of sovereign power very often work, and those subjects who submit to its ultimatums are generally rewarded with advantages relative to their peers, both in the family and on the market. Interestingly however, with the intense codification of the model-minority/model-filiality blueprint over the decades comes not only more confirmed production methods, but also more glaring inconsistencies. The standards of achievement demanded of the child are, on the one hand, uniform, fixed and specific: "My parents expected me to be the top student in school" (Lau, *Runaway*, 9); "They forbade me to write unless I brought home straight As" (11). It is in self-conscious response to these monolithic standards (shared, presumably, by any of their Asian American readers), that Liu's narrator makes certain to establish herself— within the first paragraph of the memoir—as having been a "very bright scholarship student [. . . at an] Ivy League" institution (Liu, 2), the "place whose prestige so pleased [her] family" (154); and though the comment is oddly gratuitous, seemingly out of context with her other remarks within the topic of its paragraph, Lau's narrator is also quick to report that "at seven [she] was judged smart enough by the teachers . . . to be promoted from grade one to grade three" (*Inside*, 202), and that "[her] name was on the honor roll every year" (*Runaway*, 11). Despite these tangibles, both girls come to feel that, on the other hand, "Nothing was ever enough" (Liu, 282): that "no matter what I did, I could never justify being alive and being their daughter"—"And that was what it was all about" (*Runaway*, 12). That there should be a rigid formula, and yet that fulfilling the stipulations of that formula term by term should prove nonetheless inadequate, exposes the stark incongruities of sovereign power: its sham of fairness and its insatiable appetite.

This contradiction reveals, however, an important truth: that "model" children and their counterparts—the "failures," the dissidents, the writers—

emerge not from two different paradigms of parenting, but from one and the same. The incessant product comparisons, whereby market benchmarks and filial baselines are discovered and set, run on perpetual projection and deferment: the "model" child is always someone else's child, not the parent's own. Evelyn reports being told that, "my cousins in the States are getting straight A's in school and, at my age, already deciding which university they're going to attend. . . . Model youth" (131).[26] Meanwhile, Liu's narrator, as she is likewise flagellated with the achievements of her rivals and counterparts, realizes that "These [the children of my parents' friends] were children to whom I was once presented as a model of exemplary behavior: I did so well in school, and my Chinese was so good. I was so quiet and well-behaved, so little Americanized, so plain and demure" (Liu, 285; see also 301). Or, in an alternate and marvelously economical approach, the child may be pitted against herself: "Later, my father would tell anyone who cared to listen . . . that I was the perfect child until the age of fifteen. After that, he had no idea what happened; I became bad" (286). A variant on the usual form, this revisionist refrain confers model status upon a bygone figure of the daughter, only now that her present self may pale in comparison. In truth, meeting the fixed academic and professional terms of obedience makes the subject eligible for an ever-deferred approval: a relative and rhetorical endorsement effective for disciplining another child or even the subject herself, but of no inherent value or defense against the sovereign; under these conditions, the child remains categorically and unconditionally "unfilial," perpetually guilty and deficient.

Nevertheless, to say that the logic of power permits no such thing as restfully "model children" is not to deny any real difference between those children who go on to become the doctors and lawyers their parents wanted, and those like Evelyn and Catherine who insist upon choosing otherwise. To discover when and why the same type of conditioning should produce one response over the other is something of a "what if" problem, inviting sociological investigation beyond the literary-critical and theoretical project at hand. But, while Lau's and Liu's texts will not yield such data, they do allow us some productive conjecture. One might hypothesize that those who "fail" to follow the charted course are inherently indisposed toward the few permitted professions, and that "investment" pressure to adhere to medicine or engineering pays off, or not, subject to the child's ability and aptitude. Surely this must explain some cases; it does not seem, however, to explain either of our narrators. Neither narrator indicates having struggled with any particular subjects or skill sets. They evince inclinations toward literature but, with

no intellectual or practical impediments to pursuing the career paths designated to them, could feasibly, as Catherine's mother advised that she do, have
arranged merely to "write on the side." Arranging themselves in opposition
to the model children they could have been, Lau's and Liu's literature-bound
personas—like the Asian American academics, artists, and activists of Viet
Nguyen's formulation—seem to declare allegiance to dissent and, "align[ing]
themselves with . . . the nonmodel minority, form the population of bad subjects *by choice*" (Nguyen, 21; emphasis added); this is a choice both deliberate
and perverse. Notably, both young women draw the ideological correlation
between model minority status and an uncritical devotion to the powers that
be, in specific distinction from themselves: Lau's narrator speaks of her parents' disapproval of her involvement in the peace movement (*Runaway*, 11),
and Liu's narrator expresses her disaffection with her "very expensive, very
fancy" undergraduate institution, an aversion born both out of insubordination to her parents' power-smitten values (its "prestige so pleased my family"), and out of an alienated distaste for that very cultural hegemony: "I met
Wasps there for the first time in my life. I learned about Wasp traditions and
Wasp habits, Waspy accents and the power of money, especially old money"
(Liu, 155). It would seem that a critique of familial domination can operate
in conjunction with a critique of social and political domination, and indeed
that one may animate the other.

◆ your cultural capital is no good here

Where does the difference lie, then, between the family's defective product and
its successfully turned-out model minority, if both are produced as the unfilial
child? The accounts Evelyn and Catherine give of their childhoods suggest that
when the production line of child-as-investment grinds to a halt, this outcome
is wrought by the weight of its own methods. To illustrate this, we begin with
what may seem to be a facetious choice of case-in-point: the pronounced and
distinctively Asian American mania for playing bourgeois, Western classical
instruments. The pattern has tipped into cliché that every immigrant family
in the upper-middle class, or looking so to be, must enroll its children in classical music training—a seemingly Extravagant monetary expenditure without
direct future financial return, for children who are slated to become lawyers or
engineers. Indeed, as a form of traditional symbolic capital, classical music's
canonical place in Western high culture makes it a curiously anachronistic
investment for a model minority ensconced, as we've established, within the
very pragmatic New Class. Its appeal must be understood to lie partly in the

immigrant's aspirational rather than achieved self-positioning in racial and class hierarchies: "the desire of many Asian parents to have their children study music is at least driven partly by notions of symbolic distinction and . . . the aspiration for assimilation and upward mobility" (Yoshihara, 147). That this should be the single symbolic investment overwhelmingly adopted by the model minority, however, suggests furthermore that its practice generates some manner of value for the professional-managerial class. Droll though this unoriginal (parental) choice of extracurricular activities may be, it captures succinctly the tension between the immigrant's discerning pragmatism and, in its anachronism, his potentially costly misreading of cultural capitals.

As a practice—one requiring endless hours of repetition and immobility daily inside a room—the learning of classical instruments supports exceptionally well the overarching parenting principles of discipline and confinement:

> If after five hours I had done my homework inside out, then for two more I would have to study for some future test that would never materialize. If that was over, I would spend another four hours hunched over the piano. And if by then it wasn't late at night and therefore bedtime, well there were always kitchen floors to be swept and washed, dishes to be done, carpets to be vacuumed. (Lau, *Runaway*, 163)

Thus, as a *technology of power* within the household, training in the piano or violin works in hitchless tandem with the host of other regimes producing the docile, laboring, and potentially gendered body. According to Mari Yoshihara in her study of Asians and Asian Americans in classical music, "The discipline of music [and] practice regimes . . . all worked together to define women's place and responsibility as the home"; "in Asia . . . [and] the West, this musical education was intended not to train professional performers but rather to produce properly domesticated women" (Yoshihara, 102). Finally, as a mode of developing character proficiencies in addition to skill proficiencies, classical music can prove quite a "competence necessary for the performance of [the New Class'] specialized functions" (Guillory, 263): "Indeed, students who have had rigorous music training acquire discipline and focus that often lead to academic and professional achievement in fields *other than music*" (Yoshihara, 147; emphasis added). Classical training may be regarded additionally, then, as a form of *cultural capital* coterminous with any of the more technical forms valued by the professional-managerial class. It is, in other words, not play, but work.

The tensions threatening this seemingly well-integrated machinery, however, surface in descriptions of the lived experience of such music practice, characterized by the child's misgivings of isolation, social dysfunction, and fear: Evelyn recalls herself as "the twelve or thirteen-year-old . . . sitting lonely on the piano bench . . ., hiding behind the drapes when people walked by outside. . . . I was the hidden-away Chinese girl whom the other kids in school had ridiculed and put down mercilessly, who had been beaten by her parents in hopes of giving her a better life" (Lau, *Runaway*, 251). Households like Evelyn's and Catherine's, in which children are confined like prisoners to the bedroom to study or practice interminably, overlook major components in the qualifications required for the professional-managerial class. While the kind of academic credentials and technical knowledge it is possible to acquire in virtual isolation may be of great potential market value, they comprise only a portion of the cultural capital needed in order to be "capable of acceptably fulfilling [one's] roles at the pragmatic posts required by [capitalism's] institutions" (Guillory, 82). If the emergent techno-bureaucratic class is one which has been "fully integrated into mass culture," a consumerist media culture "mediating the desires of every class and group" (263), then by that token, a subject fully integrated into the New Class system must be able to marshal and circulate the appropriate markers of that social identity—in this case, not an esoteric cultivation of canonical arts, but a full participation in the mass culture of consumerism. It is counterproductive, then, that

> the very pursuit of classical music often marginalizes students in American schools where classical music is definitely outside mainstream youth culture. In environments where the "popular kids" typically excel in sports, play in rock bands, or are savvy in popular culture trends, classical musicians accumulate no cultural capital. (Yoshihara, 87)

In the manufacture of the model minority child, a system of production that privileges ascetic isolation and discipline—to the disregard and dismissal of social identity—is at odds not only with a "mainstream" sensibility, but with its own ends: "The model minority identity is an identity that is testimony to the Asian American ability to be a good citizen, productive worker, *reliable consumer*, and *member of a niche lifestyle* suitable for capitalist exploitation" (Nguyen, 10; emphasis added).

It is thus as a model minority subject *disabled by her own production* that Liu's narrator comes into crisis. Catherine finds that, as a consequence of having spent her childhood in a box, when she sets out for her Ivy League college she is not a functional member of the society she is to enter: "I was afraid of people . . . [R]aised the way I was, I emerged into the world totally unprepared for human interaction" (Liu, 153). Significantly, she interprets this point of leaving her parents' jurisdiction as being "finally allowed to enter into American culture," and begins an aggressive program of remedial cultural self-training—in the very specific form of "work[ing] three jobs at a time [to begin] to finance my consumer desires" (154). In a strikingly similar moment, Lau's narrator agonizes that "I never developed any social skills before leaving home because my parents refused to let me go out" (Lau, *Runaway*, 243), and that as a result she *still* "cannot do something like go out with a friend without a great deal of stress" (259). Evelyn asks herself, "How can I do anything ordinary, like going to a movie, without tranquilizers to get me through the evening?" (243; emphasis added), and the example she chooses is revealing, because it specifies the act of "going out" (in its very phrasing antithetical to her captive upbringing) as an act of *cultural consumption as group formation*: A truly enfranchised member of society must be able to leave the walls of the home and associate with like others in a ritualized mass culture. Even after Evelyn has run away, her mother is "genuinely puzzled" by that cultural practice—apparently another activity which is not only perverse but unintelligible to filiality: "Going out tomorrow night?" she asks her daughter; "Where is there to go?" (134).

"Going out" involves "eating out," or other various forms of ceasing work and purchasing pleasure, and yet as a middle-class ritual and social convention, it constitutes such Extravagance as a kind of Necessity. After all, "[t]he cultural-ideological project of global capitalism is to persuade people to consume above their 'biological needs' in order to perpetuate the accumulation of capital for private profit" (Sklair, 345). The "cultural logic" of "limitless consumerism" which late capitalism produces (Santa Ana, 16) is essential to its continuation—indispensable, if the capitalist system is "to ensure that [it] goes on forever" (Sklair, 345). This means, however, that the ability to signify and comfortably to negotiate consumer culture amounts to an *evolution* of symbolic capital, as much "organic to the constitution of the professional-managerial class" as technical expertise. It is conversance not with philosophy or Schubert but with *contemporary* leisure which makes for a constitutive form of cultural capital—but capital requiring a mode of production fundamentally antagonistic/disruptive to the larger systems of discipline by which the model minority is tooled.

This is not to claim that your average Asian immigrant family cannot recognize the social function of conspicuous consumption; as Lisa Park's work demonstrates, many such families are quite adept at precisely that. Rather, it is to speculate that some families run a better shop than others: Those parents who fail to "buy in" to the values and markers of cultural participation, and to engage their children in the same, may find their methods for producing the model minority subject falling short in the end. The trouble with a disregard for cultural participation is that, no less now than in its "traditional" form and context, symbolic capital performs the vitally important work of class *identification*. Without the proper markers of proficient consumption, an Asian American aspiring to the model minority can neither signify as nor be identified as a member of the New Class; to lack these markers is to be dis-integrated.

> It wouldn't have been difficult for my parents to buy me a pair of jeans and a sweatshirt. Instead, I arrived at school each day in ridiculous attire dug out of my mother's trunk . . . From the moment I stepped into the schoolyard, I was ridiculed mercilessly till I left in the afternoon. I used to pray every night for hours that I would die in my sleep, so I wouldn't have to face the same thing the next day. My parents wouldn't listen to my pleas. (Lau, *Runaway*, 10)

To have come by one's clothes by rooting through the attic is precisely not to have partaken of that consumerist compulsion at the core of our social order: Going Shopping. The resulting unsuitability of Evelyn's self-presentation is profoundly distressing to her because it forms the basis of a decisive social ostracism. Her clothing need not reflect great wealth, high fashion, or individualized sensibility; it needs rather to be utterly *normal* vis-à-vis mass culture, to signify belonging, or at least its possibility. The narrator later recalls a party at which her mother's shoes, "cheap and ungainly," were "ridiculed by a child" (*Inside*, 209). It is in *this* moment that Evelyn's view is expanded to see her parents "as they appeared to others": "Two small people in the world: two scrawny, *poorly dressed* Chinese immigrants with no power over anything" (208; emphasis added). Power is conveyed in the language of attire, and her parents' inability to signify membership marks them as undesirable and ineffectual. Power is circulated through social networks, but without the minimum conduits, they languish in disconnect: "They sat on the sofas, looking shy and tongue-tied, *plain* and *out of place*" (209; emphasis added). And if the mother's clothing is a sign of powerlessness and of cultural unassimilability, then it stands to reason that to make the daughter wear the same outcast garments is in effect to have her inherit the associated cultural handicap: inadvertently to reproduce rather than redeem the parents' failed middle-class aspirations. Whether in the purchase of clothing or movies—going shopping or going out—mass culture embodies the indoctrination of play as consumerism, and consumerism as play. Evelyn carps that she "was never allowed to play much as a child" (*Runaway*, 86): her hours structured as endless work, by parents opposed to both unproductivity and extravagance. Unfortunately, to be awkward or incompetent at consumer culture signals an incriminating failure or unwillingness to share the ideals of capital. One who cannot play in the prescribed ways is thereby capitalism's bad subject, not its model minority. To be forcefully thwarted, by the same authorities, from the very means to achieve the ambitions one is forcefully obliged to adopt and pursue, is a recipe for frustration and defeat all around. And as the narrators' repeated references to depression, insanity, and suicide suggest, the stakes of disappointment can be high. Though both based on principles of disciplinary formation, there is a line between school and prison, a difference between enclosure and its furthest application of captivity; and for power to lose the distinction is to confuse whether it is making docile bodies for a profitable citizenry, or simply breaking them down.

∿ no telling where it hurts

Yet, even when it is legitimate to say that the child's position in the model minority machinery is an unreasonable or unbearable one, her condition is materialized in terms so frivolous as to be an impossible grievance to present. However articulate they may be, the narrators of Lau's and Liu's texts are constrained to talk about their distress in terms of not being able to play or go shopping, see movies, or kiss boys, because they were always vacuuming or practicing the piano. Like Jade Snow and Maxine before them, Catherine and Evelyn find their narratives hard-pressed to meet the task of critiquing the paradoxes and hypocrisies of a power instantiated in such underwhelming details. Indeed, for their parents, insistence upon the triviality of the daughters' troubles is instrumental as a silencing strategy. Scolding her, Evelyn's "father kept emphasizing that [she] had an 'easy life'"; her response is immediate and sarcastic—"Oh? Where is it, then? I must search for it among my possessions" (135)—a sharp rebuttal to the inference that one's welfare may be judged by material means alone. Catherine's father, likewise, "liked to tell us that we had it easy because of him. He let us go to school. . . . We had enough food to eat. We got more than one set of clothes a year" (Liu, 128), but extends the inference further, to undermine his daughter's claim specifically to literary expression: "My father told me that it was only through suffering and experience that a writer would find his material" (258), and that "I would never be able to write anything of real value because my stomach was always full" (259). Maxine's throat-seizing anxiety that she "would never be able to talk with" her elders because she had "no stories of equal pain" (Kingston, *Men*, 207) is here transcribed onto the written page, a paralysis for the hand and pen. Not only does the apparent pettiness of their accounts undercut the force of Catherine's and Evelyn's critiques; it threatens their right to write at all.

Accused of having a life not worth writing, Liu's narrator learns to yearn for suffering which may be more justifiably documented: something with physical evidence, historical scope, epic drama—suffering with a good plot. "As a child, I dreamed of being on the [Long] March because it seemed that suffering for the [Communist] Revolution made sense, whereas the suffering I experienced was totally meaningless" (Liu, 148).[27] Lau's narrator recalls as a child drifting inside depression for months or even a year at a time, a state which found her "wishing [she] had some physical explanation" (Lau, *Inside*, 28) for her "unfocused sense of impending doom," which was "made more unbearable because it was without cause" (29). She describes depression as "a difficult state to tolerate in another. There is no visible wound to bandage, no doctor's pronouncement of a terminal illness with which to sympathize" (41); "And though [to the depressed] their suffering is as real to them as a severed limb, it cannot help appearing to the observer like an affliction of the spoiled and wasteful, like the behavior of an anorexic or bulimic would seem to the starving in Africa" (42). The recurring allusion to Third World poverty here is revealing. In this imaginary, poverty is a thrillingly physical reality, in which people who eat their leather belts to survive have direct access to meaning and value, and which exists only beyond the seas. Evelyn and Catherine judge themselves against and through the eyes of the imagined Third World poor, because it is that subject position the parents claim as their own, and leverage against the girls. Unable to measure up to this standard of legitimacy, the narrators exhibit a kind of masochistic envy: for a recognized and validated hurt, something very bad, and something that, having been identified, can be treated. Suffering that cannot be instantiated with material injury, privation, or palpable trauma is ill-addressed not only within the family but within the legal and social apparatuses of the state—a Western state with which the parents then demonstrably share a common rather than alternative logic, a materially privileged rather than inherently Third World perspective: "I think of [the social workers] who tried to help me but could not find one gigantic bruise or one long scar they could point to triumphantly and say, 'This is what they did to her, take her away'" (Lau, *Runaway*, 163). Even while still in her adolescence, Evelyn is able to recognize that her afflictions are "much more *insidious*" (emphasis added) than what the system needs to find, and therefore that it cannot see to help her.[28] Such "insidious trauma" defies the telling, because it is foreign to the vocabulary of its place and time:

> Our experience as children had been so peculiar, so *uncommunicable . . .* that strange, *inaccessible place, more remote than China, more geographically isolated* than the Himalayas, more temporally distant than the ancient Chou dynasty—our Chinese suburban childhood, a nonplace whose main characteristics were utterly absent from any forms of representation, popular or literary. (Liu, 185; emphases added)[29]

Without vehicles for representation, experience so incommensurable can become elusive even to the subject herself: "What did my parents do to me, if anything? My mother screaming, my father lecturing and criticizing my existence . . . But what if there's nothing wrong with that?" (Lau, *Runaway*, 152).

That both narrators confess to an assortment of variously self-destructive acts is consistent with, and demystified by, their felt need for a culturally recognized hurt, an empirically verifiable injury. It is with a certain savor of optimism that Liu's narrator, at a young age, searches out clinically diagnosed forms of mental illness she might have, in order to explain her situation:

> I read every book I could about mental disorders in the young adult section of our public library. I began to think I was crazy. If I was being treated so badly and it was my fault, perhaps I was not simply selfish, incompetent, mean, impatient—that is, flawed in a modest and normal way—perhaps I was actually mentally ill. I started to read books like . . . *Three Faces of Eve*, and *Sybil* with feelings of dread and fascination. (Liu, 151)

When they get older, both girls take up drug habits—a problem for which there are rehabilitation clinics and hotlines, informational pamphlets and medical procedures, even a national ad campaign. Both enter high-risk lines of sexual work, tempting infection or attack with every encounter: Catherine as a stripper and Evelyn as a street hooker.[30] And of course, Evelyn runs away. In one of the first events of her journal, she is committed to a brutal psychiatric ward, and finds that institutionalization is not the blessing of legitimized suffering one might hope. "If this experience has taught me anything," she says, "it's not to do anything later in life that would result in hospitalization or imprisonment. It's just not worth it" (Lau, *Runaway*, 32). Yet, as soon as she finds out that her parents have come to retrieve her, she panics and fights to stay: "I would almost rather stay in the psych ward scumhole than live at home and didn't [sic] understand why I was being kicked out like this" (33). In its two-year run, the diary chronicles countless episodes of harrowing physical danger: illness, rape, and beatings; relentless scavenging for food and shelter from one cold night to the next; all experiences sharpened by a never-distant fear of death. But as Evelyn compiles these pages, each incident narrated in grim, harsh detail, she is able to say,

> the pain of what I have gone through since leaving home is far less than the pain I experienced at home . . . (252)
>
> Do you think that being on the streets is anything more than a physical flogging? If I wanted to wreck myself inside I'd go back to my parents, bring home straight-A report cards, do all the housework and smile. (81)
>
> I am happy. I work hard, but whenever my jaw aches or my arms fall asleep, whenever a man takes forever to come, I tell myself it is much better than vacuuming the house for my parents—which would be my "day off"; in the evening I'd be confined to the bedroom studying again. (260)
>
> Still, I believe that dying out here "free" is better than perishing mad and alone inside a bedroom. (56)

The comparison she makes—that this diary, written after she leaves the family home, is "no different from all the . . . diaries preceding it—it is a story of survival" (12)—is explicit, but it allows her to make an argument which is strategically *implicit*, in that she is able to refer to the horror she can describe, horrors we as a society are prepared to recognize, *in place of* the horror she cannot find words to make us understand. The comparison does its work for her, and she is relieved of the need to *prove* in logic and in detail that home was awful, because the proof lies in the default, that she would prefer even this.

bloodletting ∾

In using acts of self-destruction as means of self-preservation, Lau's and Liu's narrators corroborate Michelle Massé's psychoanalytic account of masochism as a (problematic, but nonetheless viable) form of agency. In opposition to readings which would cast the masochist either as sole agent of her solicited injury, or passive victim of another's domination, Massé argues that masochism is in fact an "adaptive behavior" (Massé, 51) whereby the relatively powerless seek to avoid further grief. "The masochist offers her own fantasy to ward off a worse dream or reality. By presenting herself as spectacle, she asserts that she always/already has paid enough" (47). Hence, the "pain she may inflict upon herself," in this case epistemologically verifiable harm, is applied as a "technique of control" (46) with hopes of "warding off [what she perceives to be] more dangerous external threats" (51):[31] harm which is incommunicable and culturally unrecognized. Through masochism, furthermore, a child may be able to retool victimization into "an *attack* ([i.e.,] 'suffering is my revenge')" (46; emphasis added)—both, for example, as in Evelyn's vengeful embrace of banishment, and in the sense that "conspicuous and silent suffering can shout an accusation at her tormentors" (47). Such suffering, then, is intended for the reception of an audience other than the tormentor, whether society at large, or a literary reading public. "It's said," and I would like to quote, "that in Chinese society a young woman's suicide was often investigated, and publicly perceived, as a sign of family abuse, and so suicide was the ultimate form of protest available to young women" (Chu, 154). This is not to posit a cultural causality, but to draw a parallel: that "what appears to be pain-dependent behavior turns out to be a vehicle of power for the weak" (Massé, 50), those who will not otherwise be heard or believed. Suicide is an option Evelyn invokes often—as evidence of the unbearable pressure her family places on her ("Once in Grade 5, I received 89 percent on an exam. I couldn't go home with this imperfect mark and frantically told a friend that I was going to commit suicide" [Lau, *Runaway*, 10]); as an act which would bring "disappointment," shame, and embarrassment to her parents (10, 11); and as an out which she eventually chooses, in alternate forms at once more passive and no less active: Falling into drug addictions to which, by definition, she surrenders control, Evelyn concludes, "It was a symbolic suicide, each pill, each cup of methadone" (226). And, most simply, a 14-year-old girl who decides to live on the streets places herself *in harm's way*; it is as if she were to step out onto a target range and wait to be shot, rather than pull the trigger herself: "Maybe tonight will be the night that something terrible happens" (*Inside*, 15). The more passive aspect of these acts, their deferral of accountability, is of course itself richly symbolic. Ironically enough, self-destruction incriminates, because it implies causality and responsibility on someone else's part.

Insanity and suicide recur, often as paired terms, not only in Lau's and Liu's texts but in Asian American women's literature more broadly. One or both of these terms is to be found in Kingston's *Woman Warrior*, Tan's *The*

Joy Luck Club, Janice Mirikitani's "Suicide Note," Fae Myenne Ng's *Bone*, and Lisa Park's "A Letter to My Sister," to name a few. The genre's investment in these markers of self-destruction arguably constitutes a kind of "protonarrative, a private or collective narrative fantasy" (Jameson, 115), which presents an "imaginary resolution of the objective contradictions to which it thus constitutes an active response" (118). In this context, to slit a wrist or drop out of school is to split open "the façade of a dutiful, high-achieving daughter from a hard-working immigrant family" (Lau, *Inside*, 92); the breach rent in one's flesh or life thus makes public family failures—in other words, it publishes them. Literature may well be not only the earliest of Catherine's and Evelyn's acts of disobedience, but perhaps even pattern for the rest, because their ensuing acts of self-destruction share with their pursuit of literature its terrible ambivalence as an effort to survive. Like reading and writing, insanity and suicide are ways for the subject to arrange that her body be in the room but the rest of her is not; as modes of escape, all are severely troubled by the indistinctiveness of success and failure, of critique and capitulation. Moreover, literature, as it turns out, prefigures madness and suicide in masochism. In reflecting on her attachment to writing, Evelyn recalls:

> A woman I know who used to write poetry says she's glad she stopped. "I don't know how I would have coped if I'd kept going. It took me to a very difficult place. I think eventually it would have destroyed me."
> *Who would choose to be destroyed?* (106; emphasis added)

This self-implicating question leads immediately into (sets up or is answered by) the memory of that conversation in which she insists on rejecting medicine for literature; *equating* the harrowing process of writing with self-destruction, the narrator *frames* her understanding of disobedience in such a way that the three terms dissolve into a single act: To write is to resist is to be destroyed. To publish an indictment of one's parents is therefore masochistic precisely in that the writer inflicts harm upon herself as an act of aggression against her family. However, the annihilation of self, as in death or madness, is privileged in Evelyn's and Catherine's imaginations as an end to which one is credibly driven, not a state one may frivolously seek: "Somehow I knew that if I didn't [leave], I would kill myself or go crazy" (*Runaway*, 12). It is that validating lack of choice—the strange prerogative to disavow agency and assign accountability elsewhere—that makes self-destruction, in a context of limited options, not only a rejection of indebtedness to power, but also an expressive deployment of pain, even a compelling mode of discourse.

✌ dear reader

Asian American critics displeased with Lau's representation of the family have been known to slight her narrative as having an Agenda: to sell copies, by selling out her culture. I have no doubt that this diary, the bulk of which details hard living and risk-taking, sold far better than would have the earlier diaries she lost, pages filled with bitterness over piano practice. But that is very much to my point here: It is a sensationalistic story, to be sure; worthy of a television special. But its sensationalistic elements do not include her family life, the writer's "culture." Indeed, accounts of her life at home occupy a tiny fraction of the book, primarily as a frame for her decision to leave, and make no claims out of the ordinary. In fact, it is the very unsensationalistic nature of the domesticity she does recount that commentators such as Lien Chao and Jan Wong target: "expecting one's daughter to become a doctor or lawyer may not be an outrageous demand by parents in any culture," yet "Lau paints her mother as a dictator who tries to impose ancient Chinese discipline on her: 'rapping a ruler impatiently against her palm and forcing [her] to recite the answers to textbook questions'" (Chao, 162). By these belittling measures, Lau's narrative is ranked as "self-indulgent" (J Wong, A11) and ethnically treasonous:

> To most Canadian readers, the behavior of Lau's parents appears unreasonable and unaccountable. The only possible explanation for that could be their inappropriate Chinese cultural baggage. . . .
>
> By presenting her parents as the perpetual cultural Other, the narrator makes sure the reader can see through her parents who "are so obvious, clumsy, revealing all the more starkly what they are trying to hide" [218]. Later the narrator even borrows the power of her psychiatrist . . . , who compares her parents metaphorically to the permanently fixed, unchangeable sign on his car: " . . . no matter how much he talked to it or yelled at it, the letters would never change. 'F-O-R-D.'" [135]. Through a continuous process of Othering, Lau's parents are fossilized as the forever opposite of the narrator. (Chao, 163)

But the terms of Chao's critique, as well as her roughshod disregard of evidence,[32] expose the critic's adherence to an Agenda of her own. Through her charges of Orientalism and her distancing reference to a majority readership, Chao firmly establishes her position in antagonism to white cultural hegemony; by defending Evelyn's parents against their daughter's attack, she aligns herself with the immigrant generation. In her dismissive interview of Lau,[33] journalist Wong draws like allegiances when she declares, "But I'm a parent now," and seals her personal contrast to Lau with a History-pegged value judgment: "Now, I left my comfortable Montreal home at 19 to voluntarily haul pig manure in China during the Cultural Revolution" (J Wong, A11).

However, the trouble with communal criticism of this vein, as Tomo Hattori argues, is its inability to "confront the capitalism of its own logic" (Hattori, 229); invested in promoting the oppositional theories and politics which "are the currency that enables its institutionalization and survival" (Nguyen, 14), such ethnic nationalism "disavows the model minority status of many Asian American intellectuals themselves" (144)—and of the subjects with whose positions they identify. Having collected, even briefly, just the kind of experience that Catherine's parents claim for themselves, Wong leverages it in the same manner, to legitimate herself as one who, having known important suffering, has direct access to righteous politics and may now dispense judgment. Both Chao's and Wong's pieces betray a desire, in fact, to fossilize Evelyn's parents as forever the opposite of white capitalist America (as if having been a materially deprived Chinese native makes a subject automatically and henceforth politically subversive), and to color themselves "bad" by association. But to paraphrase Kingston, one's family is not necessarily the Third World poor to be championed; in a confusing state of affairs, any of these purportedly bad capitalist subjects might well have found themselves prosecuted as owning class by agents whose motivations were themselves suspect. And certainly, it is difficult to sustain the case that scores of would-be first-generation Americans or Canadians are now or were ever motivated to immigrate out of a desire *not* to gain access to "the washer, the dryer, the brown indoor/outdoor wall-to-wall carpeting, the microwave oven, the toaster, the big color TV that had shows on it twenty-four hours a day, and, on top of it all, the VCR" (Liu, 86), as if the dream of these things did not figure into their intentions.[34] As Hattori argues, "the romance of the Oriental Girl conceals," for the white men who mail-order an Asian bride, "the reality of a Third World woman with the blunt economic ambition and vulgar materialist drive of a capitalist" (Hattori, 240). Ironically, cultural nationalist Asian American critics cherish a parallel fantasy: the romance of the Third World subject, which likewise enables their own agendas by concealing the same (unheroizable) drive to assimilate to capitalism.

Given the capital-investment mentality Catherine's and Evelyn's parents apply toward leveraging their children into the professional-managerial class, they represent quite the reverse of the contestatory principles or "refusal to be assimilated" that Chao, and a wishful ethnic scholarship behind her, try to ascribe to the Asian immigrant subject (Chao, 165; Koshy, 160). They are instead very much a driving force behind their children's assimilation, setting their sights on Harvard, M.I.T., Google, Goldman Sachs, Neiman Marcus, Mercedes Benz. The narrators' grievances against their parents are a function not of the latter's cultural otherness, but of their relentlessly capitalist determination. This is not to say that the parents themselves suffer no oppression under the social and economic systems to which they wish to be incorporated. Both Lau's and Liu's narrators are perceptive to their parents' positions of relative powerlessness in the world outside their homes (Liu, 114; Lau, *Inside*, 208), and understand that discriminatory practices enacted upon their fathers, as the primary breadwinners, impact upon the financial as well as emotional welfare of the family. Liu's narrator observes her father's fear of "Americans" (Liu, 130), his "bowing and scraping . . . before those more powerful than him," and makes the connection ethnic nationalist scholarship itself has made, to the intimidation and tyranny he levels at her:

> Outside of the family, with his superiors, . . . he could be deferential to the point of absurdity. Inside the family, he demanded from us his own brand of servility. (128)

> [M]en of color who have been abused in a white society are often tempted to restore their sense of masculinity by venting their anger and self-hatred against those who are even more powerless. (Cheung, 108)

Certainly, there are historical contexts and identifiable, contributing factors to which one may point, to situate the family and its manner of inhabiting power. It does not then follow, however, that behind the domination there is no personal investment. Unlike ethnic nationalist criticism, Catherine is not tempted by extenuating factors to harbor the hope that whatever violence the family inflicts upon its own is not "meant" (Liu, 114). Rather, she comes to question whether "being Chinese, being a child in war-torn China," or even being an immigrant, racial other in the United States, "could excuse the antics and excesses of the Fat Man" or his wife (128). As Massé argues of patriarchal domination, not only does "being oppressed . . . not make one a de facto nice person," but the oppressed may very well become in their turn oppressors who, in replicating their subjection, "aim . . . not to deny or resist the self-destructive aims of [dominant] ideology but *to close the gap between self and the dominant other . . . by full merger*" (43; emphasis added). When a system of subjugation fails to create resistance, and furthermore forms oppressors in its own image, then a scholarship of oppositional intent does ill to defend, much less to align itself with, the enlisted agents of such power, for in doing so it will perpetuate the ideologies and acts of domination.

Asian American studies has thus far shown itself, nevertheless, to be mainly invested in a defense of immigrant parents against their reproachful daughters. And yet, between the intellectual class of the Asian American left and the writer figures of Lau and Liu or their narrators, there is arguably more similarity than difference.

> [This class, including our] academics, artists, activists, and nonacademic critics, is a part of the realm of cultural production that finds its basis in . . . the economic world reversed. . . . In this reversed world, it is not economic capital, that is, money and its investment, that matters as much as *symbolic capital*, other things besides money that we invest with value and which eventually generate an economic return. (Nguyen, 5)

It is very much like Evelyn and Catherine that, not only does this class shun the lucrative professions of the model minority, but the authors of literary criticism in particular have opted for careers in the pursuit of literature— careers the traditional symbolic capital of which immigrant parents do not recognize and are not apt to grace with approval. The emphatic contrast that critics such as Chao and Wong seek to draw between themselves and "bad daughters" such as Catherine and Evelyn must then be viewed in light of their actual parity. May I suggest that what is at stake in such vigorous disavowal of intergenerational conflict can be both personal—a fear of the brazenly unfilial act—and political: a fear of association with insufficiently oppositional politics, politics which would then devalue their own institutional stock. In either case, a mounted defense of the first-generation parent is strategic: For one, to detail at length the extent of another's disloyalty to the family is to make use of the tools of filiality itself but to flip the direction of comparison—and defer failure by projecting it onto someone else's child, not one's self. For another, Catherine's and Evelyn's avowals of thirst for consumer culture are profanity in leftist communities of activism and academics. To denounce Lau's and Liu's narrators is to disavow one's own good capitalist consumer compunctions—the self-unacceptable contradictions of "an academic intelligentsia that is both the most vocal advocate of radical Third World emergence and a reliable middle-class consumer of Third World sweatshop products" (Hattori, 243). In either case, that which endangers the critic's position and prompts attack is not otherness but dangerous proximity—a likeness which makes her aggression then suggestively masochistic in nature: self-(pre)serving and self-destructive all at once.

Butler maintains that where power not only subordinates but functions in the first place to form the subject, "providing the very conditions for its existence and the trajectory of its desire" (Butler, *Psychic*, 2), resistance will necessarily risk the dissolution of the subject in challenging the conditions of its social existence.

> [T]he power [the subject assumes then] remains tied to those conditions, but in an ambivalent way; in fact the power assumed may at once retain and resist that subordination. This conclusion is not to be thought of as (a) a resistance that is *really* a recuperation of power or (b) a recuperation that is *really* a resistance. It is both at once, and this ambivalence forms the bind of agency. (13)

Such an admission of ambivalence is meant not to evacuate or foreclose possibilities of dissent, but to enable such honesties as Nguyen urges of criticism. To own that, as Asian American intellectuals, we "can frequently occupy both [model minority and bad subject] situations simultaneously or, at the very least, alternate between them," and that our positions are constituted by such "mutual interdependency" (Nguyen, 144), is to enable more accurate responses to subject positions which threaten by mirroring us, and perhaps to imagine more effective courses of action. For those who would style themselves unruly subjects, critics, and opponents of power, for whom compromise looms as a worrisome or threatening thing, it is interesting to consider, as Hattori suggests, subjects who are not hounded by a standard of nonexistent political purity. Be it in words or on their bodies, the narrators of Lau's and Liu's texts perform a heady mixture of accommodation and resistance, in the service of dissent and survival. If *The Woman Warrior* and *Fifth Chinese Daughter* track the paradoxes of power, *Runaway* and *Oriental Girls Desire Romance* can be said to trace the paradoxes of resistance—their attempts to defy power built on a structure of ambivalence, manifested in the duality of masochism: forever and irresolvably suffering and struggle, oppression and choice. And yet, if agency may be defined as "the assumption of a purpose *unintended* by power, . . . that operates in a relation of contingency and reversal to the power that makes it possible, to which it nevertheless belongs" (Butler, *Psychic*, 15), then Catherine's and Evelyn's exploitation of their subjection as a strike against power may never be free, but is nevertheless agency.

Desirable Daughters

Fae Myenne Ng, Elaine Mar, Chitra Divakaruni

Despite all the prohibitions and injunctions surrounding the
sexual behavior of Oriental girls, or perhaps because of them, I
had sex. . . . I felt like I was trying some forbidden drug, and this
made things exciting. I kept it all to myself, and did it as much as
I could. I proved to myself that I could do what I liked, but I felt,
nevertheless, that I was doing something terrible, something for
which, one day, I would have to pay. I continued anyway, despite
my fears, which were very, very real. I was afraid of boys, I was
afraid of people, I was afraid of my parents, but I pressed on.

Catherine Liu, *Oriental Girls Desire Romance*

Sexuality must not be described as a stubborn drive, by nature
alien and of necessity disobedient to a power which exhausts itself
trying to subdue it and often fails to control it entirely. It appears
rather as an especially dense transfer point for relations of power:
between men and women, young people and old people, parents
and offspring, . . . an administration and a population. Sexuality
is not the most intractable element in power relations, but rather
one of those endowed with the greatest instrumentality: useful
for the greatest number of maneuvers and capable of serving as
a point of support, as a linchpin, for the most varied strategies.

Michel Foucault, *The History of Sexuality*, Volume I

Among the three ill-fated daughters of Fae Myenne Ng's *Bone*—"one
unmarried, another who-cares-where, one dead" (Ng, 24)[1]—there is a suicide
to be sure, but there is also a disownment. When Nina, pregnant and unmarried, decides to abort, she decides also to inform her parents of these develop-

ments. The disclosure is unnecessary on any legal or logistical level—bound to do no good, then, but to prompt her expulsion from the family; it is both baffling and intelligible to her eldest sister for that same reason. As their parents curse Nina, sure enough, to suffer and die abandoned and alone in this life and the next, Leila understands that the pregnancy, and the telling, were her sister's "way out" (51). Nina leaves the home from which she is now barred, and it is unclear how or whether any notions of familial responsibility or filial obligation apply to her thereafter. It is commonly recognized that the story told in *Bone* begins after Ona's suicide and moves backward, looking for answers, straight past that crucial moment of her death and into the sisters' childhoods. But if Ng's narrative deliberately "misses" the point of origin and explanation for which its characters search, it is equally true that the narrative misses a turning point for which they do not even think to look, and do not bother to explain. The story begins its telling long after Nina has been expelled from the home, and skips right over any moments of her sexual initiation, pregnancy, abortion, or disownment, to continue investigating her sister's death and life. While the characters obsess over their responses to Ona, worrying the past for indications of what they might have done differently—how to read what happened, Ona's decisions and their own—neither they nor the narrative pause to consider whether *Nina's* actions might have produced a different reaction, why *these* events took the shapes they did, and what these shapes might mean.

This same family narrative is first told in "A Red Sweater," the short story from which *Bone*, the novel-length development, presumably grew, with subtle but provocative variations. In this earlier version, the second daughter's suicide is quickly announced and quickly sets the scene, but like an abandoned subplot, is carried neither forward nor backward along with the narrative; twice it is made known that the middle sister "jumped," but in just that stark, seemingly traumatized way, devoid of remark or the least speculation. This is noteworthy because in the novel, while mostly absent, Ona is a constant preoccupation, yet here it is as if the narrative has no further interest in her. Of course, should one care to speculate, her narrative abandonment may have any number of causes or implications, ranging from the intriguing to the very mundane; for my purposes, I find it interesting to think about the neglect of Ona's counterpart as a by-product of the short story's markedly different focus from the novel. Whereas in the latter, suicide eclipses disownment, in the former it is the disowned daughter who takes precedence. And though the shorter piece does not grant answers any more than the novel, we are led by its alternate focus not to speculate about Ona, but to wonder along with Nina's character "if there wasn't another way" (Sweater, 359) for her relationship with her parents to have turned out. Despite the press given in *Bone* to the whys of Ona's death, it is provocative to consider that the underlying impulse of its story may lie instead with Nina—not with the character who, in the story's conceptual origins, slips out of mind and narrative like a fine point or fleeting pretext. It is Nina's counterpart who narrates "A Red Sweater," and as she proceeds to relate memories of her childhood, by midway through the short story, those memories seem as if populated by only two girls; repeatedly the language makes room for only the narrator and her eldest sister: "How many times did my sister and I have to hold them apart? . . . Was it *she or I* who screamed?" (367; emphasis added). In the *novel's* earliest memories, as it were, in the characters' psychic lives, there is no Ona whose death to answer, and the pressing anxiety is actually to sound out the relationship between the youngest and her oldest sister, to discover how one tells the difference between them.

Leila and Nina occupy opposing positions, as "the daughter who takes care of the parents" and "the daughter who has been banned from the home." And yet, unsurprisingly, the boundaries between good and bad daughters here are more fluid than firm—as demonstrated by the very reversal of roles between Ng's texts: In *Bone*, it is Leila who narrates, Leila who observes her sensually beautiful (rebellious) sister; in "A Red Sweater," the table is turned, and Nina's character narrates, yet it is the dutiful oldest sister whom Nina watches for her beauty. The physical description of the chosen "beautiful" sister in each of these parallel scenes is, in fact, identical in language ("[X] is reed-thin and tall. She's got a body that clothes look good on. [X] slips something on and it wraps her like skin. Fabric has a pulse on her"), but the characters' names are neatly swapped (*Bone*, 27; Sweater, 362). This astonishing moment exposes the identities themselves to be fundamentally unstable: partially interchanged, partially interchangeable. That these qualities of body (markers of distinctively sexual valence) could alternately characterize both daughters, and that in *Bone*, furthermore, *both* young women are in fact and *to their parents' knowledge* sexually active, together dislodge any tidy conceptions of what makes a daughter sexually "obedient" and what makes her sexually transgressive. Thus, to take up the question of whether, for Nina's short story counterpart, there might have been "any other way" than pregnancy and disownment, is to consider what it is that she was trying to accomplish, and what role sex played therein.

Though it may seem something of a logical commonplace that a sexually active girl "rebels" against her restrictive upbringing, this chapter begins by asking why rebellious girls have sex. More specifically, it asks what complex of meanings is deployed when an Asian American daughter chooses, as in so many literary instances she does, to take up with boys in defiance of her immigrant parents. I draw up this question advisedly, in order to avoid having first or comprehensively to answer why it is that families restrict their daughters' sexual activities far out of keeping with their sons'. *What is it about daughters* that, even in an age of contraception, a girl's engagement in sexual activity could cause her to be discarded, said to be forgotten as if she had never been born? *What is invested in female virginity* such that a family should insist upon keeping its reputation between its daughters' legs, and what purpose would such an ill-advised arrangement serve? As that Ur-story exceeds the compass of our literary texts, it extends also beyond the sights of our line of inquiry. This chapter will hazard no theories of origin, but limit its examinations instead to current uses, being in one sense but an extension of Foucault's argument in *The History of Sexuality* against the "repressive hypothesis": The point will be made here that the prohibition against sex for the second-generation daughter is a productive one; in this iteration, we will be interested in the prohibition's production of the Asian American daughter as a particular gendered subject. Taking a discursive rather than ethnographic approach, this chapter will look to literary narratives for the stories we tell ourselves about sex—as glimpses into a cultural imaginary about how to raise proper Asian American womanhood. Referencing works by Chitra Divakaruni, Gish Jen, and Elaine Mar as well as Kingston and Ng, this chapter will address fiction and nonfiction equally, as equal players in the perpetuation of discourse.

In chapter 3 I argued that second-generation sons and daughters had reached a potential parity in their economic value to, and therefore in their treatment within, the family; this chapter complicates that claim by recognizing standards, and investments, which are unmitigatedly gender-specific. Girls are singled out to be threatened with and trained on cautionary tales of other daughters who stray from the paths of sexual purity and meet some combination of madness, death, or disownment; their lives and bodies are routinely ordered and restricted by measures to which their brothers are never subjected. These gendered practices produce a relationship to power, articulated through sexuality, specific to women. As other post-structuralist feminist arguments have pointed out, "Women, like men, are subject to many of the same disciplinary practices Foucault describes," but we are subject also to "disciplines that produce a modality of embodiment that is particularly feminine" (Bartky, 64). Training a young girl to be properly circumspect about her sexuality, power seeks to produce in her not only the correct mind-set and courses of action, but a specifically female docile body. Indeed, each of the above—character and embodiment—implicates and constitutes the other, as the corollary of an exercise of power in which discourse and discipline are themselves mutually constitutive.

However, while this chapter is interested to address familial standards and investments explicit to the construction of femininity, it does not take gendering authority to be synonymous with patriarchy or the patriarch alone. Such exclusive attribution of power requires too much systematic omission, when so much of the work of producing the "model daughter" via sexual prohibition is conducted through discursive technologies traditionally under the purview of female authorities: the round of gossip, the cautionary tale. It is worth remembering that the *Woman Warrior's* most bitter struggle to define a "feminist" subjectivity is articulated in that text which pits Maxine not against her father, but against her mother. This is not to suggest that patriarchy is not a system of male advantage, surely; but it is to take into account other cultural configurations of power with arguably equal investment in the control of young women, sexual or otherwise: power structured around interests including but not limited to gender hierarchy. Certainly, individual women who perpetuate destructive gossip may well be said to act out of an investment in short-term or limited benefits allowed to them within a patriarchal system; subjects can and commonly do act as guardians of systems which do them fundamental disservice, and a mother may energetically support a patriarchy which oppresses all women in order that she herself or her own daughters may thrive within its rules, relative to other women. Male domination alone, however, is too monolithic an explanation to account for power differentials among women who vie—not only across institutional units—but within one: mothers and daughters, aunts and nieces, and so on. What other configurations of social relation obtain here, such that the interests of one member, male or female, may be placed over or empowered to determine the interests of another within a single family? This chapter bids us consider seriously that, if authority figures both male and female take such an active investment in perpetuating the system, then authority figures both male and female must stand to gain from the successful production of a specifically gendered daughterly subject.

∿ gossip mongers

We begin with "No Name Woman," the cautionary tale that sets the stage for *The Woman Warrior*. As Maxine's narrative of her mundane childhood and upbringing, the book makes a revealing choice in opening on the primal stuff of folklore: pregnancy, death, and the powerful maternal injunction that "Now that you have started to menstruate, what happened to her could happen to you. Don't humiliate us. You wouldn't like to be forgotten as if you had never been born" (Kingston, 5). The aunt's story, a discursive framework used to fashion Maxine's own reality, belongs to a genre of like tales which share both its formal and its functional qualities. In Chitra Divakaruni's "The Word Love," for instance (a short story written in the second person, for an effect that is both detached and interpellating), the protagonist recalls

... a story your mother told you when you were growing up:

There was a girl I used to play with sometimes, whose father was the roof-thatcher in your grandmother's village. . . . She was an only child, pretty in a dark-skinned way, and motherless, so her father spoiled her. He let her run wild, climbing trees, swimming in the river. Let her go to school, even after she reached the age when girls from good families stayed home, waiting to be married. . . . He would laugh when the old women of the village warned him that an unmarried girl is like a firebrand in a field of ripe grain. She's a good girl, he'd say. She knows right and wrong. He found her a fine match, a master carpenter from the next village. But a few days before the wedding her body was discovered in the women's lake. We all thought it was an accident until we heard about the rocks she had tied in her sari. . . . Who knows why? People whispered that she was pregnant, said they'd seen her once or twice with a man, a traveling actor who had come to the village some time back. Her father was heartbroken, his good name ruined. He had to leave the village, all those tongues and eyes. Leave behind the house of his forefathers that he loved so much. No, no one knows what happened to him. (Divakaruni, 64; italics in original)

Discourse of this nature, as I have sought to show in my earlier discussion of Kingston, plays no small part in constructing the formative logic of daughterhood; in such representations is the entrée for "gain[ing] control of the individual . . . : the representations of his [sic] interests, the representation of his advantages and disadvantages, pleasure and displeasure" (Foucault, *Discipline*, 127). These narrative representations encode the most elemental knowledges of gender and familial relations, including the information that, for a girl, there is a price for sex, and it is family. However, reading the cautionary tales we see here for their con*text* as well as for their con*tent* reveals them to be no generic oral history but a specialized variety of discourse: whispered between intimates, about an absent third party of some association to the speakers, in order to consolidate the relationship between those present (Sze, 62). Both of these stories are, in other words, stories fundamentally *about gossip*, which also *participate in the circulation of gossip*—and are, therefore, a form of gossip themselves: "More attention to her looks than these pullings of hairs and pickings at spots would have caused gossip among the villagers" (Kingston, *Warrior*, 10); "People whispered that she was pregnant, said they'd seen her once or twice with a man, a traveling actor who had come to the village some time back," "There was a girl I used to play with sometimes, whose father was the roof-thatcher in your grandmother's village . . ." (Divakaruni, 64); "Don't let your father know that I told you" (Kingston, 5).

Gossip is worth considering at length here, because it may well be the definitive disciplinary mechanism by which female sexuality is regulated. In her article on *Bone*, Julie Sze argues plausibly for the positive value of gossip: in its constructive social functions, gossip forges community, gossip "heals relationships between" gossiping individuals (Sze, 64), gossip "offer[s] an interpretive and explanatory framework" for events where originally there was none (67). Lest it be valorized unduly, however, let us be very clear that gossip establishes community *on the basis of exclusion*; that it cannot have its insiders without creating its outsiders. "By agreeing about their evaluation of someone else," Sze suggests, "people reinforce their shared values and world views'" (63)—or, indeed, they demarcate values to be shared and propagated. The interpretive frameworks gossip offers are not merely a community's attempts to understand tragic events after the fact, but attempts to construct social reality *such that* tragedy is a necessary outcome of certain acts. Whether directly, as when gossip stirs a community to attack a pregnant girl's family, or indirectly, as when it merely makes life unlivable for certain of the community's occupants, gossip moves via the closing of alliances between some against others. Exclusion is both its mechanism and its product, its means and its end. As discourse, the cautionary tale is attended with habitual violence: it threatens the young girl, and lays waste the young woman. Each cautionary tale about the community's ostracism of selected individuals redoubles, in its telling, the othering of the transgressive female figure by exploiting her as a "bad example" to be abhorred and shunned by the teller and listener in turn. Thus, exclusion is also both its principle (intrinsic to gossip) and its motivation: to ban from the child certain behaviors and identities. But exclusion itself has a divided nature here. In order to keep the child inside the space of community, it is necessary for gossip to *keep* its others outside, meaning that the pregnant girls of these stories are not forgotten once and for all, but constantly re-invoked as having been forgotten, that they may be excluded over and over again. Thus, they are erased *as persons*—stripped of their personal names—but renamed as the unnamed and unspoken, never released by the community to oblivion but suspended in the sovereign ban: "at once excluded and included, removed and at the same time captured" (Agamben, 110). Even after having been "forgotten," the young women still circulate as silence, a silence which is, as Maxine realizes, not passivity but a sustained action: "People who can comfort the dead can also *chase after them* to hurt them further" (Kingston, 16; emphasis added); Brave Orchid directs her daughter *not to repeat* the story she herself is telling, yet repeats that directive three separate times.[2] Interestingly, the community's procedure of insistently disavowing the sexually transgressive daughter recalls Foucault's description of the administration of sex itself, in "a society . . . which speaks verbosely of its own silence, [and] takes great pains to relate in detail the things it does not say" (Foucault, *History*, 8): She is the thing that everyone says no one talks about. By that paradox, the unmarried daughter is conceivably less the subject of repression she first appears, and more the subject of intense administration and discursive management, disciplinary regulation and scrutiny.

She who is passed around in whispered conversation is also (must first, and will subsequently be) passed under the gaze of the speakers, whose observation produces "knowledge" about her, and whose narratives produce frameworks for her observation. Villagers need to have seen, as a young Brave Orchid herself noticed, that No Name aunt's belly had started to grow—examination of her body setting off talk and speculation, and further scrutiny so close as to include the counting of months, and in that counting further talk, until at last they yield the day when her body will give birth. The pretty roof-thatcher's daughter is watched by village women long before her coming-of-age, predictions about her made, spying and speculation done around her interactions with men, such that after her death, community narrative leaves room for no other explanation but illegitimate pregnancy and an inevitable ruin. The engine of gossip feeds the gaze to narrative and words to scrutiny such that, in its effect, gossip is as much a mode of surveillance as of discourse. Inextricable from itself, gossip enlists subjects to act in both capacities at once. And because it is arguably an "egalitarian" discourse—"in that anyone who speaks, listens, or is involved in an informal social network, can participate" (Sze, 60)—the potentially universal membership of the gossiping community also means, with more sinister implications, a frightfully unrestricted form of watching. In her study of the disciplinary production of femininity, Sandra Lee Bartky addresses this radical distribution of the gaze when she explains, "The disciplinary power that inscribes femininity in the female body is everywhere and it is nowhere; the disciplinarian is everyone and yet no one in particular" (Bartky, 74). It is Bartky's contention that the disciplinary formation of femininity is qualitatively distinct from the production of obedient workers, students, or inmates. Unlike these, the disciplinary power that acts to regulate the female body is "institutionally unbound as well as institutionally bound" (75). Femininity is not the sole charge of designated authorities within a specified enclosure: it is not a girl's parents alone but the casual acquaintance or virtual stranger who may police her comportment and character—monitoring her use of her body, its form and bearing, for any sign of slippage. This would look something like the difference between Bentham's Panopticon and the Wachowski brothers' Matrix, between a structuralist and post-structuralist model of power: Though in either case authority is pervasive, unindividuated, interchangeable, the Panopticon does keep rigid distinctions between guard and subject, and rigid divisions among subjects (such that they are not permitted to see, much less are they expected to watch, one another); within the Matrix, however, any subject may at any time become an agent of police, turning in that moment from object of observation to disciplinarian, authorized to supervise and even penalize other human subjects. While gossip does have faces—in *Bone*, the "sewing ladies," infamous gossips; the old women of the brief story above; the mothers relaying each cautionary tale—gossip is *also* faceless, anonymous by virtue of being so global as to lose any meaningful specificity. Thus, the undifferentiating expressions often used to refer to the producers of gossip: "everyone knew our story. . . . 'People talking. People jealous'" (Ng, *Bone*, 3). The roof-thatcher is chased from the village not by individuals but by a collectivity distilled to a multitude of "*tongues* and *eyes*" (Divakaruni, 64; emphasis added), and the villagers who attack the No Name Woman wear masks in order to be truly faceless, indistinguishable. But equal-opportunity surveillance means that the gaze of power may always shift. Because everyone may be conscripted as disciplinary authority—each subject an object of surveillance, each an agent of police—the partition is arbitrary and provisional, requiring constant shoring and always in danger of collapse or, worse yet, of repositioning. In this context, the idea of the game is to keep the roving searchlight focused elsewhere, away from one's own body and business.

Of course, this is not to suggest that all members of the community share a uniform vulnerability to surveillance; while a girl is observed for the prettiness of her features and the shade of her skin, the men of her acquaintance, from father to fiancé to supposed lover, are identified by occupation alone; and while the villagers watch the curves of No Name aunt's belly slowly lower and widen, her partner remains unnamed, effectively without body or face. Unlike women, then, men are not visible to power in certain ways: no regulating discourse of sexuality circulates about them, and thus they are not watched, and therefore no knowledge is produced to circulate about them. This does not mean, however, that they are immune to gossip—only that they are constructed as being vulnerable to such gossip *through their women:* thus the father who is forced out of the home of his forefathers, and the brother whose family home the villagers raid, for the perceived indiscretions of their female kin. Interestingly, then, the regulation of a young woman's body is presented as a matter of her male relations' well-being—specifically of their "good name." When the teenage Elaine in the memoir *Paper Daughter* begins to engage in sexual activity, she is sternly admonished by her aunt that "You'll destroy your father's life. It's *his* name, you know, not your own. . . . [I]f you are shamed, it's not 'Elaine' who's talked about . . . It's the Mar girl, the daughter of Yat Shing. That's the person the community will refer to. It's his reputation you need to protect" (Mar, 228; emphasis in original). This is, of course, the very definition of patriarchy, to subsume its women under a male lineage. However, while clearly such a system comprises a domination of women which contravenes their interests, it is important to recognize that this familial configuration *also* ironically binds its men's and women's interests indissolubly to one another, and that as a result, contrary to appearances, the *family's* interests are not identical with its male members' only, but a tricky composite.[3] If the community organizes its members into groups whose fortunes are directly linked—punished or praised as one entity—then these are the *operative units of self-interest* in that social order. At the modular level, the community is made up of familial networks, and it is not as men versus women or women versus men but within *familial* structures of alliance that its members struggle daily for resources, advancement, and survival. Indeed, anthropological work on the regulation of virginity has consistently taken the family for its unit of analysis, and exerted itself in sorting out the nature of the family's interest in that project. Even the control over female sexuality (a tug of war in which team stakes would seem to be unequivocally gender-based) is implemented through the institution of the family, and therefore it is *between and within families* that its power is exercised and contested, and either prevails or fails its mark. Thus, gossip pits each family against the others in their relative control of their daughters, and pits daughters not only against fathers, but aunts and mothers—that generation claiming authority to define what the family's interests are, and to dictate its members' behavior accordingly. What begins for Elaine as an argument between father and daughter "about" female sexual activity is soon conducted by niece and aunt through arguments about individual rights and the family good. This suggests that the investments and ordering principles of the family as community institution need to be fully incorporated into a cultural account of virginity, since a family's pressing concern, however male-headed, is not to maintain the world historical defeat of women; rather, the family's main interest lies in its own welfare, its continuation, and most vociferously of all, in its prestige.

As the social distillation of a family's well-being, prestige (alternately termed "'social honor,' or 'social value'" [Ortner and Whitehead, 13]) encompasses but extends beyond economic advancement or control of resources. Prestige structures are cultural systems "with properties not directly reducible to relations of production . . . nor to material power" (15), which organize communities into social hierarchies, through "beliefs and symbolic associations that make sensible and compelling the ordering of human relations into patterns of deference and condescension, respect and disregard, and in many cases command and obedience" (14). When, as is rampant in the discourse produced around female sexuality, a child is accused of "bring[ing] shame upon our family, you act this way. What do you think people think of us?" (Jen, 45), it is in an attempt to manage and assure the family's position within a hierarchy of prestige. Such watchful management is necessary, however, because prestige is not a tangible which may be positivistically secured, nor a quality inherent to the individual: As sociologist Ruth Horowitz finds in her work on honor in another ethnic-immigrant American community,[4] "Honor cannot be measured by tests or money" (Horowitz, 22). Rather, honor and shame, the dual poles of prestige, are a function of public opinion, contingent in their fluctuation on the tides of gossip. Furthermore, no distinction is made between prestige as a *measure* of well-being and well-being itself: Insofar as status is a socioeconomic phenomenon, for a family to have lost status in the public eye is paradoxically for it to have suffered grievous material injury; honor *is* well-being and vice versa. As a consequence of this logic, the family's very "worth" may be invested in and reliant upon communal discourse. The preservation of that worth against the devaluations of "shame" therefore becomes a survival imperative, and "honor" a consummate mechanism of social control. What child, faced with the false dilemma between her own will and her family's welfare, can justifiably choose dishonor? And yet if "honor can be maintained only by following particular norms and being evaluated by others as having done so successfully" (23), then it is the crystallization of social obedience. The rhetoric of honor is therefore the darling of a disciplinary technology—whereby a community, having internalized such a value structure, disciplines itself by disciplining each other; but it is also a favorite in the arsenal of sovereign power, in that it is broadly applicable "without signifying" (Agamben, 52). At the same time that it legitimizes all manner of obedience, honor reifies social law and familial dictates into a shifting threshold of communal acceptability.

Given a network of families, each angling for higher status in a community predicated on exclusion, each family unit's investment in prestige is necessarily an investment in social competition. In a disciplinary economy, after all, where positive attainment of the ideal is categorically withheld, subjects are conditioned to perceive the hierarchy as having inherent value, differentials in prestige acting as a kind of ranking where "Rank in itself serves as a reward or punishment" (Foucault, *Discipline*, 181). Thus the commonly vicious nature of gossip. Since hierarchy is only relative, gossip serves (literally, in the No Name Woman's case) as an assault on persons and character, which enhances the speakers' social standing by degrading that of others. Studying the regulation of female sexuality within the community, Horowitz observes that "Even a young woman who rarely goes out must be exceedingly careful in her dealings with men in order to maintain her [public] identity as a virgin because *there are always people who may try to discredit her* sexual identity" (Horowitz, 119; emphasis added). No wonder, then, that parents command silence: "They were always saying, Don't tell this and don't tell that. Mah was afraid of what people inside Chinatown were saying" (Ng, 112). In this context it is key to limit the circulation of information about oneself and one's family—not only because of what may be true, but because of what may be conjectured. Any information is invitation to detractors to speculate, to narrativize, and herein lies the ironic futility of managing a girl's sexuality: In the arena of community discourse, "It is *the public perception* of [a young woman's] sexual purity that reflects upon the parents," not actually the fact of the matter; "If she is perceived as a nonvirgin, the family's honor is questioned" (Horowitz, 70; emphasis added). Indeed, within gossip "what is fact and what is fiction is nearly impossible to discern" (Sze, 60), because for its purposes the distinction is immaterial—even useful, to ignore.

Little wonder, then, that parents also clamp down on their daughters' conduct and movement. Horowitz finds that it is only with "complete parental control over [their daughter's] behavior" that a family may hope to "minimize" (but not, even then, to eliminate) "the risk of her being perceived as a nonvirgin or of actually losing her virginity" (Horowitz, 70). This means to counter the community's broad and anonymous surveillance with a familial surveillance that is institutionalized and enclosed—to confine her to the home as much as possible. Families in Horowitz's community have their daughters "maintain that image [of purity] by rarely being seen in public and by spending most of their time outside school or work at home" (119); one mother "timed her daughter's return from school every day; it took eight minutes to walk home and if her daughter was not home within twelve minutes after the last bell, the mother went out looking for her" (69). These descriptions of confinement and surveillance sharply recall Jade Snow, Evelyn, and Catherine, in accounts of their upbringings from previous chapters and other contexts. They are, all three, daughters who "never went out, helped with the housework, had no boyfriend and few friends"—girls who lived "stuck for hours and hours inside [their] bedroom[s]" (Lau, *Runaway*, 12). The privations and restrictions they complained of take on added meanings and motivations here, as when Jade Snow finds, by the age of 11, that she

> could hardly find a moment of her life which was not accounted for . . . by Mama or Daddy. She had not yet been allowed to visit any friend, of any age or sex, unaccompanied. . . . When she was old enough to go alone to school, to the barber shop, or to the grocery, she either took Younger Sister, or was allowed exactly enough time to accomplish her purpose and return without any margin for loitering on the streets. (JS Wong, 65)

Moreover, if it is the *perception* of virtue that matters, then a hyper-vigilance must be exercised over the daughter's body for those times it must nonetheless be seen, lest by looseness in appearance or comportment it connote to harsh critics that it has already been sexually despoiled. Disciplinary technology thus comes to bear on every aspect of the female body, including "rules of body-disguising dress and of modest demeanor; [rules for] expression, communication, and movement" (Ortner, 19), "not only so that [that body] may do *what* [power] wishes, but so that [it] may operate *as* [power] wishes" (Foucault, *Discipline*, 138; emphases added): in other words, that it may behave like "a body which in gesture and appearance is recognizably feminine," obedient, and chaste (Bartky, 64). Foucault contends that, with the advent of disciplinary power, the docile body leaves the realm of signs (as in ritualistic gestures of submission, e.g., genuflection), and enters the realm of efficiency: "the object of control . . . was no longer the signifying elements of behavior or the language of the body, but the economy, the efficiency of movements, their internal organization; constraint bears upon the forces rather than upon the signs; the only truly important ceremony is that of exercise" (Foucault, 137). However, this account overlooks other applications of discipline wherein the body is still foremost conditioned to produce signs—wherein the movements and language of the body are not ceremonial but indeed an internal and semiotic organization of obedience. Bartky details at length the ways in which, through disciplinary power, "Feminine faces, as well as bodies, are trained to the *expression* of deference" (Bartky, 67; emphasis added): to sit with legs closed, eyes downcast; to move with constraint and meekness. In those expressions of deference or docility, the female body is required to *signify* submission to feminine norms such as chastity, in order that surveillance may be appeased.

∾ the uses of chastity

Yet soberly considered, what rationale would hold for turning such a vast apparatus of surveillance and training on a young girl's conduct? "The surveillance of an adolescent girl," anthropologist Alice Schlegel points out, "is a burden to her family, which must begin to socialize her in childhood and monitor her behavior until she is married"; detail-oriented and exhaustive, time-consuming and labor-intensive to maintain, these practices are "not a burden families are willing to assume unless they profit from doing so" (Schlegel, Management, 182). In previous chapters, such measures of control were exposed as being economically driven: efficient use of time, better cultivation of investment. At this juncture, we may begin to bring these elements together: obedience, profit, sexuality.

Anthropological literature on the management of sexuality has long been interested to produce explanatory sociocultural schema for the regulation of virginity. These accounts are many, extensive, and somewhat at variance with one another, but they do seem to share a commitment to underscoring the *economic* bases for the veneration of virginity—and to take the family as an economic unit, without disaggregating parental interests along gender lines. Whether the theory be that women constitute a scarce and contested resource (Schneider); that the circulation of women in marriage partakes in gift-giving, as one of the most archaic forms of both economic and social commerce (Levi-Strauss); that in a class-stratified society, a patriarchal family may hope to improve its status by marrying its daughters up (Ortner); or a combination of variations upon these, these anthropological projects have extensively demonstrated strong material imperatives in each political economy for the sexual control and circulation of women. This consensus on the economic underpinnings of intimate power is unquestionably welcome here, but (how) does it hold when the economic substructure has itself drastically shifted? Developed from the study of village or agrarian systems, these anthropological theories are hard-pressed to explain the relevance of chastity when none of the clear economic incentives truly obtain. Regarding sexuality in Western industrial contexts, Schlegel observes that,

> With readily available contraception and abortion, extramarital sexual relations do not have to result in pregnancy or illegitimate birth. [Sexual relations, in other words, do not need to result in kinship relations.] . . . Equally important, the dowry has lapsed in most European and European-derived cultures. Parental investment in daughters is increasingly in the form of education, not dowry. Furthermore, the daughter's choice of a husband does not have the significance for the family today that it did in earlier times. For most people in the industrial world, there is little in the way of a family estate to preserve [or obtain]. Even among the rich, a rebellious daughter and her husband can be cut out of the will . . . Thus, a daughter's choice of husband is not critical to the well-being of the family and the maintenance of its assets. (Schlegel, Status, 732)

From this apparent discrepancy in technological and material conditions, vis-à-vis social structure, Schlegel reasons that "As marriage transactions disappear and social status is gained more through achievement than through the family into which one is born or marries, . . . the virginity of daughters loses its salience." In other words, cultural values and social relations will automatically change to reflect current material conditions; what appears to be incongruity is just a little lag time.

Furthermore, even where historical or ethnographic work on female sexual regulation has expressly examined modern U.S. contexts, explanations of conservative sexual practices have hung upon this notion of incomplete cultural adjustment, lagging assimilation: Describing working-class families, both native-born and (white) immigrant, in California in the early twentieth century, Mary Odem traces "concern with female chastity" back to "the patriarchal structure of preindustrial societies" in which "fathers had controlled the labor and sexual lives of wives, children, and servants in ways that best supported the family economy"; to the extent that she explains why the "code of honor that linked family reputation to the morality of wives and daughters" should still apply in the new industrial society, it is that (in essence) Necessity makes it so: "Out-of-wedlock births threatened the limited economic resources of the family" (Odem, 51). This explanation is identical to that proposed in the narrative of Kingston's No Name Woman—brought uninflected from the village and agrarian context, even as Odem describes families in which daughters earn wages in department stores, offices, and even Hollywood's entertainment industry. In her study of New York City South Asian families in the 1990s, meanwhile, Sunaina Maira states quite clearly that "traditional dictates about gender norms are not etched in stone but are variously interpreted and contested"; subjected to the demands of immigration, "ideologies previously taken for granted can be reconsidered, denaturalized, and recreated. Gendered expectations that are presumably cultural or social also have a material dimension that is highlighted by changes in the family's labor and consumption practices" (Maira, 160). For instance, she points to "the expectation that daughters should have educational credentials, such as a college degree," as a new wrinkle in the family's "material and political practices"—but also then repairs to the notion of disjunction, to explain sexual ideologies specifically: "Yet the social control of female sexuality is not always mitigated by these new labor patterns or expectations of class mobility but often comes into conflict with them, particularly in the second generation." Such explanations grant sexual regulation a curious, exceptional status: as having a particularly high immuno-resistance to material influence, or out of all the interlocking components of gender ideology, being singularly ahistorical.

I would like to remind us, alternatively, that if gender institutions are indeed more than vulgar superstructures, then they are not limited to being the direct functions or effects of reproductive technology and exchange systems; versatile productions, they can be put to new uses, and in their full promise usher in rather than only follow from material realities. Sexually regulatory practices seem less the quaint anachronism when taken to be instrumental, rather than symptomatic. If this alternative has not presented itself more strongly to the studies above, it may be because they apply themselves to giving extensive account of the social structures within which women are circulated; they are less attuned to the subjectivation of those women. By this, I do not mean simply to complain that scholarship ought to attend more to the psychic or subjective dimensions of cultural theory. Rather, I mean that for women to circulate like currency, like land, like symbols, like bait, like gifts, is *not* for them to circulate as community *objects,* but to circulate as a particularized "kind" of community member: *subjects who have been commended to themselves as objects.*[5]

the self-producing subject ❧

As we know, a prisoner, student, worker, or daughter who behaved "well" only when being observed would not be a disciplined subject, and a system that needed to exercise direct surveillance over its subjects at all times would not have successfully applied disciplinary technology. A daughter who has been properly disciplined, however, has learned as a subject to take charge of herself as an object: to police her self as a body which operates, in comportment and deed, in obedience to authority at all times, such that the functioning of power is automatic within her (Foucault, *Discipline,* 201). From this Foucauldian standpoint, control is evidently not merely a question of power's acting upon the subject by means of "rules" and "restrictions" for its bodily concealment and confinement (Ortner, 19), but a question of inspiring in that subject an ever-active involvement in her own management. Unable to read Chinese as a child, the narrator of *Paper Daughter* recalls asking her mother the contents of the Chinese-language newspaper to which her family subscribed, and having been told each time something to the effect that "It tells all the Chinese in Denver, in America, about your misbehavior! Everybody in Denver knows that you don't keep your clothes clean. They know you don't listen to your mother. I'm so ashamed that I'm afraid to go out in public!" Elaine describes the effect of this response on her as follows:

> Her words made me nervous. I flipped through *Sing Tao* furtively, looking for my picture and name. Although they never appeared, I couldn't be sure Mother was lying. Perhaps I'd looked on the wrong page, I thought, or perhaps I'd missed an issue. . . . [S]hyness settled in my bones and ossified my voice box. I watched guests covertly, studying their gestures for evidence of my badness. If I couldn't hear a conversation, I assumed that it criticized me. An ambiguous comment was a negative one. I acquired a paranoia that never quite left. (Mar, 162)

This is an instructive passage for the function of gossip in subject formation, because it shows how profoundly the subject is immobilized by the smoke and mirrors of surveillance. Everywhere she is enjoined to imagine watchers, and thus enlisted to search out and imagine all the ways in which she might be an object of knowledge—to watch the watchers such that she may conjecture how it is she might be seen and spoken of. Passive submission to the directives of authority is insufficient; for her, obedience must be active, a constant effort to imagine and approximate authority, because while her kin may share in her shame, she alone is responsible for her guilt. In this context, virginity may be seen not only as the evidence of a subject who has successfully safeguarded her body against her own depreciation, but as a sign that she takes ownership of the duty to regulate herself as her family requires. Less wonder then that it is ever the girl's task to protect her virginity, and never the boy's to help her do so; and that it is the appearance of virginity rather than its fact that matters, if its primary function is not as economic resource but as a symbolic product of willing accommodation to power.

Furthermore, it is true, as the above passage suggests, that gossip and surveillance attend not only or exclusively to the sexual; the feminine body is constructed to be docile in infinite respects—unlimited, precisely because unspecified. And yet, while the surface of gossip is not necessarily sexual in nature—in the end, it always is. As the roof-thatcher's daughter is observed for the shade of her skin and her climbing of trees, or the No Name aunt for stray hairs on her brow, there is no non-sexual detail in a cautionary tale; all personal qualities are only indicators of an eventual ruin. For the young woman, all conduct is framed through the sexual—because it is only through that interpretive process that every detail can take on such enormous weight. All gossip winds back to sexual conduct. In this non-agrarian/ no-dowry context, one might say it is not that gossip functions to regulate female sexuality—but that the regulation of female sexuality functions to generate gossip.

Consider the implications of sexual control if its use-value actually lies in the effects of gossip on subject-formation. It now follows that even where a daughter's sexual purity has no exchange value, the regulation of chastity may still be salient to her upbringing as a self-disciplining subject.[6] Correlations have been observed between the geographic and intergenerational "closeness" of families and the sexual mores of their children (Horowitz; Berger and Wenger), giving rise to the supposition that parents whose offspring live at home are better able to enforce and transmit a heavy cultural emphasis on female chastity. I would like to suggest, however, that the cause-and-effect sequence here may very well be reversed: that parents (especially those of girls) who place a heavy emphasis on virginity are better able to keep their daughters at home. Within an ideology of virginity, young women "are said to be *in danger*, justifying [patriarchal] protection and guardianship . . . they are said to be [sexually] pure, and to need defending" (Ortner, 26), from both physical and verbal attack. It is ostensibly *for her own good*, then, that a young woman—like Jade Snow, Evelyn, Catherine, or Elaine—is locked inside the house.[7] The discourse of virginity, in other words, has its uses: "when there is a situation of inequality in some significant social realm, 'ideals are used as weapons in these struggles, both to unify status communities and to justify power interests'" (Berger and Wenger, 666);[8] it is both part of and justification for a system of intensive surveillance, confinement, and control of young women. To keep tabs on the sexual status of a young girl who had no particular commitment to staying a virgin would, indeed, be a costly endeavor. However extensive a network of gossip, within the community "everyone is aware that most women can escape the watchful eyes of their kin"; "families are concerned with the movements of their daughters but cannot completely restrict their activities": chaperoning resources are limited, and girls must leave the house at least to go to school (Horowitz, 67).

However, when anthropological or sociological studies neglect the interpellation and subject formation of unmarried daughters, they also overlook how very easy that project of surveillance can be. The ultimate success of disciplinary technology rests on its internalization: "So to arrange things that the surveillance is permanent in its effects, even if it is discontinuous in its action; that the perfection of power should tend to render its actual exercise unnecessary" (Foucault, *Discipline*, 201).[9] To recognize the psychic role of gossip is to realize that, when a young woman has been effectively enlisted to be her own keeper, the payoff to power is great. A paranoid daughterly subject need trouble her family very little to punish or restrict her; she has learned to anticipate the strictures of power such that she will seldom even ask for permission to do that which she suspects power might disallow. After all, the very inquiry after an uncertain object, even prior to or without its pursuit, is apt to be itself an infraction, when a subject is made responsible for knowing and fully obeying all possible permutations of obedience and guilt. Where a request for more than what she *knows* to be allowed stands to gain her nothing, but would thereby reveal potentially punishable desires, a daughter may very well choose to *assume* that anything questionable is off-limits to her, and that she is best off not wanting these things, much less trying to have them. Thus, she watches herself far more comprehensively and preemptively than any flesh-and-blood community, or any mechanism of external observation, could manage to do.

It is to a family's advantage to raise a daughter within this system, because it need then do absurdly little to maintain her at all, and such a self-disciplining female subject has *the most value* within the familial economy, whether as a bride and daughter-in-law, or simply as a daughter. In chapter 3, I make the argument that to the Asian immigrant family, the model child is a profitable one: a hard-working and uncomplaining member of the "professional-managerial class" (Guillory, 263), a doctor or lawyer preferably, who dutifully repays parental investors with large cash dividends and prestigious consumer goods. In the case of daughters, this profitable subject is, with proper training, also an especially inexpensive one. For "her own good," she returns herself home from school each day, where she may be applying herself toward a lucrative profession, and when she is not further honing her math and science skills in homework, she is thoroughly occupied by housework. Evelyn describes her life at home as having consisted of the following three required elements: "bring home straight-A report cards, do all the housework and smile" (Lau, *Runaway*, 81)— that is, to be a creditable capital investment and future worker, to be an able domestic laborer so as to maximize her surplus value for the family, and to like it, so that she need not be policed into doing what she is expected to do. Like Evelyn, who helps with dinner (116), sweeps and mops and vacuums and does dishes (163), Mona and her sister mow the lawn, vacuum the living room, wash the storm windows, and help out at the restaurant—an arrangement that Jen glibly refers to as "slave labor" (26) but of course is not. By whatever "historical and moral element" in a capitalist system the wife and not the husband may be deemed the party who will provide the unpaid household labor needed to reproduce the laboring class (Rubin, 164), not a son but a daughter can be hailed to take over the duties of that reproduction of the family.[10] Thus Catherine vacuums, and watches her "brother playing with his friend in the backyard through the glass doors of the living room" (Liu, 274). And a worker who will docilely, for the cost of room and board, promise the returns of a future six-figure income while performing the bulk of those tasks necessary to her own physical upbringing *and* to the maintenance of her family, is a subject worth producing indeed. When Evelyn comes home late from an afternoon volunteering at the community paper, and is accused of being a "lying, whoring, ungrateful, uncontrollable daughter" (Lau, *Inside*, 202), this is not because her mother actually suspects her of having spent the afternoon in sexual intercourse, paid or free. The "whoring" component is key, however—included not merely for rhetorical but for discursive effect: to construct the daughter as a subject who, noncompliant in any measure, is imaginably guilty of the kind of transgression which calls for the full weight of disciplinary machinery to be set upon her.

❧ the impossible daughter

The high stakes of sexuality are thus of no little service to the parent who would have a daughter trained to regulate herself *as if willingly*: "the parent who cannot tolerate the child's attempt to do things independently will make the child feel that the price of freedom is aloneness . . . Thus if the child does not want to do without approval, she must give up her will. This usually results in the 'choice' to stay close to home and remain compliant" (Benjamin, 34). Though there is a deep irony in the practice of keeping one's daughters close to home by exploiting a sexual narrative based on disownment, the family's administration of sexuality is only that much more like its other exercises of sovereign power for being rife with paradoxes. The regulation of the girls' chastity aligns with the larger discourse of filiality and filial obligation, in being essentially the rational implementation of irrational ends. That a young woman should be required to maintain an ideal of sexual purity which it is ultimately in the power of discourse to strip from her *regardless* of the truth of her actions, is another permutation of designated failure; not a viable endpoint of exercise, chastity acts as a norm always for the subject to abide by and never up to her to realize. Itself contradictory, this discourse of sexuality holds together a system in which that family member who is ever being threatened with exile is the embodiment of the family's honor—one in which a subject who has no name (a daughter's name being not her own, but her father's) can singlehandedly destroy it.

Yet perhaps these irrational combinations will begin to look like reason if we consider that the paradox, once granted, is not without balance: Precisely in her liminal status, the daughter figure may be the inverted image of the very sovereign, who himself[1] constitutes a threshold: "the sovereign is the point of indistinction" between the order of law and violence, at which one passes over into the other (Agamben, 32). It may be said of the sovereign equally as of the daughter, though in just the opposite sense, that he is not quite *of* the family, and yet simultaneously embodies the family in himself: "the sovereign, having the legal power to suspend the validity of the law, legally places himself outside the law. This means that the paradox can also be formulated in this way: 'the law is outside itself,' or 'I, the sovereign, who am outside the law, declare that there is nothing outside the law'" (15). As a consequence of this perplexed liminality, attempts to define the relations of law and membership in family will often offer more slippage than surety: When Mona relates that "this is what it means to be a family member: There is nothing so small but that you've got to ask the parents' permission"

(Jen, 26), it would seem that only children can be considered "members" of the family, for being removed from the obligation to seek higher authority, the parents are its sovereigns and not its members. And yet, in that passage as well as in the following, from *Paper Daughter*, parental will and familial will are one—the sovereign *is* that of which he is not a *part*: "You can't make these decisions for yourself, you're part of a family. . . . This is what it means to be an adult—you learn . . . to follow your elders' lead. . . . You use your brain [only] to judge what [your elders] will think is right. You take care of your family. That's who you are—your family" (Mar, 228). Furthermore, the daughter's own "membership" within the family, however adamantly it may be asserted, is categorically unassured. Each passage instructs the girls to set aside their selves, decisions, minds, because *that is what family means* for them: By definition, the logical set which is "family" is derived either without reference to (if passively) or through the exclusion of (if actively) the term "daughter" which is one of its members. In other words, the daughter is *part* of that which she is *not*.

If sovereign and daughter share like (but reversed) positions at the unresolvable thresholds of the family, they also share like (and reversed) symbolic functions. Within a given order, the sovereign is defined by his "power of proclaiming a state of exception and, therefore, of suspending the order's own validity" (Agamben, 15). Meanwhile, within the order of the family, the figure which inhabits that exceptional state of "inclusive exclusion" (21) is that of the daughter, singularly poised or designated for abandonment. And if the very marginal person of the daughter is so disproportionately weighted with the system that expels her, this is less strange in consideration of her exceptional status. Within sovereign law, the exception "is that which cannot be subsumed; it defies general codification, but it simultaneously . . . 'explains the general and itself. And when one really wants to study the general, one need only look around for a real exception'"; "The exception does not only confirm the rule; the rule as such lives off the exception alone" (15–16). In a fundamental sense, sovereign and exception are each invested with the order to which they cannot be subsumed, and in relation to which they are both inside and outside.[12] This convoluted liminality may be itself irresolvable, but that paradoxical basis, once granted, affords the positions which hinge upon it both symmetry and sense. As "the exception is the structure of sovereignty" (28), both sovereign and daughter are known by their relation to the structure of law. For the sovereign, this is a relation of projection: his is to determine the form and content of the order, and to inscribe that structure through control of its exception. For the daughter, this is a relation of reflection: hers is to express the order upon herself, to be the body upon which sovereign law may be read. That a daughter's primary directive should be to regulate herself in active approximation of authority—modulating her inclinations in order to compose of her body and mind a smooth reflective surface—and thereby to safeguard herself as an object of value, follows from this relation without contradiction. While the sovereign is that term entrusted with the family as "subject"—to be its judgment and its will—the daughter is commended with the family as object: to embody its reputation as a "thing" which circulates.

It may seem necessary to object that the state of exception can hardly be considered constitutive of a subject who has not been consigned to it (being yet unbanished), but such an objection would overlook the work of subjectification, which starts young. The successful cautionary tale must begin by interpellating its listener—initiating its intended subject into an impossible position: a daughter must be *implicated* by the banished figure within the story for it to have effect. She must share the fallen woman's subject position and vulnerabilities, and *also* participate in her reviling. These stories elicit from their intended audience, before all else, an act of identification, in answer to the "You there!" which establishes the child as a daughter—and bids her assume her guilt. [13] Certainly, it is understood that any cultural authority will necessarily proscribe certain modes of sexuality, identity, and embodiment in order to prescribe others as normative; but what's more, and more interesting, this polarization must be preceded by yet another psychic process. (I draw here an instructive analogy from Butler's schematic of the conditioning of heteronormative sexuality, though knowing that the domain of the "culturally impossible" queer identities she theorizes [*Bodies* 111] will not lend itself wholly to this analysis. The important distinctions will become relevant presently. Meanwhile, what holds true is as follows.) Within such a psychic mechanism, the rejection of abjected subjectivities (queer or, in this case, fallen) can itself "take place only *through an identification with that abjection*, an identification that must be disavowed, an identification that one fears to make only because one has already made it, an identification that institutes that abjection and sustains it" (112; emphasis added). This means that a daughter charged to be filial and "chaste" must defend against the taint of "vice" all the more because she has been produced in such a way as to embrace and internalize it. In this context it is worthwhile to note that the heroine of a cautionary tale is, as a rule, pretty: rewarding to imagine and appealing to inhabit. *In a cautionary tale*, the specific narrative and cultural convention of ascribing beauty to the fallen daughter has no other apparent purpose but to facilitate the girl child's identification with guilt, and her conditioning to the state of exception. It is no wonder, then, that both Kingston's and Divakaruni's narrators project themselves into the dishonored daughters' places—in their extended fascination with the other young women's physical beings, imagining what it would be like to inhabit such delinquent bodies:

> . . . my aunt, my forerunner . . . I see her life branching into mine . . . (Kingston, *Warrior*, 8)

> She brushed her hair back from her forehead, tucking the flaps behind her ears. She looped a piece of thread, knotted into a circle between her index fingers and thumbs, and ran the double strand across her forehead. . . . Then she pulled the thread away from her skin, ripping the hairs out neatly, her eyes watering from the needles of pain. (9)

> When you fall asleep, you dream of a beautiful dark girl knotting stones into her *palloo* and swimming out to the middle of the dark lake. The water is cool on her heavying breasts, her growing belly. . . . Before she goes under, she turns toward you. Sometimes her face is a blank oval, featureless. Sometimes it is your face. (Divakaruni, 64)

In this way are the girls recruited into a subjectivity which obliges them fastidiously not to "show." (Butler, *Bodies*, 112)

However, while this normative femininity may share with normative (hetero)sexuality that initiating identification with abjection and subsequent disavowal, where femininity is concerned the sequence evidently does not take place at the same subconscious depth of psychic processing as what Butler describes. Its daughterly identifications are readily available to the subject's perusal, and the process of disavowal more likely a conscious effort (if that) than a matter of repression. That this "abjected subjectivity" should be not repressed but rather most freely represented—within cultural forms and familial discourse, as well as by the subject herself—would seem to indicate that *unlike* queer identities (there being no genre of cautionary tales about the girl or boy who went queer), the position of the dead wayward daughter may not be very "culturally impossible" at all.[14] Quite to the contrary, it may abound in cultural representation precisely because it is highly "possible": culturally *taken into account*, yes, and also culturally *cooperative*. For it so happens that even that reviled and abjected subjectivity with which a daughter is made to identify is in fact a self-punishing one! The young women of each cautionary tale are daughters who, having failed, feel so very dreadful about it that they cannot permit themselves to live, and so give up all they have in seeming atonement (however ineffectual) for their families' shame. In their own fashions, they are obedient to the end. The moral a young listener may glean from these stories is that she must either exist in subordination or surrender her existence,[15] making these daughter figures reasonably "safe" choices for identification after all.

That the transgressive should turn out to be quite culturally "possible" is in keeping with the logics of both sovereign power and disciplinary technology. As we have seen (in the child who is produced as guilty, named a whore long before any sexual act), transgression is not only expected but indeed moot. Appropriately, then, Ng's entire pantheon of daughters in *Bone* is composed of fallen women: whether good, bad, or dead, each has—as designated— "failed" the sexual ideal. Likewise, in the universe of sovereign power, guilt has no need to be ascertained, as it is a function of being subject to the law and the very condition of being managed by power. It is in this context that the actual administration of female sexuality can afford, if it so chooses, to be unpredictably inconsistent: As is the prerogative of sovereign power, it regulates when and where it will,[16] without being bound to reliability in judgment, because its decisions refer to a subject to whom it is not accountable. Mona's mother will not allow the girls the use of tampons, yet astounds both daughters by giving the older one a sex education pamphlet; Mona will be firmly banished when she is discovered having sex, but her parents having treated her boyfriends with such expansive benevolence, their unyielding displeasure dawns on her by surprise; Nina's parents disown her for her pregnancy, yet allow Ona and her boyfriend to make out in the laundry where their families are working, and permit Leila's boyfriend to spend the night in her bed. While the administration of sexuality may suggest certain patterns of allowable or banned behavior, *there is no rule which holds* across the entirety of the field, because there is no rule to which power may be held. Given such radical inconsistency, however, there is precariously little difference to discriminate between failures or, by extension, between daughters: between Nina and Leila, for instance.

Leila's boyfriend Mason sleeps over at the family home because her mother has judged it "Better for the neighbors to see [his] car in the morning and wonder than for them to [see him leaving] in the middle of the night and know" (Ng, *Bone*, 183); and when her mother advises her, "You shouldn't sleep with him so much" (190), the warning is likewise strategic (that Mason not get bored with the ease of access) rather than reproachful in intent. Yet this apparently liberal bedroom policy is belied by Leila's fear, the dread she experiences when she tells her mother that she and Mason will move in together: "For a minute I expected the worst, that she'd slap me, hit me with a hanger, call me names" (191)—names, perhaps, along the lines of "rotten, no-good, dead thing" (Sweater, 360), or epithets Leila would recognize as meaning "something lowly, despised" (*Bone*, 25), such as were inflicted on Nina. What it is that makes the narrator's sexual acts and disclosures unobjectionable to her parents, where her sister's are utterly unacceptable, is neither clear nor reliable to Leila, who might at a minute's notice find herself in Nina's place. Moreover, in her short-story incarnation, the Leila/Lisa character *is* in Nina's place: Images reversed across the dinner table, the sexually charged Lisa is described openly as long having "wanted out" of her role in the family (Sweater, 367)—whereas Nina's character, who has forced her own "way out," "imagine[s] what it would be like to take her [sister's] place" taking care of their parents, and remarks, "It will be my turn one day" (366). This slippage across the state of exception reveals that that threshold is not the edge of power, but its axis: subjects are managed back and forth across that line and, played against each other, become part of the regulating mechanism.

∾ the high cost of living

Where there are no "good" subjects—where failure is produced and punished, *within* the normal parameters of obedience—the distinction between Leila and Nina cannot be their relative success or failure, as clearly those positions may shift beneath their feet. As we have seen, the meaning of a daughter's sexual conduct is determined not by the features of the act, but by the whim of the sovereign. What sets the filial and banned daughters apart, then, may lie in the direction of intent rather than content: what, indeed, they were trying to accomplish, and what role sex played therein. To return to the question of Nina's sexual choices, we excavate the following moment in the character's backstory: an exchange between the short-story counterpart and her parents, leading up to her disownment.

> "Get an abortion" [Mah] said. "Drop the baby," she screamed.
> "No."
> "Then get married."
> "No. I don't want to."
> I was going to get an abortion all along. . . . Now I can see how I used it as an opportunity. (359)

The altercation is intriguing because, contrary to expectations, the speaker is not "confessing" to transgressions for which she subsequently "receives" banishment; she is endorsing whatever transgressions will yield her desired results. In heaping meaning onto the discourse of virginity, the family makes sexual activity a particularly privileged semantic system with which to spell submission or resistance; it is as a direct but unintended result of this that Nina's character may treat sexual conduct as a kind of lexicon of the body, from which to choose her own speech acts: in this case, defying, daring, even bluffing power—in provocative counterpoint to the parental bluff of disownment itself. It would seem, in other words, that unlike Leila, who waits and sees where Mah will place her, Nina conducts herself across the axis wherever it should land. There is nothing essential about this choice; Leila may make the same later, and in the short story, Nina indicates that she expects to change her mind. But for the moment, the two daughters are mirror images: Both are commended with the family's value as object, but where Nina holds that value hostage, to make the family pay, Leila holds herself as hostage, and pays for her own safekeeping.

The essence of the exchange between Nina and Mah above is its subtext: information not about the wayward daughter or her pregnancy, but about the scope of casualties which she is willing both to inflict, and to endure. Nina's refusal to abort or marry communicates a willful determination to blight the parents' interests—even at great cost to herself: The threatened acts of noncooperation would encompass months of unsupported pregnancy, years of raising a child alone, and loss of considerable options in a future that is, after all, her own. As a social unit in which, we must remember, members' interests not only compete but are complexly bound, the daughter who embodies familial value threatens that hostage only by threatening herself. And the family that governs by disownment wagers its own dissolution: routinely casting out its good name, in hopes of assuring greater return. This makes the nuclear destruction of incited disownment a kind of bilateral pyrrhic victory, because it is unclear whose winning blow it is, or whose loss is greater. The prolonged tolls of Nina's hypothetical future are intrinsic, not incidental, to the choice it represents, for ironically like its opposite, disobedience is an exercise never done and over with, but requiring constant upkeep. It is not once but every day that one is a writer instead of a lawyer, a runaway or dropout instead of a valedictorian, a single mother instead of a culturally sanctioned wife; not in the single moment of conflict but in the unnumbered moments before and after, that a daughter sleeps or lives with a man—forcing her parents to know of it, or hoping to get caught.

It is common to assume that a daughter has sex in defiance of her parents because the rewards of sexual relations or activity are such as to outweigh for her the cost of her family's grief. But our body of texts suggests that neither half of that assumption is true. Preservation of the family's well-being having been core to the doctrine of social obedience, the infliction of grief is less unfortunate by-product than naïve logical inversion: one must protect the family to be filial; one must harm the family to be free.[17] Moreover, what stands out about the sexual choices described by Liu, Lau, Mar, and Divakaruni's narrators—with whom and under what circumstances—are not their rewards but their potential to be profoundly (self-)punishing. *Paper Daughter's* Elaine seeks out the ruinous in sexuality; for her, its pleasures are laced with fear and discomfort, and its social effects are to enclose her in a more complete isolation, estranged not only from her family but from even her "American-normal," teenage society: Following her frantic gropings with a (white) boy,[18] she observes that "My sexuality pushed me deeper into the nether regions, a private life I couldn't explain in my hours on the phone with [my best friend]" (Mar, 231). Her imagination dwells on the details of cautionary tales: "horror stories about sex, conjuring violent, graphic images—pelvises breaking under a man's weight, ripped vaginas being sewn shut, pregnant girls dying in childbirth, their shame bleeding out for all the world to see" (229). But neither these visions of bodily horror nor real social costs being a deterrent, her absorption with them suggests that they may instead be a draw.

In this context, the shapes that sexual expression often takes are those prone to ravage not only the family but the subject herself:

> I had sex. I was, however, looking for something else. Most of the time, what I found was a brief, unsatisfying contact high. I started in secret, with boys my age. I felt like I was trying some forbidden drug, and this made things exciting. I kept it all to myself, and did it as much as I could. I proved to myself that I could do what I liked, but I felt, nevertheless, that I was doing something terrible, something for which, one day, I would have to pay. I continued anyway, despite my fears, which were very, very real. I was afraid of boys, I was afraid of people, I was afraid of my parents, but I pressed on. (Liu, 153)

In this striking passage, Liu describes not gratification (the act is "unsatisfying"), but a compulsion to keep moving in the direction of felt danger—harmful to the user first and foremost, with or without external penalties exacted by authority. It is not by random chance that Evelyn becomes a prostitute and Catherine a stripper. In what other mode of rebellion is harm to the family's prestige so sure—and yet dangers to the self so rife and so varied? Rape, pregnancy, disease . . . the subject may pick between poisons as quick as murder or as quiet as harassment, exploitation, and ill-use. Divakaruni's narrator chooses a lover who does not care enough to hide his cheating from her properly, a white man whose racial condescension is uncompromising and whose selfishness is cruelty, such that to be with him is to subject herself to emotional pain: "You try to tell yourself that he wants to hurt you only because he's hurting" (Divakaruni, 58). Thus, sexual rebellion winds back to the masochism of the previous chapter, recalling the psychic and economic investments in suffering and suicide which characterized each of Evelyn's and Catherine's acts of insubordination.

This anticipatory pursuit of pain resonates uncomfortably with the familial sentiment at the core of every cautionary tale, and plainly spoken from time to time in narrative:[19] that an "unfilial" child *should* suffer, that surely the world will not countenance a daughter to flout parental will and meet no misery. It is a parental edict, an invocation, a curse: "Defy us and you will pay." Elaine seems at first to refute that edict when, confronted by her parents for her trysts, she defends her sexual activity as a kind of self-preservation: "It's my life."

> They said that I was too young for boys, and besides, he should have been Chinese.
> Father demanded that I end the relationship.
> I said no.
> Father screamed, "How dare you disobey? You've disgraced the family!"
> "It's my life!" I shouted . . . I was sick of living for my family. (Mar, 228)

Yet when their conflict boils over into crisis, her language converts to that of self-sacrifice, self-destruction: "I held a broken glass over my wrist. 'Go ahead! Hit me! Beat me! . . . *I'll kill myself for you!*'" (236; emphasis added). As Elaine's chilling outburst suggests, self-preservation may contain within itself a bargain with power—a transaction made on the basis of not only self-punishment, but even self-destruction. Whether the child pays for disobedience in lump sum after the fact, or in ongoing installments as it happens, this transaction of self-hood for pain makes the edict of karmic retribution an implicit contract of exchange. If the provisionally good daughter "repays" her parents' suffering in material goods, the incumbent bad daughter but abides by alternate terms of exchange in the same economy: She repays not only the sacrifices of her birth in self-immolating potlatch, but the suffering she inflicts for her freedom with synchronous suffering of her own. This means, however, that "defiance" operates not solely as a way out of power; it may be that where lived compliance is intolerable, paying for small hits of resistance makes it easier to bear.

Ultimately, true to her founding identification with the figure of dutiful suicide, the child who actively conducts herself across the line may be brought by her own transgressions to even greater indebtedness, and atonement. When, the boyfriend gone, the crisis has abated, Elaine gives herself over to remorse and a compulsive penance—meaningfully enacted by disciplinary measures of mortification, upon the body:

> I was angry at the way [my family] judged me, but convinced that their pronouncements were correct. . . . *Mother was right,* I decided. . . .

> I worked to perfect myself. When I tucked my shirt into my pants, I measured the spaces between the folds to make sure they were even. I scraped my scalp raw parting my hair in perfect, straight lines. I stopped smiling because my teeth were crooked. I thought that if only I were a better person, my family would be happy again. (245)

Even her disobedience is thereby susceptible to a self-incrimination that will, in the end, make her only all the more aggressively obedient a subject. In a comparable variation, the narrator of Divakaruni's story subjects herself to a harrowing exercise of obedience within the very (daily) act of misconduct:

> The first month you moved in with him, your head pounded with fear and guilt every time the phone rang. You'd rush across the room to pick it up [in case it was your mother calling] . . . (You'd made him promise never to pick up the phone.) At night you slept next to the bedside extension. You picked it up on the very first ring, struggling out of layers of sleep as heavy as water to whisper a breathless hello, the next word held in readiness, *Mother.* . . . But it was never her. . . .

> And so you grew less careful. . . . Or was it that you wanted her, somehow, to find out? (Divakaruni, 62)

When she is in fact discovered, and disowned, her immediate response is to abase herself desperately in repentance, and to fixate on suicide: She dwells on the roof-thatcher's daughter, the bottles of pills at her disposal, and her mother's possible forgiveness when she has given up her life in expiation. Interestingly however, in the last few paragraphs of the story Divakaruni's narrator changes her mind, deciding to *stop* seeking reacceptance as daughter in the family home, and instead to begin a "new life, the one you're going to live for yourself." In the narrative, this refashioned subject, "hollow, clean, ready to begin" (68), is seemingly new-born in a baptism of rain that washes away the birth-blood of family and past, conditioning and guilt—but importantly, it is right here on "begin" that the story ends. The daughter who emerges from her birth "clean" and unbound cannot be imagined beyond absence—as being "hollow" or empty, because nothing in this culture of power would have produced her, prepared (for) her, or given her substance; which is to say, she cannot truly be imagined, not by the system nor by the daughters it does turn out. Like a Foucauldian case in point, this thinking subject shows herself the effect of power, "created as the delimiting field of possibility for all thought" (Bersani, 3). Likewise with Nina's character: the short story no sooner introduces her as a bad subject but she is already caught in repentance. Granted, she is later recast in the novel as a figure of such seeming autonomy as to lack all remorse or even compassion for her family; as a daughter immune to remorse, however, the character ceases to be told in the first person, and becomes instead a remote projection for the narrator: a figure whose interiority cannot be fathomed, a hollow. Be it cautionary tale or literary production, cultural narrative seems at a loss to assign psychic reality to a subject whose guilt (whether in the constitutive or transgressive sense) does *not* move her to suicide or other self-mortification, inspired by an emotional endorsement of the family's honor or shame, its pronouncements and declarations. If "ingratitude" is a state of being resistant to the call of debt—the ability to receive without acknowledgment or return—then it does not describe the disobedient daughter any better than the obedient one. They but settle their debts in different ways. In other words, it is finally *ingratitude* which comprises the culturally impossible—with all due irony, that offense of which a daughter is always accused but which she does not know how to commit.

sexual acts ❧

The logical trajectory from sexual defiance to self-destruction bears some additional unpacking, however, precisely because of the rhetoric of pleasure and liberation, even of health and life, by which the notion of throwing off sexual repression is surrounded. If sexuality is not the "natural" act of liberation it is touted to be for the Western subject, it is even less "natural" and more discursively overproduced for the Asian American female subject, whose sexual acts take place in an overtly overdetermined social context of sexual/racial/cultural ideologies. What Foucault calls the sermon of sexual liberation, a production of the dominant culture, dovetails neatly into an opposition between freedom (West) and repression (East), between women's rights and misogyny, between individual and family. To have (unrepressed) sex then takes on the connotations of all those elements on the left-hand side of the opposition, as if an Asian American woman follows her rights and her pleasure right out of the family. And yet, however ideologically objectionable or even fallacious these oppositions may be, I suggest that this logic motivates much of a rebellious Asian American daughter's sexual practices: her overly enunciated sexuality/promiscuity,[20] her penchant for partners outside the race.[21] "Out-marriage" comes to express the above logical opposition in exponential form: multiplied by itself across sex, race, and culture. In this sense, out-marriage is literal: a means for the subject to get "out" of the Asian American family by banishment—and by ensuring that she cannot reproduce it. In her resolve to resist the conditions of her formation, the daughter expresses at once a desire for self-preservation (insofar as she resists conditions and structures of power that subjugate her), and for self-obliteration (insofar as preventing the replication of the Asian American family ensures that a subject like herself, racially and culturally, will not be produced again). Thus, once again in her putatively liberating sexual practice, the subject navigates that fine line between self-protection and self-hatred: in the same irresolvable act asserting her subjectivity, and pursuing its exploitation or erasure.

The practice of sexual activity is nothing if not loaded, with meanings and with potential avenues of self-destruction. The daughter who seeks release through sexuality chances an extraordinary wealth of injury, risking not only disownment but the kind of disease, pregnancy, heartbreak, attack that could devastate a life—defile the body and raze the mind. And this richness of possibilities, we must recognize, is integral to its appeal. Awash in the rhetoric of self-determination and the rush of pleasure, sex allows the subject to invite damage with a singular abandon: a mixture of control and surrender peculiar to the gambler, the suicide, the player of Russian roulette. She dances, she teases, she lies back, and the violence that misses her today may find her tomorrow. Suicidal sexuality is a most insidious thing, because the subject need not know her own purpose—performs it all the better the more oblivious she is to her desire to self-destruct. When unsafe sex is defiance, death is a promise, misery never far, and neither ever entirely the subject's own fault.

But it speaks eloquently to the condition of a subjectivity always threatened with annihilation, that the subject learns to look for destruction much like a shoplifter scans for loot: almost unconsciously and everywhere. The trinket that may hold beauty, might hold ruin, and it is to its potential that she gravitates, pocketing one after another by impulse. What carefree sex holds for the failed daughter, the bad subject, is the security of feeling that one's "out" is never far from hand, the consolation of sensing that release may come in any form or face or day, the half-formed expectation that some point of suffering will be enough. Such carelessness with life can be a way to persist in one's being, to comfort oneself for continuing to live.

Afterword

The Ending

Even
After
All this time
The sun never says to the earth,
"You owe
Me."
Look
What happens
With a love like that,
It lights the
Whole
Sky.

Hafez, "Sun Never Says"

Ingratitude goes to press something like a decade since its first pencil outline, and it's strange to see how predictive that outline truly was. Though what I could not at that time have predicted, what would have confounded the imagination then, is the present. In which living is not a debtor's prison, and one's most cherished wish is not escape. But this book ends on a bridge. Which is why it is important that I finally say to my sisters, whom I do not want to abandon at that wind-whipped railing: the heroine lives. There is a happy ending. Yet typing these words has me curled weeping over my keyboard, because to get dishes washed and classes taught one simply cannot remember how breathlessly expensive it has been to unlearn reflexes . . . to retrain posture, hunger, contentment, and guilt. So I will not pretend that shift "happens" in some natural course of things—not the coming of age, nor of grandchildren, much less in a sudden rebirth; nor can I point to any literary examples of it being convincingly done. That I offer no model from here is perhaps because (I've always thought) Tolstoy had it backwards: *unhappy* families are all alike; every happy family is happy in its own way. I would presume to tell no one on her ledge which ending to choose. But it must mean something to know that payment is not every option.

I put down this book with inevitable thought to other things it might have been and done. For one, I likely would have built into the spine of the argument a number of recently published texts, had they been available a decade ago. They include Jhumpa Lahiri's short story "Only Goodness" (2008), Sheba Karim's novel *Skunk Girl* (2009), and Samantha Lê's fictional memoir *Little Sister Left Behind* (2007). Notably, the families they feature hail from "humble" Bengali, "middle-class" Pakistani Muslim, and refugee Vietnamese backgrounds, respectively—yet each of these texts might have lifted passages, paragraphs, even whole pages from our heavily Chinese American archive without a hitch in the narrative. Tropes of filiality and the model minority replicate with compelling faithfulness across these seemingly imposing ethnic-national differences.

Though these writers' daughter-protagonists take different paths and the stories differing plots, the discursive and disciplinary universe they occupy is very much the same.[1] We find, in each, intense pressure for educational overachievement, up to and including that familiar assimilationist adulation of the Ivy League: "When Sudha was fourteen," Lahiri writes, "her father had written to Harvard Medical School, requested an application, and placed it on her desk" (Lahiri, 129). Meanwhile, Karim's young protagonist quips, "'One daughter at Harvard, one at Yale.' If my parents had a theme song, this would be the chorus" (Karim, 70). And like Lau's and Liu's narrators, Lê's offers up earnest proofs of her academic cred: "Armed with high grades; honor classes; college courses; a high SAT score; along with a long list of club, athletic, and after school activities . . ."; "I had already been accepted into all the universities to which I applied" (Lê, 202, 209).

In due course, we find the disciplinary use of gossip and prestige, as Lahiri's Sudha sighs, "For years they had been compared to other Bengali children, told about gold medals brought back from science fairs, colleges that offered full scholarships" (Lahiri, 129). She is echoed by Lê's narrator: "The straight A's, the achievement awards, and the after-school activities were always quickly overshadowed by the graduation of so-and-so's son from law school or the marriage of so-and-so's daughter to a doctor" (Lê, 198). And their thoughts are finished by Karim's Nina: "The way my mother acts sometimes, you'd think What Everyone Will Say is the force that rules the universe. . . . Gossip is one of their favorite pastimes"; "It's as though there's an unofficial Pakistani prestige point system." In her mock point system, Nina also rattles off professional-managerial tracking, extending even to the aligning of literary endeavors with failure and self-destructive inactivity:

+5 if you're a doctor . . .
+3 if you're a businessman, a lawyer (the money-making kind), or an engineer . . .
-4 if you're an artist, musician, poet, or anything else in the creative fields . . . (Karim, 68, 78)

Both Lê and Lahiri chime in: "I was also to aspire to be a professional, i.e., a doctor, engineer, lawyer, etc., no matter what my passion or dreams were" (Lê, 198); as proof of her brother's precipitous fall from the ranks, Sudha mentions not only his now C-level grades at Cornell, but that he "had dropped biology and organic chemistry and taken up film and English literature instead" (Lahiri, 139).

Next up, for gendering the docile body, we find sexual regulation, captivity, and surveillance: Sudha confides that she "had waited until college to disobey her parents. Before then she had lived according to their expectations, her persona scholarly, her social life limited to other demure girls in her class, if only to ensure that one day she would be set free" (Lahiri, 129). With more humor but less equanimity, Nina speculates that "the only two types of people who spend their Friday nights in high school at home [are] Pakistani Muslim girls and future serial killers." She continues,

Though I suppose some Indian and maybe even some Asian parents might be as strict with their kids. . . . I bet we [she and some Indian girl would] be allowed to spend our Friday nights together, memorizing vocabulary words or something.
Whenever [my father] talks about what will happen if I let go of my Muslim values I always end up being a street hooker on drugs. (Karim, 28, 36)

Lê's narrator, meanwhile, takes us to the bleakest version of this place:

"No boys." . . . Everything came back to this rule.
Phone conversations to girlfriends were randomly monitored. Then if all that spying wasn't enough, since I lived in the dining room where everything I did was within viewing distance, Father could simply sit on the couch and watch me as if I were an animal in a cage. (Lê, 205, 206)

The comparables run far longer than we'd wish to follow them here, so we wrap with that essential rhetorical complex of hopeless inadequacy, (lack of) suffering, and irresolvable debt: Sudha reflects that "Her father . . . never let his children forget that there had been no one to help him as he helped them, so that no matter how well Sudha did, she felt that her good fortune had been handed to her, not earned" (Lahiri, 140). Once again, with a little more angst, Nina: "The dread I'm now feeling [of failing to measure up once again] is a culmination of years of dealing with . . . repression, suppression, exclusion" (Karim, 7). And lastly, with anger:

> Everything that I did, everything that I was, and everything that I achieved was, in one way or another, never quite enough. The bar from which I was measured would suddenly be raised just as I thought I had finally stretched myself far enough to leap over it. (Lê, 198)

Moreover, Lê's narrator realizes that should she fail, as her father predicts, "he would have proof that I was no good—an ungrateful, morally loose, stupid daughter who had no idea just how lucky she was that her father was so noble and generous as to put a roof over her head" (212). Clearly, these texts approach their themes with varying gravity: Karim's young adult novel, like Jen's work, trends more toward levity than desperation, more success than suicide, while Lê's narrative mirrors Lau's in anguish. Whether within the more recent South- and Southeast-Asian American set or alongside their Chinese American predecessors, an overview of texts indicates that families applying these systems don't necessarily do so with uniform severity. But if the question is whether these daughterly narratives equally know the model minority and model filiality as a common paradigm, then—incredibly across ethnicity, class, religion, and immigration decade—I believe the answer would have to be yes.

The model of the Asian American immigrant family this book has distilled from such stories is uncompromising, no doubt. To make a case as unwelcome as this, I have believed, its champion must yield no quarter. It has also been my hope, however, that the hard line drawn here may allow for greater latitude in later analyses of intergenerational conflict, such that future scholarship may theorize the family's structure of feeling as fully as its structures of power; may engage with a character's humor, and sometimes endearing self-deprecation; may take this model outside the lab of prose and page, to test in the messiness of interpersonal relations. This next stage of necessary scholarship may be more possible with the security of knowing the academic collectivity is now on notice: that administering childhood by the family prestige index is not ideologically defensible parenting, that the professional-managerial model child costs us something incalculable to make.

Notes

NOTES TO INTRODUCTION

1. In the Omi and Winant sense.

2. As has received increasing media attention in recent years, "suicide is the leading cause of death among Asian American women aged 15–24 (Centers for Disease Control and Prevention, 2003) and . . . Asian American women aged 15–24 and over 65 have the highest female suicide rates across all racial/ethnic groups (National Center for Health Statistics, 2003)" (Noh, Suicide, 88). This is revealing especially when compared to the suicide rate for the Asian American population as a whole, which is half that of the general American population. In discussing these statistics from a perspective outside of Asian American studies academia, Dr. Aruna Jha from the Asian American Suicide Prevention Initiative cites the complicity of the community (including that of her own South Asian) and the family in enforcing model minority standards upon their children, thereby contributing to the mental distress of their daughters. "[T]he model minority stereotype . . . that's a stereotype that the Asian community is also buying into, because it is a source of pride" ("Confronting Suicide: Asian-American Women," Tell Me More, NPR, May 21, 2007).

3. Nor, of course, should dismantling the public/private binary mean reducing the family to "public" motives. This project means not to deny the affective nature of intimate bonds, but to remember a far more difficult truth: that, as within passionate attachment itself, love and self-interest are often one and the same. In other words, "Your family . . . want[s] to help, but embedded in their support for you is what they want from you"— consciously, or not (N. Wong, 15). Moreover, though this book will often pitch its analysis of parental prerogative in language that suggests the willing or rationalistic exercise of power, its argument is more accurately preceded by the advisory that—if power may be "at once intentional and nonsubjective" (Foucault, History, 94)—she who operates it need not do so with all deliberateness at all times.

See also Rachel Lee's reading of *Typical American* for a critical recovery of national, class, race, and gender projects via the very seeming myopia of domestic details (44–72; esp. 52–53).

4. So much rides on the politics of these readings, that Palumbo-Liu's litmus test would split the oeuvre of a single writer. He warmly admits Janice Mirikitani's "Breaking Silence" into the fold, on the basis that a piece protesting Japanese American internment supports a "collective grievance [of the Asian American community] against the state" (409), and thus is politically copacetic. But Mirikitani's "Suicide Note" would be unwelcome in the community canon, this poem which she prefaces with the explanation, "An Asian American

college student was reported to have jumped to her death from her dormitory window. . . . Her suicide note contained an apology to her parents for having received less than a perfect four point grade average." In that selective acknowledgment of texts, Palumbo-Liu typifies the Asian American community's "collective" rejection of internal critique—averting its face from the suicide of one of its own, to validate a (wishful, and coercive) unity.

5. When Abercrombie & Fitch clothing manufacturers, for example, unveiled a line of t-shirts in April 2002 caricaturing Chinese food and laundry services, Asian America mobilized with the passion of grossly dissatisfied customers, threatened to withhold business (in activist language: "boycott"), and received lightning-fast customer service:

> The national nonpartisan APA political action committee, 80-20, received emails Wednesday from APA youths urging the organization to investigate the matter and take action. The following Thursday morning at 10:30 a.m., 80-20 President S. B. Woo called the Abercrombie and Fitch Chairman and CEO Michael Jeffries and left a message expressing the wish for Abercrombie and Fitch to withdraw the products. Two hours later, Seth Johnson, an executive of Abercrombie and Fitch returned Woo's call to inform him that the T-shirts were being pulled from the shelves. (Jennifer Lauron, "Offensive Anti-Asian T-Shirts pulled from Abercrombie and Fitch Stores," http://www.asianfortune.com/may 02/Anti-Asian%t-shirts.htm)

Meanwhile the 80-20 Initiative itself, established in 1998 with the motto "Unity is Power," was born with the purpose of wielding a swing bloc vote to "win equal justice and equal opportunity" by "help[ing] the 11 million APAs break the glass ceiling in workplaces" (http://www.80-20.to/unity1.html). 80-20's major undertaking for July 4, 2001, was a campaign appealing to APAs to fly U.S. flags as a statement of belonging—an unsolicited pledge of allegiance.

6. Thus, while it is not implausible that some similarities hold between Asian immigrant family structures and those in their countries of origin, what continuities there are do not prove this model a timelessly or universally "Asian" one; this project holds, rather, that what continuities survive across continents are selected for and culled away from a set of discontinued behaviors, because these in particular are perceived as effective not only in their original milieux, but in immigration's altered social and political context of racialization, capitalist competition, and educational opportunity.

7. A note about terms: Though as a category, the term "Asian American" is itself increasingly challenged for its ability to hold, I have adopted that term for use in this book with the understanding that it is a "working" signifier, rather than one that need pretend to positivist truth. I am persuaded by Kandice Chuh's very elegant argument for "a definition of 'Asian American' that relies not" on the empiricism of bodies and ethnic/national identities, but "instead emphasizes the fantasy links between body and subjectivity discursively forged"—for this embracing of the discursive power of the category precisely as a discursive construction can, as Chuh suggests, "provide grounds for continuing to mobilize and deploy the term 'Asian American' in light and in spite of contemporary critiques of its limitations" (Chuh, x). In opting not to turn to terms such as "Asian Pacific American" or "Asian Pacific Islander American," I support her contention that "Such adjustments, through pluralizing or through expansion, . . . are clearly corrections designed to enhance the term's accuracy, its reflectiveness as a representational sign" (21)—and that such pluralizing measures can only ever advertise their incompleteness.

I use the term "intergenerational conflict" in the sense most colloquial to Asian American cultural studies and social science: to refer to families where the parent is a first-generation immigrant, and parent-child disputes often take on the rhetoric of cultural preservation vs. assimilation, collective vs. individual interests, traditional vs. modern values—whether or not these are indeed the issues truly at stake. The book will use the term "second generation" as a form of shorthand to mean "child of the immigrant generation," though the *experientially* distinctive position to which it refers is not restricted to children technically born into American citizenship; in fact, many of the narrators in this study would be more accurately classified as immigrants or 1.5 generation, but experientially are peers with their second-generation counterparts.

8. The borders around "Asian America" are a little crookedly drawn here to include Evelyn Lau, who is of course Canadian. Yet Lau's work is so critical to the genre as to help define it, and for that reason her nationality comes to reveal more than the other texts might regarding the structural and material necessities of the intergenerational narrative: Binding these instances are capitalist nations with similar histories of Asian racialization, comparable economic structures of opportunity, and a nuclear-family immigrant formation, suggesting that this quintessentially "American" narrative may not be so confined to the United States per se. Her inclusion is thus inherent argument for the model's mobility, even as I strive to hold it still for study.

9. For South Asian examples one might look to independent film and documentaries (*Spellbound*, 2002, comes quickly to mind), and not only to mainstream but ethnic news media, in print and online. The titles of Vivek Wadhwa's "Are Indians the Model Immigrants?" (*BusinessWeek* Sept. 14, 2006) and Smitha Radhakrishnan's affirmative if critical response "The Desi Overachiever Syndrome" (PodBazaar.com, Nov. 28, 2006) speak for themselves.

10. Interestingly, recent social science studies like many of those mentioned earlier come increasingly to flex the empirical imperatives of data, and borrow from the terminology and toolbox of literary scholarship:

> [R]egardless of how little knowledge the children do possess, their *stories* are remarkably similar to each other regardless of their ethnic and class background. . . . I argue that the second generation *utilizes three variations of the classic Western narrative* in describing their parents. (LSH Park, 85; emphases added)

> [P]art of the story I tell in this book [is] how [second-generation] Chinese American students, both women and men, from diverse class and educational backgrounds *constructed a similar narrative* of Asian American parents as paramount in their children's educational lives. *The similarities lie in the language they use* to speak of this role and in the particulars they saw in the role itself . . . (Louie, xxvi; emphases added)

> As a result of the *lack of language* for suicide that moves beyond binarist discourses of victimhood or recovery, these Asian American women are forced into silence about their psychic traumas or to represent their pain in self-destructive ways. (Noh, *Suicide*, 89; emphasis added)

I suspect that it is in increasing recognition, both of the power of discourse *as* discourse, and of the distance between available language and analytical distillation, that these particular interdisciplinary moves are made.

11. While in large proportion the primary texts in this study are explicitly autobiographical in content, it is with the understanding that fiction and nonfiction (as well as commercial literature and ethnographic account) occupy a common continuum between empirically derived experience and narratively constructed fabrication—and that the genre by which each text or source announces itself does not necessarily reflect the position on that spectrum where it actually falls—that the project disregards generic classifications and considers all of its primary texts equally revealing of the discourses that we circulate.

12. This use of the dream metaphor of the political unconscious I borrow from Fredric Jameson by way of Abdul JanMohammed.

13. As a Foucauldian, it should be noted, I regard these economic models as part of a system for the administration of power rather than as its base or origin; in this way, I side in the debate over Marxist (in)compatibilities and influences in Foucauldian theory with cultural materialism at large: "If cultural materialism reduced to essentials holds simply . . . 'that cultural practices should be regarded as forms of material production' . . ., then there is much . . . in Foucault . . . that is in this generic sense 'cultural materialist'" (Milner, 107).

NOTES TO CHAPTER 1

1. By the time of Wong's writing, Asian Americans had been mired in a virulent wartime form of "Yellow Peril" discourse. Interestingly, Wong chooses to navigate her readers away from such associations precisely by skirting any intimation of the economic modernity linked with what Colleen Lye has called "American Orientalism," and aligns herself instead with the earlier and less threatening European vision of a primitive and opulent Far East. Moreover, it would seem that it is to this European vision of Oriental origins that the immigration narrative of "cultural assimilation" continues to hew—as it tells not of a crossing from Asian industry to Western modernity, but of a romantic teleology from feudalism to capitalism, ancient to modern.

2. Kingston's Brave Orchid plays fast and loose with Chinese cultural "traditions" in similar fashion, amending rules as needed to suit her interests, while trumpeting the rhetoric of time-honored custom. In inciting her sister to "demand [her] rights as First Wife" (Kingston, *Warrior*, 127) from her estranged and Americanized husband, Brave Orchid insists that her sister *both* claim the second wife's two sons as her own (ostensibly in accordance with Chinese practices), *and* that Moon Orchid "Tell [her husband] that [their] daughter, who is the oldest, must inherit his property" (131). In the latter demand, Brave Orchid exploits the possibilities of American inheritance law to argue for a daughter's entitlement to a father's property, over and above the rights of his sons—while continuing to extol this as part of Chinese cultural practices which it manifestly is not.

3. While the Confucian culturalist explanation is popular in many camps both in and outside of academia, Asian Americanist social scientists (psychologists aside) have tended to argue that there is much that a Confucian account fails to explain, including considerable "variation, both historically and in the contemporary era" (Louie, xxviii) with regard to "within-group differences in achievement" (S. Lee, 53); that "there was certainly no empirical basis for the notion of Asian Americans as academic exemplars prior to World War II" (Louie, xxviii); and that intergenerational relations in the "Confucian" homelands themselves *take different forms*: children's ambitions overseas are not funneled into medicine, and daughters are there subjected to contemporary de-professionalizing pressures in a manner that immigrant daughters in the United States and Canada are not (see Ong, 151–53).

If the Confucianist explanation is truly insufficient, however, it must be so on a stronger basis than its being reductive (for what explanation isn't reductive, finally) or politically unpalatable (steering the discussion in Orientalizing directions which we do not wish to pursue, a matter of preference rather than validity). Rather, as Souchou Yao has observed, "The problem with a culturalist explanation . . . is precisely that it does its job too well; it too quickly establishes a singular truth about 'Chinese culture' [or, about Confucianist-derived Asian diaspora cultures] and its determining effects by appealing to the power of Confucianism" (Yao, 102). While the history of Confucian philosophy and its alleged cultural influences is itself complicated and contradictory, it has been ascribed a nearly global explanatory power at every turn. At one time considered ideologically incompatible with and inhospitable to the development of capitalism, it is now commonly considered the unequivocal reason for capitalism's spectacular rise in Asian nations, as well as for the success of Asians in Western capitalist nations (see Max Weber's *The Religion of China*; Yao's *Confucian Capitalism*; and Arif Dirlik's "Confucius in the Borderlands: Global Capitalism and the Reinvention of Confucianism"). While this is not a set of debates I intend to enter into here, it is clear that "Confucianism" is no self-sufficient explanation but a selective and opportunistic deployment of ideological constructs. In other words, while seeming to explain everything, a Confucianist account actually *explains* nothing—because it is tautological in form: Confucian cultures do the hokey-pokey, and Asians do the hokey-pokey because of their Confucian cultures. While seeming to act as an explanatory mechanism, this account in actuality traps us in a closed circuit of assumptions, rendering its object of study utterly opaque. *Ingratitude* will doubtless address in the course of its analysis much that can be flagged as having Confucian overtones or origins, and to tag those elements as such is not necessarily harmful; to think that pronouncing social behaviors or formations "Confucian" is a triumph of analysis, however, is to circle inside its naturalizing assumptions. Its rhetoric plays but a support role, and is not to be mistaken for the story: "If Confucianism has a place here, it is in support of the illusionary relationship between culture and practice, so that what goes on in a Chinese family . . . is detached from the organization of power and inequality" (Yao, 81).

4. So's *Economic Citizens* counts *Fifth Chinese Daughter* among a cohort of Asian American texts preoccupied with financial activity as a means of negotiating subjecthood. Racially consigned to inhabit the economic realm, to tend "the circulation and exchange of commodities" (So, 3), these Asian American subjects strive compulsively and without

success to "translate" their value in financial terms into meaning in representative politics and legibility in social relations. This explanation of the pervasive "tropic economy" (21) navigated by and onto Asian Americans makes enormous headway in accounting for Jade Snow's negotiations of the "public sphere" (14)—but applied to the micro-economy of the narrator's home, its insights stop short. By So's standards, economic discourse must be acknowledged as no less a "private" Asian American idiom than a public one, as illustrated in the Wong family, where the language of filial obedience (i.e., familial "belonging") is as monetary as that of citizenship. Indeed, if according to So's observations, monetary and labor exchanges in the family seem to be *more* "silencing" (41), more "exploitative" (42), and more "unrecognized" (43) than work Jade Snow does for white employers, then this is a surprising assessment of relative advantage for an argument bent upon critiquing the miscarriages of capitalism not in the ethnic family per se but in the national context. May I suggest that, if Jade Snow seems to be driven by the tolls of the private sphere into financial success in the arms of the public, then our analysis needs to be able to account for the "internal tropic economy" of that familial space in both symbiotic and differentiated relation to the external tropic economy in which it operates. Restated by So's terms, if in the home (among Asians alike), the racial excess that disables the general equivalent is not an issue, then financial value *may fully* transfer into social accounts. Rather than enfranchising the financially viable subject, however, the immigrant family that governs its offspring by the general equivalent may be an even more silencing and exploitative demonstration of economic relations successfully mapping onto the social.

5. "Mopping and other housework beyond Jade Snow's physical capacity, Mama did herself, though it meant that she had to stay up one night a week until two in the morning" (JS Wong, 70). It is immediately after this remark that Jade Snow announces her base-pay, and launches into a list of *additional* chores she eagerly solicits in overtime—concluding with a triumphant tally of her total "income":

> [F]or another fifteen cents a week, [she] also cleaned Big Brother's room and changed his bed. If she had time for it, she persuaded him to let her do some of his light laundry, for which she was paid at the rate of a penny a piece. In this way she sometimes earned as much as twenty-five or thirty extra cents a week. These activities . . . gave her an income of about three dollars every month. (71)

6. "These activities, together with the twelve-and-a-half cents she saved from carfare almost every week, gave her an income of about three dollars every month" ; "her own three dollars could buy an extra sweater, a pair of new shoes, or an occasional ice cream" (JS Wong, 71)

7. Ironically, the option to *earn* democratic membership is arguably better derived, in theory and by logical extension at least, from the republicanism which premised political and social citizenship upon a minimum requirement of property ownership, and which classical liberalism replaced. In its early days, Glenn points out, this premise had permitted single, financially independent women the vote—including, in one case as late as 1807, any able to present (and potentially, to have earned) fifty pounds in currency, whether she be white or black (Glenn, 23).

8. By this point in the book, Mr. Wong has ordered himself addressed as "Daddy." For further description of this incident, please see the early pages of the Introduction.

9. Sau-ling Wong notes the "residual" psychological effect of hardship as contributing to this contradiction: "Superficial improvement in material conditions alone . . . cannot, in short order, undo the effects of a lifetime of scraping and scrimping. Expectations of further neediness are not easily overcome" (33). I suggest in addition that the logic of Necessity, its habitual bookkeeping and debt-oriented mind-set, is at odds with itself: parents who work "for" their children cannot successfully release those children from Necessity if they keep on record a debt that never expires.

10. More fully expanded, Fox's model implies a greater "freedom" attendant to social exchange, in that this variety entails "'no binding contract that can be enforced . . . through legal sanctions'"; he further claims that since "the nature of the return cannot be bargained about," it "must be *left to the discretion of the one who makes it*" (Fox, 71; emphasis added). This construction assumes, however, a context in which no other sanctions may prevail upon the debtor, or none of sufficient force to trump her discretion. We find this unworkable for, as we shall see in chapter 3, formidable extra-legal sanctions do exist in familial-social relations, such that the debtor faces an impasse wherein the obligations of return are both unspecified and non-negotiable.

11. This argument will not further address present-day debt bondage, because in its current evolution it has largely shed familial immigration structures. The fact that debt continues to be such a reliable lever in the manufacture and import of unfree labor, however, is highly suggestive of the profitable role it plays in a capitalist economy—and its heightened pertinence to the terms of Asian immigration.

12. Evelyn Nakano Glenn cites a figure of over 400,000 male contract laborers transported to Hawaii from China, Japan, and the Philippines between 1850 and 1930 (Glenn, 193); M. L. Bush cites a figure of 300,000 Chinese bonded laborers to California alone, between 1850 and 1890 (Bush, 42).

13. Indentured servitude, by contrast, bound laborers to work for discrete lengths of time, in the service of whomsoever purchased their labor contracts. Both indenture and peonage were, however, used as modes of paying immigration fare, and as previously mentioned, were often practiced in hybrid rather than pure configuration (Bush, 33).

14. Indeed, in the debate between joining with other workers across ethnic lines to unionize, or scabbing against them at the plantation owners' behest, the narrator's father takes the archetypal position of the model minority: "We should know our place and not anger them [the owners]. That's the only way we'll gain their respect" (37).

15. Disciplinary practices "produce a 'practiced and subjected' body, that is, a body on which an inferior status has been inscribed. A woman's face must be made-up, that is to say, made-over, and so must her body . . . [T]his presupposes that a woman's face, unpainted, is defective" (Bartky, 71). "Since the standards of female bodily acceptability are impossible fully to realize, requiring as they do a virtual transcendence of nature, a woman may live much of her life with a pervasive feeling of bodily deficiency" (81).

16. Kingston's shifting use of perspective and voice reflects the influence of William Carlos Williams' *In the American Grain*, a textual paradigm for what it is to imagine history through character, to lay "claim . . . in a literary way" (Islas, 16) through the projection of consciousness. In addition, especially evident in his first two essays, "Red Eric" and "The Discovery of the Indies," is that Williams handles first and third person

perspectives as if they are *direct* and *indirect* discourse, exploiting both and shifting rapidly between them to construct the subjective realities of his characters. His example demonstrates that the narrative choice of pronoun in and of itself neither dictates identification, nor enables/disables narrative projection.

17. "[Brave Orchid's] sons and daughters mumbled and disappeared—into the bathroom, the basement, the various hiding places they had dug throughout the house" (Kingston, *Warrior*,128).

18. By book's end, Jade Snow owns her own business, and declares in triumphant evidence of her changed status that, "After three months, she was driving the first postwar automobile in Chinatown" (244).

19. In her official capacity as a State Department goodwill ambassador on a cultural tour through Asia, Wong vouched for the United States—in the uncomfortable years after Japanese American internment—as a democracy proud of its Asian citizenry (Kapai, 388).

20. Though the comparison may seem arbitrary, *Ingratitude* in fact began with this entirely different set of women, and that evocative parallel: The nineteenth century gave us a strain of women's narratives, including most famously Kate Chopin's *The Awakening* (1899) and Charlotte Perkins Gilman's "The Yellow Wallpaper" (1892), in which ordinary women descend into a creeping madness, or drown themselves in the sea, because they cannot stand the underlying conditions of their lives—and no one, from the outside looking in, can fathom why. Dubbed the "marital gothic" by Michelle Massé in *In the Name of Love*, this distinctive storyline is characterized by heroines who, by any dominant cultural measure, suffer nothing. Married to caring, morally upstanding men; relieved by class status of the burdens of employment, or of tending to their children and the upkeep of their homes; these women yet undergo an unraveling customarily characteristic of grievous trauma, where no manifestation of classic trauma exists: "It was true that her husband seldom spoke harshly to her; but there were days when he did not speak at all. It was true that he had never struck or threatened her; but he kept her like a prisoner at [their home]" (Edith Wharton, quoted in Massé, 27). The roots of their disintegration are lodged within the very constitution of their positions as woman, wife, mother, and within the structures of power which form their interpersonal relations. In its sense of oppression as structural and thus imperceivable, and of the literary text as an expression thereof, Massé's concept of the marital gothic wrought for me eerie correspondences with contemporary narratives of intergenerational conflict—extending even to what she describes as "the difficulty the story has in getting itself told" (20).

NOTES TO CHAPTER 2

1. Though this chapter focuses primarily on Kingston's first book, it considers *The Woman Warrior* and *China Men* as one extended text, assuming a continuity of narrative subject position, characterization, and storytelling across the two books. Such a merged treatment I believe not only to be feasible in terms of the texts themselves, but justified given their production and acknowledged interrelation: Kingston states that, "*China Men* was almost part of *The Woman Warrior*; I wrote much of those two books at the same time. I once meant for them to be one large book. But the women's stories and the men's stories parted into two volumes . . . The Quality Paperback Club printed *The Woman Warrior* and *China Men* as a boxed set, the most correct presentation" (Kingston, *Statement*, 24).

2. The story of the No Name Woman may be likened to the "fairy tale" for several of its definitive features and functions: "[I]t is principally female figures who occupy central positions in fairy tales" (Rohrich, 4), and "In the area of law and custom the fairy tale has . . . preserved ancient material—like matriarchal inheritance and horrifying penalties—as remnants of judicial procedures" (3). In terms of its function, the fairy tale is said to be "a paradigm . . . for determining and developing individual behavior and personality within [the] community" (Bottigheimer, xii), and as such is "used to discipline children" (Rohrich, 6). Fairy tales "have generally been told neither naively nor without specific intentions" (6)—a statement with equal application to Brave Orchid's oral narration.

3. Here we may recall the very similar affirmation of parental love at the outset of Jade Snow Wong's memoir (2), as well as its overly pat conclusion: "for the first time in her life, [Jade Snow] felt contentment. . . . when she came home now, it was to see Mama and Daddy . . . smile at her, and say, 'It is good to have you home again!'" (246). It is just this closure that Bow argues is ideologically and narrative "forced." When the earlier narrative concludes by insisting on supposedly asemantic and self-evident proofs of parental affection—a mother's tears, a father's pride—critics have rightfully faulted its closure as hollow and disingenuous. We cannot then abort the arc of Maxine's own investigation of the family (the nature of its power, its logic and technologies) by proposing that her verbal acknowledgment of parental feelings be enough. Cheung's phrasing, "the feelings they do have for their own daughters" (Cheung, *Silences*, 97), invites no interrogation of the character or valence of familial "feelings," but implies that anything at all a parent feels for her child can be assumed to be a positive. Such blank assumptions are analytically disabling. It is valid and necessary to discover the particular forms and meanings of any affect, even including what we may call love—how it is interpolated by power, or power interpolated by it, as neither power nor love makes the other less true.

4. Christine So figures this deployment of historical events in particularly intriguing terms, claiming that in these narratives, such "'History' . . . function[s] as another character, an overwhelming series of challenges that generations of Chinese women confront and overcome" (So, 128). In these terms too, however, if History is a character, then for the American-born generation, she is a powerful ancestor they have never met.

5. Cheng's Preface opens, in fact, with this account: "In the 1930s, social psychologists Kenneth and Mamie Clark conducted a series of experiments . . . designed to study how African American children perceive racial difference . . . [W]hen given the choice, the majority of the African American children . . . found the brown dolls to be 'bad' and preferred instead to play with the 'good,' white dolls" (ix). Her intention in so centering the case of the doll test, she explains later, is to call attention to the fact that as a society "we hardly know how to confront the psychical imprints of racial grief," in great part because of our "tendency to rely on exclusively material or quantifiable terms to articulate that injury" (6).

6. See "An Introduction to Chinese- and Japanese-American Literature," Chin et al.:

> It is the racist truth that some nonwhite minorities, notably the Asians, have suffered less and are better off than the other colored minorities (xxv).
>
> White racism . . . did destroy a lot of [Black and Native American] bodies, and leave among these minorities a legacy of suffering that continues to this day. But they did not destroy their impulse to cultural integrity . . . and produce races of people who would work to enforce white supremacy without having to be

supervised or watch-dogged./ In terms of . . . complete psychological and cultural subjugation of the Asian-American, the people of Chinese and Japanese ancestry stands out as white racism's only success." (xxvi)

It would seem to be more meaningful homology than pure coincidence, furthermore, that the ambivalent semantics of "racist love" should, like "parental love," prove so difficult for the Asian American subject to negotiate.

7. This moment is for Cheng the literal expression of melancholic suffering, in which the young narrator is struck down by hypochondria in the place of any medically validated illness. For Cheng, Maxine's illness somatizes an internalized racial antipathy (Cheng, 68), amounting to the conviction that racial difference itself is an unlocalizable disorder in the body. Reading hypochondria as an expression of the subject's perception of the self in relation to the social world (69), Cheng frames the condition within psychoanalytic terms as "a form of melancholic self-allergy," and the "Freudian melancholic as someone hypochondriacally aware of and allergic to the abjection lodged within" (65). The utility of this model of racial injury speaks for itself, and so I will not rehash Cheng's diagnosis of "Asian American hypochondria" (69) here. I do believe, however, that her argument taps the clarifying powers of this trope too conservatively. Consider that Cheng recognizes Maxine's hypochondria to be "an illness close to, *and of*, home" (68; emphasis added): "to be with her mother and in Chinatown (literally, this narrator's biological and geographical origins) is to suffer debilitating illness; to be elsewhere is to enjoy perfect health" (66). Consider that Cheng describes this correlation as a "disturbing *affinity* between familial-ethnic origin and the anticipation of illness" (68; emphasis added)—and yet that she explores the implications of hypochondria *exclusively* as a function of the subject's social relations with "mainstream values" (69) and national models of assimilation. While Cheng's work is very much about examining "the ways in which individuals and communities remain invested in maintaining such categories [as gender and race], even when such identities prove to be prohibitive or debilitating" (7), it stops short of acknowledging that "investment" involves so much more than "maintaining" a received racism. A subject's proximity to and relations with(in) the home are not exclusively a function of public forces, even with regard to racialization; those who share our familial-ethnic origins fervently shape the form and content of those identities we impose on or receive from each other.

8. "Her fingers and palms became damp, shrinking at the ghost's thick short hair like an animal's coat, which slides against warm solidity as human flesh slides against muscles and bones" (Kingston, 69).

9. Though hypochondria is a key term in Cheng's thesis, the technical and psychoanalytic definition which informs her analysis is explicitly not the colloquial one in use here. Cheng specifies that she is "not interested in a vernacular understanding of hypochondria as an imaginary illness or in suggesting that Kingston's narrator is 'making up' her illness whenever she is at home in Chinatown" (68).

10. See the *International Handbook of Multigenerational Legacies of Trauma*, edited by Yael Danieli.

11. This assertion is tricky to uphold especially in light of the fact that, of all the personas incorporated into the memoir, her mother's is the one perspective from which Maxine never speaks in the first person. Her mother's is *specifically* the identity, then, with

which the narrator will not allow herself to merge: However intimate and proximate they may become, they are always distinctly two ("my mother"); and at times, as we have seen in chapter 1, the narrator withdraws from Brave Orchid's association completely. Even if plausibly there is some trauma passing from this mother to her daughter, there is also a real attempt on Maxine's part to break the circuit of transmission—*to refuse a forced loan*—for which the image of the daughter as pale echo or vessel for the mother's voice cannot account.

12. Jennifer Griffiths, too, has brought the concept of insidious trauma to bear in her reading of *The Woman Warrior*. Unfortunately, while Griffiths notes that "Maxine displays a kind of vigilance [around rape] associated with Root's description of 'insidious trauma,'" she then proceeds to read the narrator's "split in the nail" as indication that "the body bears an unerasable trace of trauma" passed from aunt to niece (Griffiths, 358). This campaign to locate evidence of psychic injury as a "mark" on the body seems to me misguided, as it rather undercuts or misses the thrust of a theory meant to authenticate suffering that makes no marks.

13. See chapter 4 for further elaboration on the mechanics of sexuality and disownment, interpellation, and identification in this act of storytelling.

14. I am indebted to the interventions into trauma theory made by feminist psychoanalytic critics such as Massé, Brown, and Root; in addition to this chapter's use of insidious trauma, I turn in chapter 4 to Massé's discussion of masochism as specifically conditioned by such very vague suffering, and cannot understate the importance of insights such as these:

> The victim of shell shock will not always awaken to the sound of actual bombs, nor will contemporary society deny the validity of the trauma. . . . In contrast, the heroine of the marital Gothic will always reawaken to the still-present actuality of her trauma, because the gender expectations that deny her identity are woven into the very fabric of her culture, which perpetuates her trauma while denying its existence. (Massé, 15)

In its reliance on the language of trauma, however, the work of such critics presupposes a "whole" and original self that is subsequently stripped, constrained, traumatized, which formulation stands at odds with this project's more Foucauldian model of subject formation. Furthermore, though it is vital to gain cultural acknowledgment that real subjective damage occurs in more insidious forms, I feel that to belabor the omnipresence of trauma performs an unsavory leveling of injury, evacuates the term of certain meanings which need to be preserved. Between structural domination; and rape, mutilation, terror within structural domination; there are necessary and important distinctions. I believe it is useful and politically strategic, especially in a feminist politics, to reserve some portion of "trauma" for the meaning it has attained: a "breach in the mind's experience of time, self, and the world" (Caruth, 4), a violence beyond the pale. I would opt, therefore, to maintain a distinction between trauma as a form of breach and injury which this book's later narrators in fact adopt in preference to the suffering that they habitually undergo—and the qualitatively distinct (if not necessarily quantitatively "lesser") effects of normalizing relations of power. If anything, a reading of trauma such as Massé offers us may be incorporated into the discussion of Asian American women's literature, in that such a critical stance would be arguably *symptomatic* of the very structures and narratives we study: Massé seeks, much as our later narrators themselves do, to *use* the vocabulary of trauma in order to express structural violences that defy articulation as injuries on their own terms.

15. Waverly's wry comment in *The Joy Luck Club* that "you can't ever tell a Chinese mother to shut up. You could be charged as an accessory to your own murder" (Tan, 173) is therefore accurate, if amusingly exaggerated, to the structure of disownment in sovereign power.

In this light, it is also interesting to recall Jade Snow Wong's seemingly gratuitously exoticizing characterizations of her upbringing as having operated "by the nineteenth-century standards of Imperial China" (vii), and to wonder whether such comments might actually be residual references to a vivid imaginary of cultural lore which is deployed in her childhood, but not recounted in her narrative.

16. The term "contract" is used here in partial irony (as the parent-child relation is not one formed by mutual consent, and in the literal sense is thus quite the reverse of contract), but also with reference to the more originary sense of the social contract, which may apply between parent and child or, in another instance of sovereign power, between master and slave. In this latter sense, the subject's "consent" to continue each moment in unfreedom in order to persist in life constitutes a form of perpetually renewing contract, albeit one entailing grossly imbalanced terms without the benefit of prior negotiation. Chapter 3 will return to this discussion of consent and the terms of life's continuance in greater detail.

17. Certainly, such anxieties are overdetermined, and it would be unwise to discount or dismiss the racialized content and societal context of the narrator's fears: "If I made myself American-pretty so that the five or six Chinese boys in the class fell in love with me, everyone else—the Caucasian, Negro and Japanese boys—would too" (12). Maxine's personal version of these fears takes a course not entirely rational, from incest to miscegenation, and integrates along the way such complications as the differential genderings of mainstream American versus immigrant Chinese cultures. However, for the purposes of this argument, we will limit our present concerns to the contention that this passage demonstrates the niece's anxieties to be significantly, if partially, a response to the morality tale she hears, tells, and uses.

18. See Jacques Lacan, "The Mirror Stage as Formative of the Function of the *I* as Revealed in Psychoanalytic Experience." In the classic form, the toddler upon first recognizing the reflection in the mirror as herself is jubilant at the competence and integration of this "ideal-I," which compares so favorably to her frustrated internal experience of herself as arms and legs that do not do her bidding. This moment, which inaugurates the ego, is an empowering one, but it is also a permanent fiction, whereby the new subject will henceforth and forever assign her agency to an illusion which is external to herself, and with which perfection she can never merge. In the case of this present, speculative reversal, the image embraced is equally external and inaccessible to the self, but *while being more rather than less fragmented, is also more empowering* in that it allows the subject to articulate herself to greater (political) effect. Both cases, then, entail a simultaneous and ongoing gain *and* loss.

19. While in technical immigration terms the son of this account is "first" rather than "second" generation, in terms of kinship he is Maxine's "Elder Brother" and therefore her

generational contemporary. Moreover, the narrator emphatically describes "Mad Sao" as even "more American than us" (*Men*, 171)—and she aligns him, within the parent-child divide, with her own position as the child. (His relationship with his own children is not addressed.) I use the Mad Sao account as an extension of the novels' representation of immigrant parent-child relations because the narrator, similarly, employs this account in a supplementary rather than contrapuntal relation to her own perspective.

20. The practice of comparison is an ongoing process, visible in abbreviated form at moments in both texts, as the immigrants seek to judge each others' and their children's relative hardships and merits—assessments which are ever shifting. Thus, while waiting for her sister's arrival at the airport, Brave Orchid remarks that "These new immigrants had it easy. On Ellis Island the people were thin after forty days at sea and had no fancy luggage" (*Warrior*, 115). Yet a few sentences later she comments, "Luggage conveyors fooled [new] immigrants into thinking the Gold Mountain was going to be easy" (116), implying that life in America is never that, not for old or new immigrants and perhaps, not for their children. Likewise, the same children she refers to as "Her bad boy and bad girl" (114) are later revealed to have undergone far more arduous upbringings than did the newly arrived Moon Orchid. In comparing them against her sister, Brave Orchid thinks, "Even the children could work. Both girls and boys could sew. . . . The children could work all of the machines, even when they were little and had to stand on apple crates to reach them" (137). The relative values of the family members' lives—their toil and deserts—is by no means an established ratio, but a contended margin which fluctuates on the mustering of anecdotes. Furthermore, the parents themselves may be conflicted as to the logic of this comparative economics: devaluing the merit of a child's life of relative ease when that ease, as we saw in *Fifth Chinese Daughter*, was supposedly part of their purpose in immigrating. "The immigrants could be saying that we were born on Gold Mountain and have advantages. Sometimes they scorn us for having had it so easy, and sometimes they're delighted" (205).

21. This may be in part as, in their pure forms, both rejection and acceptance leave the logic of indebtedness intact, but more so that, as we shall see, the terms "nothing," "plenty," and "not enough" are in effect equivalent.

22. Significantly, the method of her bracing is to inflict physical pain upon herself, and to imagine physical trauma. This manner of response is endemic to "insidious trauma," and will bear discussion in chapter 3.

23. This is not to imply that the difference in receptivity to debt is gendered; certainly, Mad Sao approximates more Maxine's response than those of her boy cousins. And daughters far more willing to inflict "offensive" harm against parental power will be found in chapter 4.

24. The "sacrifice" here seems at first, in the former of the mother's two statements, to refer to the family's surrender of a child for the cause, and therefore to imply a debt owed to the family (including quite possibly to the child/warrior herself) by the villagers she saves. Such a reading makes no sense in light of the latter statement, however, which distinguishes parental sacrifice from a daughterly responsibility to remember.

25. The story of Fa Mu Lan, then, returns us to the genre of the fairy tale, with which both the novel and this chapter begin. By convention, such tales are full of "the impossible task," missions or chores assigned to ordinary mortals which no ordinary mortal can perform. Their completion usually requires the intervention of an object or being of a magical order. Kingston's telling of Fa Mu Lan meets these principles: a young girl

is selected to save her country, but can do so (and win her parents' approval) only with the magical training of fairy-godparent figures. Thus, the filial trope of sending (enough) money here gains status as a mythically impossible task.

26. A statement meaningfully reminiscent of the language of sovereign power.

27. Tellingly, it is this conclusion—the single moment wherein Maxine seems to execute the seamless transgenerational transmission and channeling of her mother that Cheng suggests is true of the narrative relationship overall—which the critic herself professes to find least convincing.

NOTES TO CHAPTER 3

1. This chapter will also incorporate discussion of Lau's later memoir *Inside Out: Reflections on a Life So Far* as coupled with *Runaway*, watchful for shifts in perspective but arguing for a workable continuity across the two books, on the basis of the memoir's own candid positioning of itself as a meditation on the former text. In its opening sentence, *Inside Out* makes deliberate reference to *Runaway*, expressing both its subjective distance from the younger narrator therein, and its ongoing compulsion to revisit, and rework, the subject matter of the diary.

2. http://voices.cla.umn.edu/vg/Bios/entries/liu_catherine.html. Though the first-person narrator of Liu's novel is unnamed, to minimize confusion between the Lau and Liu texts I will refer to her for practicality as "Catherine," taking some liberty here with the distinction between novel and autobiography, but hoping to maintain the customary separation between author and narrator.

3. Like Maxine herself, Kingston's readers are suspended in epistemological uncertainty by the "extravagance" of her stories ("You won't tell me a story and then say, 'This is a true story,' or, 'This is just a story.' . . . I can't tell what's real and what you make up" [*Warrior*, 202]), such that even when she speaks of American-life routine, the possibility of fantastic hyperbole maintains an obscuring veil over the facts of her family's personal life. Meanwhile, the surfeit of subject positions permits the narrator to make multiple statements obliquely without binding her position to any single (incriminating) one.

4. Though the family's position of debt means a mathematically negative objective of making up loss rather than a positive one of bringing in gain, these are but relative positions in the economic continuum. A business is no less motivated by profit for operating in the red rather than the black.

5. This is not to say that the boys are free to be drunks or braggarts as long as they perform their function as breadwinners; rather, Kiyoshi distinguishes between "filial" sons who bully or lie, and "other" sons (*not* filial) who drink or gamble, the apparent difference between these characteristics being that conduct which detracts from the boy's income is not filial, but character traits which do not endanger the money he brings home are irrelevant–that is, beside the point.

6. It bears noting that the mouthpiece for this gender ideology is in Murayama's story not the immigrant parents but the second-generation son. This comment expresses Toshio's view of his parents' extreme injustice and poor financial management, which result in a greater load of debt and exploitation devolved upon him as a producer. As it is not possible to "invest" where there is no premise of financial return, expenditures on the girls' educations are in this schema chastised by Toshio as a form of consumption.

7. Both Jade Snow and Maxine recall selective adjustments of parental standards for traditional feminine "propriety," made to best exploit financial opportunities for women in the new country (see chapter 1 for expanded discussion). For Evelyn and Catherine, the expectation that a girl will marry out of the home and out of financial responsibility to the parental household, will have evaporated without a trace.

8. Interestingly, furthermore, while Kingston foreshadows her later counterparts in bringing up the subject of mathematics, the context, connotations, and very ambiguity of her brief allusion reveal that the meaning of this cultural signifier had then not yet been codified. In supposed response to their Hong Kong aunt's traumatic rejection by her younger Americanized husband, Brave Orchid's daughters are said to have vowed not to let their husbands stray, and "[a]ll her children made up their minds to major in science or mathematics" (160). Certainly, this last bit of a non sequitur explains little of the reasoning behind the children's choice of math (and/or science; apparently mathematics had yet to receive the singular status of a fetish item), and is more than likely ironic. Nevertheless, it is markedly different from the scene related by Lau and Liu in making no mention of parental coercion, and motioning instead at the possibility that qualities perceived as inherent to the discipline (plausibly, its strict logical nature, its freedom from emotion), rather than its lucrative promise, may have motivated the siblings' decision.

9. Taken from *The New Face of Asian Pacific America*, these data indicate that, while the greatest proportion of white Americans continue to hold high school degrees only, the percentage of Asian Americans holding advanced degrees (45%) is more than double that of Asian American high school graduates (approximately 17%). The latter figures regarding the breakdown of graduate degrees date to 1995.

10. Reminiscent of Jade Snow Wong's becoming a potter/writer.

11. In Canada, likewise, though "women had entered the . . . occupations of university teacher, physician, [and] lawyer . . . by the time World War I began" (Kinnear, 20), it was only in the seventies that they were admitted to the professions in appreciable proportions: "The 1974 [law school class] was among the first which graduated significant numbers of women" (Adam and Baer, 43).

12. As we shall see in chapter 4, however, gender discrimination adjusts but does not disappear from the labor arrangements of the immigrant family. The household "chores" that Catherine (like Jade Snow) continues to do, while her brother is excused, suggest that in contemporary configurations, while sons may have been promoted fully to the professional class, and relieved of the duties of day or wage labor, daughters, even as they are allowed and expected to achieve a comparable social mobility, continue to work the infamous "second shift" (Hochschild).

13. Kingston: "I alone devote pages of paper to her" (16); "What we have in common are the words at our backs" (53). Wong: "She discovered very soon that her grades were consistently higher when she wrote about Chinatown and the people she had known all her life" (132); "Letters of congratulations poured in . . . Her picture was printed, not only in the contest-sponsoring paper, but in all the Chinese papers, which carried translations of the main points of her essay. For the first time, Daddy and Mama had the opportunity of understanding how their fifth daughter's mind worked" (196).

14. Notably, Catherine's parents are not at one in their estimate of writing, in that while her mother finds literature thoroughly suspect, her father prides himself on his own published work in Chinese. Yet, whatever the father's personal esteem for literature, it

does not materially alter his stance in the family's investment-style child-rearing: Catherine's parents are *a unit* in their condemnation of her pursuit of a nonlucrative career in literature (Liu, 301).

15. "I never went out, helped with the housework, had no boyfriend and few friends, brought home good grades, never experimented with alcohol or drugs" (Lau, 12).

16. Notably, reading functions in very much this escapist fashion in *Fifth Chinese Daughter* as well: "During the next two years, Jade Snow found in eager reading her greatest source of joy and escape. . . . Temporarily she forgot who she was, or the constant requirements of Chinese life, while she delighted in the adventures of the Oz books, the *Little Colonel, Yankee Girl,* and Western cowboys, for in these books there was absolutely nothing resembling her own life" (JS Wong, 69). However, as literature has not at this time taken on its particularized meanings in contradistinction to the model minority/filiality paradigms, Jade Snow gives no indication of overtones of rebellion or need for deceit in her act of reading.

17. The (bed)room's contradictory valences of shelter and confinement, haven and cell, are sorely apparent in the following passage, in which Evelyn recalls as a young child having been "fascinat[ed] with small, bare, locked places—I would shut myself in a closet or bathroom and stay there, wondering, 'Would I rather live here, never to go out again, or continue the way I am (with my parents)?' The answer was always the same: I'd rather live in a closet" (Lau, *Runaway*, 89).

18. This distancing strategy recalls the narrative splittings of Wong's and Kingston's personae in *Fifth Chinese Daughter* and *The Woman Warrior*—used here as in Kingston to grant rather than deny access to threatening representations.

19. Indeed, Catherine refuses to call either of her parents by any relational terms for the span of six pages at the beginning of a chapter—referring to them instead by descriptors usually reserved for monsters out of nightmares and fairy tales: "I knew that I lived under the spell of the Fat Man and his pale, vengeful Wife" (Liu, 127). Like Wong's use of "Daddy" or Kingston's use of "Brave Orchid," such choices cannot help but represent the degree and quality of a narrator's alienation from or identification with her parents, and Catherine's choices could not convey more unequal threat than inhabits the primal face-off between a child and her archetypal demons. Evelyn, likewise, figures her mother as a monster in the dream-like language of her worst childhood fears: Upon seeing on the street a woman who physically resembles her mother, Evelyn states, "I expected her hand to grasp my arm like a claw, to be dragged back to the house where, in my mind, the drama was still being played. . . . But this woman who could have been my mother walked right past me, continued on her way, and the black spell was broken" (Lau, *Inside*, 184).

20. Her demands for "filiality" challenged by her son, Murayama's mother figure, likewise, repeatedly responds with the words "Someday you'll have your punishment" (Murayama, 45), an invocation which calls misfortune down upon her son as if his hardship would vindicate, avenge, and appease her.

21. Butler's discussion of passionate attachment is universalized to all subjects insofar as they cannot come into being outside formative systems of power and subordination. I find its workings extra-ordinarily pertinent, however, to a context in which "[t]he one who holds out the promise of continued existence [and] plays to the [subject's] desire to survive" (Butler, 7) does so persistently and explicitly rather than merely by default. The dynamics which for Butler *underlie* subjection lie on the *surface* of this relation, a

difference not of mere degree but of kind: that between the mitigation, acceptance, or exploitation of advantage.

22. Sovereign power's indiscriminate application of the ultimatum, elaborated in the previous chapter through Maxine and Jade Snow, reemerges here with something of a more abusive aspect.

23. Little wonder, then, that eating disorders such as anorexia and bulimia should make their appearances in Asian American women's literature (see Christina Chiu, Elaine Mar, Evelyn Lau). To reject the material gift that is food is at once to manage the accruing debt, and to seize control (via its destruction) of the existence by which one is indebted.

24. In provocative parallel, it is true for Asian American subjects in the national context that "racist institutions in fact often do not want to fully expel the racial other; instead, they want to maintain that other within existing structures"; "the racial question is an issue of *place*," of containment and control, of exploitation for profit, "rather than of full relinquishment" (Cheng, 12).

25. To clarify, however, it is not Butler's project, nor ours, to foreclose the possibilities of political resistance in this formulation of ambivalence, but more cautiously to enable it. She explains,

> That agency is implicated in subordination is not the sign of a fatal self-contradiction at the core of the subject and, hence, further proof of its pernicious or obsolete character. But neither does it restore a pristine notion of the subject, derived from some classical liberal-humanist formulation, whose agency is always and only opposed to power. The first view characterizes politically sanctimonious forms of fatalism; the second, naïve forms of political optimism. I hope to steer clear of both these alternatives. (Butler, 17)

26. Comparisons of this nature can also be found in Murayama's and Chin's texts, but notably not in Wong's or Kingston's, as parenting in the latter is not concerned to maximize ROI.

27. See chapter 2 for extended discussion of History-based and generationally biased valuations of suffering, as well as its implications for storyteller and narrative form; the introduction for inclusion of Lau's and Liu's narratives in that larger pattern.

28. See Sianne Ngai's *Ugly Feelings* for an important charting of the political economy of affects, in which strong and directed emotions such as anger offer political purchase, economic claim to resources, social legibility; whereas flat and undirected "moods" such as depression, with their "weak intentionality—their indistinctness if not absence of object," serve a "diagnostic rather than strategic" function (Ngai, 22), and defy insertion into conventional calculations of "grievance" (to cross-pollinate from Anne Cheng) and reparation.

29. What is illegible about this second-generation, model minority upbringing is then, very pointedly, not some essentially exotic identity, but the immigrant family's very particular form of normalcy.

30. More on sexuality, self-destruction, and revolt in the next chapter.

31. See Judith Herman's chapter in *Trauma and Recovery* on, sadly, child abuse for a clinically derived description of these same psychic maneuvers in response to a "family environment [in which] the exercise of parental power is arbitrary, capricious, and absolute" (Herman, 98).

32. It is in a moment of longing and closeness—of *identification*, when Evelyn sees her parents precisely as people who love her—that she describes them as being obvious and clumsy: "The sadness is unbearable, watching my parents try to contain themselves, try not to do anything wrong or alienate me again. Yet their attempts are so obvious, clumsy . . . Their efforts fall short but are efforts nonetheless, and it makes me feel immensely sad" (Lau, *Runaway*, 218). Chao's use of this moment to characterize Lau's work as a "ruthless" act of sellout objectification shows a rather appalling lack of respect for either text or analysis (Chao, 172). Her subsequent example of the Orientalism of Lau's depiction, furthermore, strains piteously against the sheer American impact of the evidence she musters: few cultural references could evoke more good-old-fashioned American capitalism, and less ancient China, than Henry Ford.

33. See epigraph to Introduction.

34. See Claire Kim's *Bitter Fruit* for a discussion of Korean immigrants' pre-arrival ideological investments.

NOTES TO CHAPTER 4

1. Leila, the unmarried, is eldest; Ona, the suicide, is second; Nina, disowned, is third.

2. "You must not tell anyone" (3); "Don't let your father know that I told you" (5); "Don't tell anyone you had an aunt" (15). See also the comparable use of a disavowed daughter in Christina Chiu's *Troublemaker*. Here, too, the girl's name is repeatedly referenced *as having been crossed out*, to keep the family's other daughters in line. "At the mention of her name," her grandmother admonishes its speaker, a girl cousin, to "Hush." "One look and [the speaker] silences. She knows: To be forgotten is a terrible thing. Terrible; it could happen to her. She's had fair warning" (Chiu, 67).

3. Marxist-feminist Michele Barrett makes a similar point in her discussion of gender roles in the political-economic organization of the household: "while men undoubtedly do wield considerable power in the household and the relations of domestic labour are incontrovertibly oppressive and restricting for women, it is not clear to me that the 'breadwinner's' position is as [unilaterally] privileged as" others would suggest (Barrett, 217).

4. Horowitz's research explores the interface between honor systems and capitalist ideals within an inner-city Chicano enclave in the 1970s. While it is beyond the scope of my current project to perform a comparative analysis of the specificities between the Asian and Chicano communities in question, and certainly the contextual differences are many, it is possible to say that on a theoretical level, Horowitz's observations, especially with regard to familial honor as a function of female sexuality, are substantially consonant with my own.

5. This distinction evolved out of Gayle Rubin's observation that "The exchange of women does not necessarily imply that women are objectified, in the modern sense, since objects in the primitive world are imbued with highly personal qualities" (174). I extrapolate from her point to argue that women in such economies are not evacuated of subjectivity as such, but conditioned to assume a specifically feminine subjectivity as objects.

6. The instrumentality of chastity is somewhat analogous, then, to the utility of classical music training discussed in chapter 3—the point of each being not their ends but their means.

7. In this light it is interesting to consider, with new care, the phrasing that describes the roof-thatcher's mistake, in Divakaruni's story: "He let [his daughter] run wild, climbing trees, swimming in the river. Let her go to school, even after she reached the age when girls from good families stayed home, waiting to be married." (By way of more than coincidence, the parental figures in Jen's *Mona in the Promised Land* bemoan their prior putative laxity in the same language: "No more go out, go out . . . From now on, Mona stay home. . . . No more let the kids run wild" [246].) In these terms, a girl who "runs" wild is literally one who is not domestically confined, but has (unsupervised) mobility in the geography outside the home. Furthermore, such a girl acquires, it would seem, a familiarity with uses of her body which are themselves regarded with suspicion: to run, swim, or climb are bodily practices little suitable with the physicality entailed in the body language of feminine docility.

8. In Sau-ling Wong's "Ethnicizing Gender: An Exploration of Sexuality as Sign in Chinese Immigrant Literature," a situation of unequal "Americanization" by gender among Chinese immigrants is found to give rise to a semiotic system of cultural ideals ("Chineseness" and "Americanness"; "femininity" especially with regard to sexual norms) which are variously unifying (constructing a cultural "community" of sexual inadequacy) and marginalizing (constructing a threatening and yet enviable foreignness via sexual prowess and "excess"). Questions of cultural propriety and gender impropriety of course come into play as characters struggle to define their own sexual places and, however thwarted in their efforts, to contain or control the sexuality of others.

9. And indeed, per the logical endpoint of the Panopticon, the surveilling community is ultimately a fiction: there need be no one in the watchtower. When Elaine's or Mona's mothers bring up "the community" and its opinion of the family—"I'm so ashamed that I'm afraid to go out in public!" (Mar, 162); "What do you think people think of us?" (Jen, 45)—these are *invented communities*, selectively applied. Both families live in regions distant from gatherings of Chinese immigrants: The newspaper Elaine's mother uses to scare her is "published in San Francisco" (161) and arrives by mail to Denver in sporadic fashion. And "Chinatowns . . . are" likewise "alien to non-Cantonese refugees like [Mona's family], who live in the suburbs without extended families ('Community? What community?' asks Ralph . . .)" (SL Wong, Mona, 10). Isolated from any functional network of surveillance, what information may circulate about their families is most likely limited to gossip they themselves disseminate. Whatever the details of this fabricated gossip—"The information about me varied, but it was always the bad, never the good" (Mar, 162)—obedience is its bottom line: "They know you don't listen to your mother."

10. Thus, the docile wife's domestic labor is relieved only by the successful production of a docile daughter. See Christine Delphy's arguments regarding the "domestic mode of production": "There are two modes of production in our society. Most goods are produced in the industrial mode. Domestic services, child-rearing and certain other goods are produced in the family mode. The first mode of production gives rise to capitalist exploitation. The second gives rise to familial, or more precisely, patriarchal exploitation" (Delphy, 69)—though, of course, I would not here qualify familial exploitation as being exclusively patriarchal.

11. For expediency, clarity, and consistency with Agamben, the singular male pronoun will be used here to designate the sovereign, although as previously established in my argument, that position may be occupied in the family by either or both parents.

12. If it can be said of the daughter that "That's who you are—your family," then it might be said of the sovereign that "That's who your family is—yourself."

13. Anne Cheng describes this implicating moment via a related, though perhaps more passive, mechanism: "the child, just by listening, has already been drawn into a contract and is already at fault—a double bind that works much like Derrida's favored example of the sign 'Do not read this.' . . . [T]he impossibility of the injunction (to hear it is to transgress it; to obey it one has to be already guilty) tells us about how law works. . . . The moment the narrator hears and is exiled from the story of the No Name Aunt, she is conscripted into a relation with the aunt as the same and not the same" (Cheng, 85).

14. The regulatory systems for female chastity and sexual orientation do, however, bear more than passing similarities to one another, and for good reason. They share not only initially parallel psychic structures, but comparable effects: Transgressions of heteronormativity—whether by sons or daughters—can trigger disownment with a force and speed comparable to (if not surpassing) transgressions of female chastity, because both forms of sexual deviance threaten the reproduction of the model minority family: "Upward mobility that will increase the economic and social capital of an immigrant community depends on the assurance not only that the next generation will move into well-paying professions but also that they will marry and reproduce the heterosexual family structure" (Maira, 170). Though this project will not be engaging with the familial management of sexual orientation specifically, such convergences in the regulatory production of the (grand)child bear noting as potentially useful avenues for further theorizing the immigrant family.

15. In their suicides, these cultural figures literalize, demonstrate, and reinforce the terms of passionate attachment, wherein a child learns to accept as her only alternatives that "I would rather exist in subordination than not exist" (*Psychic*, 7). Having failed to exist properly in subordination, these female figures seem dutifully to concede their lives as forfeit.

16. In this respect, Leila's puzzlement that her parents could not even be considered "strict" answers to the very definition of sovereign power: "To me, strict implies order and consistency, some sort of agreement./ Mah and Leon had no such thing. They made up rules as they needed them, and changed them all on a whim" (Ng, *Bone*, 111).

17. Thus the almost malicious timing of Nina's impulse to announce her sexual transgressions (cohabitation with a strange man) to her parents in the immediate aftermath of her sister's suicide—before Ona had even been buried (*Bone*, 113): she would make them confront the added weight of disgrace, in a moment of already dire weakness, not *despite* but *for* the added impact.

18. The racial factor within this and other of the daughters' sexual relationships is of course meaningful, but as I will address presently, it is not necessarily the determining factor in the struggle. Indeed, as the "besides" in even this brief quote suggests, the issue is sex; the racial problem is additive rather than primary or distinctly complicating.

19. "Go. You will one day tell us sorrowfully that you have been mistaken" (JS Wong, 130); "Someday you'll have your punishment" (Murayama, 45); "It was their fantasy to find me overdosed one day . . . They seemed to find some kind of morbid satisfaction from the idea that I was becoming a depraved human being" (Liu, 68); "She [Nina]'d die in a gutter without rice in her belly, and her spirit . . . wouldn't be fed. They [Mah and Leon] forecast bad days in this life and the next" (Ng, 25).

20. See Mei Ng's *Eating Chinese Food Naked*, or Tanith Tyrr's "Sacrament."

21. A penchant more than prevalent, even in the literature alone: besides Fae Myenne Ng's Nina, Mar's Elaine, and Divakaruni's unnamed protagonist, Jen's Mona as well as second-generation women in the foregoing Mei Ng and Tyrr texts, Christina Chiu's *Troublemaker*, and Tan's numerous works all choose non-Asian men (white or, in Chiu's case, black) to date or marry.

NOTE TO AFTERWORD

1. Interestingly, the first 180 pages of Lê's novel are far enough off-formula that early in reading it I did not anticipate the book's ultimately keen relevance for this project: Much of the early narrative is set in Việt Nam, and family dynamics prior to immigration evoke little to nothing of the classic intergenerational conflict. Once in the United States, the narrator's parents separate, making for yet another departure from the parameters within which this project expects to find its purest form. Yet in its last third, *Little Sister Left Behind* turns into a classic narrative of the unfilial daughter, on par with the texts of this book's third chapter. The late turn to classic intergenerational conflict is surprising—as well as suggestive of the power of that model to overcome considerable material differences.

Bibliography

Adam, Barry D., and Douglas E. Baer. "The Social Mobility of Women and Men in the Ontario Legal Profession." *Canadian Review of Sociology and Anthropology* 21 (1984): 21–46.

Agamben, Giorgio. *Homo Sacer: Sovereign Power and Bare Life*. Translated by Daniel Heller-Roazen. Stanford: Stanford University Press, 1998.

Barrett, Michele. *Women's Oppression Today: The Marxist-Feminist Encounter*. New York: Verso, 1988.

Bartky, Sandra Lee. "Foucault, Femininity, and the Modernization of Patriarchal Power." In *Feminism & Foucault: Reflections on Resistance*, ed. Irene Diamond and Lee Quinby. Boston: Northeastern University Press, 1988.

Benjamin, Jessica. *The Bonds of Love: Psychoanalysis, Feminism, and the Problem of Domination*. New York: Pantheon Books, 1988.

Berger, David, and Morton Wenger. "The Ideology of Virginity." *Journal of Marriage and the Family* 35:4 (1973): 666–76.

Bersani, Leo. "The Subject of Power." *Diacritics* 7:3 (1977): 2–21.

Berthrong, John H., and Evelyn Nagai. *Confucianism: A Short Introduction*. Oxford: OneWorld Publications, 2000.

Blinde, Patricia Lin. "The Icicle in the Desert: Perspective and Form in the Works of Two Chinese-American Women Writers." *MELUS* 6:3 (1979): 51–71.

Bottigheimer, Ruth B., ed. "Preface" and "Silenced Women in the Grimms' Tales: The 'Fit' Between Fairy Tales and Society in Their Historical Context." In *Fairy Tales and Society: Illusion, Allusion, and Paradigm*, xii–xiv and 115–31. Philadelphia: University of Pennsylvania Press, 1986.

Botting, Fred. *Gothic*. New York: Routledge, 1996.

Bow, Leslie. *Betrayal and Other Acts of Subversion: Feminism, Sexual Politics, Asian American Women's Literature*. Princeton: Princeton University Press, 2001.

———. "Cultural Conflict/ Feminist Resolution in Amy Tan's *The Joy Luck Club*." In *New Visions in Asian American Studies: Diversity, Community, Power*, ed. Franklin Ng et al., 235–47. Pullman: Washington State University Press, 1994.

———. "The Illusion of the Middle Way: Liberal Feminism and Biculturalism in Jade Snow Wong's *Fifth Chinese Daughter*." In *Bearing Dreams, Shaping Visions: Asian Pacific American Perspectives*, ed. Linda A. Revilla et al. Pullman: Washington State University Press, 1993.

Broude, Gwen. "The Cultural Management of Sexuality." In *Handbook of Cross-Cultural Human Development*, ed. Ruth Munroe et al., 633–73. New York: Garland STPM Press, 1981.

Brown, Laura. "Not Outside the Range: One Feminist Perspective on Psychic Trauma." In *Trauma: Explorations in Memory*, ed. Cathy Caruth, 100–112. Baltimore: Johns Hopkins University Press, 1995.

Brown, Wendy. *States of Injury: Power and Freedom in Late Modernity.* Princeton: Princeton University Press, 1995.

Bush, M. L. *Servitude in Modern Times.* Cambridge, UK: Polity Press, 2000.

Butler, Judith. *The Psychic Life of Power: Theories in Subjection.* Stanford: Stanford University Press, 1997.

———. *Bodies That Matter: On the Discursive Limits of "Sex."* New York: Routledge, 1993.

Caruth, Cathy. *Unclaimed Experience: Trauma, Narrative, and History.* Baltimore: Johns Hopkins University Press, 1996.

Chang, Ching-Fei. "Homecoming." In *Making More Waves: New Writing by Asian American Women*, ed. Elaine Kim and Lilia Villanueva, 43–53. Boston: Beacon Press, 1997.

Chang, Juliana. "Melancholic Remains: Domestic and National Secrets in Fae Myenne Ng's *Bone.*" *Modern Fiction Studies* 51:1 (Spring 2005): 110–33.

Chao, Lien. "From Testimony to Erotica: The Split Subject and Oedipal Drama in Evelyn Lau's Prose/" In *Beyond Silence: Chinese Canadian Literature in English*, 156–84. Toronto: TSAR Publications, 1997.

Chen, Ying. *Ingratitude.* New York: Farrar, Straus and Giroux, 1998.

Cheng, Anne. *The Melancholy of Race: Psychoanalysis, Assimilation, and Hidden Grief.* New York: Oxford University Press, 2001.

Cheung, King-Kok. "Introduction" and "Paul Stephen Lim." In *Words Matter: Conversations with Asian American Writers*, 1–18 and 40–57. Hawai'i: University of Hawai'i Press, 2000.

———. *Articulate Silences: Hisaye Yamamoto, Maxine Hong Kingston, Joy Kogawa.* Ithaca: Cornell University Press, 1993.

Chin, Frank. "The Year of the Dragon." In *The Chickencoop Chinaman and The Year of the Dragon: Two Plays by Frank Chin*, 67–142. Seattle: University of Washington Press, 1981.

Chin, Frank et al. "An Introduction to Chinese- and Japanese-American Literature." In *Aiiieeeee! An Anthology of Asian-American Writers*, ed. Frank Chin et al. Washington, DC: Howard University Press, 1974.

Chiu, Christina. *Troublemaker and Other Saints.* New York: Berkley Books, 2001.

Chopin, Kate. *The Awakening: An Authoritative Text.* New York: W. W. Norton, 1994.

Chow, Rey. *The Protestant Ethnic and the Spirit of Capitalism.* New York: Columbia University Press, 2002.

Christian, Barbara. "The Race for Theory." In *The Nature and Context of Minority Discourse*, ed. Abdul JanMohamed and David Lloyd. New York: Oxford University Press, 1990.

Chu, Patricia. *Assimilating Asians: Gendered Strategies of Authorship in Asian America.* Durham: Duke University Press, 2000.

Chuh, Kandice. *Imagine Otherwise: On Asian Americanist Critique.* Durham: Duke University Press, 2003.

Conde, Mary. "An Interview with Evelyn Lau." *Canadian Studies* 21:38 (June 1995): 105–11.

Dafoe, Chris. "Nowhere to hide from the success of *Runaway.*" *The Globe and Mail* 14 October 1993: C.

De Bary, Wm. Theodore. *The Trouble with Confucianism*. Cambridge: Harvard University Press, 1991.

Delphy, Christine. *Close to Home: A Materialist Analysis of Women's Oppression*, translated and edited by Diana Leonard. Amherst: University of Massachusetts Press, 1984.

Derrida, Jacques. *The Gift of Death*. Chicago: University of Chicago Press, 1996.

Dirlik, Arif. "Confucius in the Borderlands: Global Capitalism and the Reinvention of Confucianism." *boundary 2* 22:3 (1995): 229–73.

Divakaruni, Chitra. "The Word Love." In *On a Bed of Rice: An Asian American Erotic Feast*, ed. Geraldine Kudaka, 57–68. New York: Doubleday, 1995.

Donzelot, Jacques. *The Policing of Families*. Baltimore: Johns Hopkins University Press, 1997.

Dyrberg, Torben Bech. *The Circular Structure of Power: Politics, Identity, Community*. New York: Verso, 1997.

Edelman, Lee. *No Future: Queer Theory and the Death Drive*. Durham: Duke University Press, 2004.

Eng, David, and Shinhee Han. "A Dialogue on Racial Melancholia." In *Loss: The Politics of Mourning*, ed. David Eng and David Kazanjian, 343–71. Berkeley: University of California Press, 2003.

Eng, Phoebe. *Warrior Lessons. An Asian American Woman's Journey into Power*. New York: Pocket Books, 1999.

Fitzpatrick, Peter. "Bare Sovereignty: *Homo Sacer* and the Insistence of Law." *Theory & Event* 5:2 (2001)

Foucault, Michel. *Discipline and Punish: The Birth of the Prison*. New York: Vintage Books, 1995.

———. *The History of Sexuality: An Introduction*. Volume I. New York: Vintage Books, 1990.

Fox, Alan. *Beyond Contract: Work, Power and Trust Relations*. London: Faber and Faber Limited, 1974.

Fuchs, Victor. "Are Americans Underinvesting in their Children?" *Society* 28:6 (1991): 14–22.

Gates, Hill. "The Commoditization of Chinese Women." *Signs* 14:4 (1989): 799–832.

Gibson, Margaret. *Accommodation without Assimilation: Sikh Immigrants in an American High School*. New York: Cornell University Press, 1988.

Gilman, Charlotte Perkins. "The Yellow Wallpaper." In *The Norton Anthology of American Literature*, 5th ddition. New York: W. W. Norton, 1998.

Glenn, Evelyn Nakano. *Unequal Freedom: How Race and Gender Shaped American Citizenship and Labor*. Cambridge: Harvard University Press, 2002.

Godelier, Maurice. *The Enigma of the Gift*. Chicago: University of Chicago Press, 1999.

Goellnicht, Donald. "Tang Ao in America: Male Subject Positions in China Men." In *Reading the Literatures of Asian America*, ed. Shirley Geok-lin Lim and Amy Ling, 191–212. Philadelphia: Temple University Press, 1992.

Griffiths, Jennifer. "Uncanny Spaces: Trauma, Cultural Memory, & the Female Body in Gayl Jones's *Corregidora* and Maxine Hong Kingston's *The Woman Warrior*. *Studies in the Novel* 38:3 (Fall 2006): 353–70.

Guillory, John. *Cultural Capital: The Problem of Literary Canon Formation*. Chicago: University of Chicago Press, 1993.

Gunew, Sneja. "Operatic Karaoke and the Pitfalls of Identity Politics." In *Literary Pluralities*, ed. Christl Verduyn, 254–62. Orchard Park, NY: Broadview Press, 1998.

Hafez. *The Gift: Poems by the Great Sufi Master*. Trans. Daniel Ladinsky. New York: Arkana, 1999.

Hattori, Tomo. "Model Minority Discourse and Asian American Jouis-Sense." *differences: A Journal of Feminist Cultural Studies* 11.2 (1999): 228–47.

Heng, Geraldine, and Janadas Devan. "State Fatherhood: The Politics of Nationalism, Sexuality, and Race in Singapore." In *Nationalisms and Sexualities*, ed. Andrew Parker, Mary Russo, Doris Sommer, and Patricia Yaeger, 343–64. New York: Routledge, 1992.

Herman, Judith. *Trauma and Recovery*. New York: Basic Books, 1992.

Ho, Wendy. *In Her Mother's House: The Politics of Asian American Mother-Daughter Writing*. Walnut Creek: AltaMira Press, 1999.

———. "Mother/Daughter Writing and the Politics of Race and Sex in Maxine Hong Kingston's *The Woman Warrior*." In *Asian Americans: Comparative and Global Perspectives*, ed. Shirley Hune et al., 225–37. Pullman: Washington State University Press, 1991.

Hochschild, Arlie ,with Anne Machung. *The Second Shift: Working Parents and the Revolution at Home*. New York: Viking, 1989.

Horowitz, Ruth. *Honor and the American Dream: Culture and Identity in a Chicano Community*. New Brunswick, NJ: Rutgers University Press, 1983.

Hwang, Caroline. *In Full Bloom*. New York: Plume, 2004.

Islas, Arturo. "Maxine Hong Kingston." In *Women Writers of the West Coast: Speaking of Their Lives and Careers*, ed. Marilyn Yalom, 11–19. Santa Barbara: Capra, 1983.

Ito, Robert B. "Philip Kan Gotanda." In *Words Matter: Conversations with Asian American Writers*, 173–85. Hawai'i: University of Hawai'i Press, 2000.

Jameson, Fredric. *The Political Unconscious: Narrative as a Socially Symbolic Act*. Ithaca: Cornell University Press, 1981.

JanMohamed, Abdul. *The Death-Bound Subject: Richard Wright's Archaeology of Death*. Durham: Duke University Press, 2005.

———. "Negating the Negation as a Form of Affirmation in Minority Discourse: The Construction of Richard Wright as Subject." In *The Nature and Context of Minority Discourse*, ed. Abdul JanMohamed and David Lloyd, 102–23. New York: Oxford University Press, 1990.

Jen, Gish. *Mona in the Promised Land*. New York: Vintage Books, 1997.

Kapai, Leela. "Jade Snow Wong." In *Asian American Novelists: A Bio-Bibliographical Critical Sourcebook*, ed. Emmanuel Sampath Nelson, 387–89. Westport: Greenwood Publishing Group, 2000.

Karim, Sheba. *Skunk Girl*. New York: Farrar Straus Giroux, 2009.

Karodia, Farida. "Crossmatch." In *Story-wallah: Short Fiction from South Asian Writers*, ed. Shyam Selvadurai, 129–55. New York: Houghton Mifflin, 2005.

Kessler-Harris, Alice. *In Pursuit of Equity: Women, Men, and the Quest for Economic Citizenship in 20th-Century America*. New York: Oxford University Press, 2001.

———. *Out to Work: A History of Wage-Earning women in the United States*. New York: Oxford University Press, 1982.

Kibria, Nazli. *Becoming Asian American: Second-Generation Chinese and Korean American Identities*. Baltimore: Johns Hopkins University Press, 2002.

Kim, Claire. *Bitter Fruit: The Politics of Black-Korean Conflict in New York City*. New Haven: Yale University Press, 2000.

Kim, Elaine. "Defining Asian American Realities Through Literature." In *The Nature and Context of Minority Discourse*, ed. Abdul JanMohamed and David Lloyd. New York: Oxford University Press, 1990.

———. *Asian American Literature: An Introduction to the Writings and their Social Context*. Philadelphia: Temple University Press, 1982.

Kim, Suki. *The Interpreter*. New York: Picador, 2004.

Kingston, Maxine Hong. "Personal Statement." In *Approaches to Teaching Kingston's The Woman Warrior*, ed. Shirley Geok-lin Lim, 23–25. New York: The Modern Language Association of America, 1991.

———. *The Woman Warrior: Memoirs of a Childhood Among Ghosts*. New York: Vintage International Press, 1989.

———. *China Men*. New York: Vintage International Press, 1989.

Kinnear, Mary. *In Subordination: Professional Women, 1870–1970*. Buffalo: McGill-Queen's University Press, 1995.

Koshy, Susan. "Morphing Race into Ethnicity: Asian Americans and Critical Transformations of Whiteness." *boundary 2* 28.1 (Spring 2001): 153–94.

Lacan, Jacques. *Écrits: A Selection*. Translated by Bruce Fink, Héloïse Fink, and Russell Grigg. New York: W.W. Norton, 2002.

LaCapra, Dominick. "Trauma, Absence, Loss." *Critical Inquiry* 25.4 (Summer 1999): 696–727.

Lahiri, Jhumpa. "Only Goodness." In *Unaccustomed Earth*. New York: Alfred A. Knopf, 2008.

Lai, Eric, and Dennis Arguelles, eds. *The New Face of Asian Pacific America: Numbers, Diversity and Change in the 21st Century*. San Francisco: *AsianWeek*, 2003.

Lau, Evelyn. *Inside Out: Reflections on a Life So Far*. Canada: Anchor Canada, 2001.

———. *Runaway: Diary of a Street Kid*. Toronto: Coach House Press, 1995.

Lê, Samantha. *Little Sister Left Behind*. San Jose: Chusma House Productions, 2007.

Le Espiritu, Yen. "Changing Lives: World War II and the Postwar Years." In *Asian American Studies: A Reader*, ed. Jean Wu and Min Song. New Brunswick, NJ: Rutgers University Press, 2000.

———. *Asian American Panethnicity: Bridging Institutions and Identities*. Philadelphia: Temple University Press, 1992.

Lee, Katherine. "The Poetics of Liminality and Misidentification: Winnifred Eaton's *Me* and Maxine Hong Kingston's *The Woman Warrior*." In *Transnational Asian American Literature: Sites and Transits*, ed. Shirley Lim et al., 181–96. Philadelphia: Temple University Press, 2006.

Lee, Peter, and Yu-Wen Ying. "Asian American Adolescents' Academic Achievement: A Look Behind the Model Minority Image." In *Psychosocial Aspects of the Asian American Experience*, ed. Namkee G. Choi, 35–48. New York: Haworth Press, 2001.

Lee, Rachel C. *The Americas of Asian American Literature: Gendered Fictions of Nation and Transnation*. Princeton: Princeton University Press, 1999.

Lee, Stacey. *Unraveling the "Model Minority" Stereotype: Listening to Asian American Youth*. New York: Teachers College Press, 1996.

Leong, Russell. "Foreword: Unfurling Pleasure, Embracing Race." In *On a Bed of Rice: An Asian American Erotic Feast*, ed. Geraldine Kudaka, xi–xxx. New York: Doubleday, 1995.

Levi-Strauss, Claude. *The Elementary Structures of Kinship*. Translated from the French by James Harle Bell, et al. Boston: Beacon Press, 1969.

Li, David Leiwei. *Imagining the Nation: Asian American Literature and Cultural Consent.* Stanford: Stanford University Press, 1998.

Lim, Shirley Geok-Lin. "The Tradition of Chinese American Women's Life Stories: Thematics of Race and Gender in Jade Snow Wong's *Fifth Chinese Daughter* and Maxine Hong Kingston's *The Woman Warrior*." In *American Women's Autobiography: Fea(s)ts of Memory*, ed. Margo Culley. Madison: University of Wisconsin Press, 1992.

Ling, Amy. *Between Worlds: Women Writers of Chinese Ancestry*. New York: Pergamon Press, 1990.

Liu, Catherine. *Oriental Girls Desire Romance*. New York: Kaya, 1997.

Louie, Vivian. *Compelled to Excel: Immigration, Education, and Opportunity among Chinese Americans*. Stanford: Stanford University Press, 2004.

Lowe, Lisa. "Heterogeneity, Hybridity, Multiplicity: Asian American Differences." In *Immigrant Acts: On Asian American Cultural Politics*, 60–83. Durham: Duke University Press, 1996.

Lye, Colleen. *America's Asia: Racial Form and American Literature, 1893–1945*. Princeton: Princeton University Press, 2005.

Ma, Sheng-mei. *Immigrant Subjectivities in Asian American and Asian Diaspora Literatures*. Albany: State University of New York Press, 1998.

Maira, Sunaina. *Desis in the House: Indian American Youth Culture in New York City.* Philadelphia: Temple University Press, 2002.

Mar, M. Elaine. *Paper Daughter: A Memoir*. New York: HarperCollins Publishers, 1999.

Massé, Michelle. *In the Name of Love: Women, Masochism, and the Gothic*. New York: Haworth Press, 1990.

Mauss, Marcel. *The Gift: The Form and Reason for Exchange in Archaic Societies*. New York: W. W. Norton, 1990.

May, Simon. *Nietzsche's Ethics and His War on 'Morality.'* New York: Oxford University Press, 1999.

Mazumdar, Sucheta. "General Introduction: A Woman-Centered Perspective on Asian American History." In *Making Waves: An Anthology of Writings by and about Asian American Women*, ed. Asian Women United of California. Boston: Beacon Press, 1989.

McLaren, Margaret. "Foucault and the Subject of Feminism." *Social Theory and Practice* 23:1 (1997): 109–27.

Milner, Andrew. *Cultural Materialism*. Carlton, Vic.: Melbourne University Press, 1993.

Mirikitani, Janice. "Suicide Note." In *Shedding Silence: Poetry and Prose*. Berkeley: Celestial Arts, 1987.

Motooka, Wendy. "Nothing Solid: Racial Identity and Identification in *Fifth Chinese Daughter* and 'Wilshire Bus.'" in *Racing and (E)Racing Language: Living with the Color of our Words*, ed. Ellen J. Goldner and Safiya Henderson-Holmes, 207–32. Syracuse: Syracuse University Press, 2001.

Murayama, Milton. *All I asking for is my body*. Honolulu: University of Hawaii Press, 1988.

Ng, Fae Myenne. *Bone*. New York: HarperCollins, 1993.

———. "A Red Sweater." In *Charlie Chan is Dead: An Anthology of Contemporary Asian American Fiction*, ed. Jessica Hagedorn, 358–68. New York: Penguin Books, 1993.

Ng, Mei. *Eating Chinese Food Naked*. New York: Washington Square Books, 1998.

Ngai, Sianne. *Ugly Feelings*. Cambridge: Harvard University Press, 2005.

Nguyen, Viet Thanh. *Race and Resistance: Literature and Politics in Asian America*. New York: Oxford University Press, 2002.

Nietzsche, Friedrich. *On the Genealogy of Morals*. Translated by Walter Kaufman. New York: Random House, 1989.

Noh, Eliza Sun. "Asian American Women and Suicide: Problems of Responsibility and Healing." *Women & Therapy* 30:3/4 (2007): 87–107.

———. *Suicide among Asian American Women: Influences of Racism and Sexism on Suicide Subjectification*. PhD Diss., University of California, Berkeley, 2002.

Odem, Mary. "Teenage Girls, Sexuality, and Working-Class Parents in Early Twentieth-Century California." In *Generations of Youth: Youth Cultures and History in Twentieth-Century America*, ed. Joe Austin and Michael Willard, 50–64. New York: New York University Press, 1998.

Omatsu, Glenn. "The 'Four Prisons' and the Movements of Liberation." In *Asian American Studies: A Reader*, ed. Jean Wu and Min Song, 164–96. New Brunswick, NJ: Rutgers University Press, 2000.

Ong, Aihwa. *Flexible Citizenship: The Cultural Logics of Transnationality*. Durham: Duke University Press, 1999.

Ortner, Sherry. "The Virgin and the State." *Feminist Studies* 4:3 (1978): 19–36.

Ortner, Sherry, and Harriet Whitehead. "Introduction: Accounting for Sexual Meanings." In *Sexual Meanings: The Cultural Construction of Gender and Sexuality*, ed. Ortner and Whitehead, 1–27. New York: Cambridge University Press, 1981.

Palumbo-Liu, David. "Appendix: Model Minority Discourse and the Course of Healing." In *Asian/American: Historical Crossings of a Racial Frontier*, 395–416. Stanford: Stanford University Press, 1999.

Park, Lisa. "A Letter to my Sister." In *Making More Waves: New Writing by Asian American Women*, ed. Elaine Kim and Lilia Villanueva, 65–71. Boston: Beacon Press, 1997.

Park, Lisa Sun-Hee. *Consuming Citizenship: Children of Asian Immigrant Entrepreneurs*. Stanford: Stanford University Press, 2005.

Pecora, Vince. *Households of the Soul*. Baltimore: Johns Hopkins University Press, 1997.

Radway, Janice. *Reading the Romance: Women, Patriarchy, and Popular Literature*. Chapel Hill: University of North Carolina Press, 1991.

Root, Maria P. "Reconstructing the Impact of Trauma on Personality." In *Personality and Psychopathology: Feminist Reappraisals*, ed. Laura Brown and Mary Ballou, 229–65. New York: Guilford Press, 1992.

Rohrich, Lutz. "Introduction." In *Fairy Tales and Society: Illusion, Allusion, and Paradigm*, ed. Ruth Bottigheimer, 1–9. Philadelphia: University of Pennsylvania Press, 1986.

Rubin, Gayle. "The Traffic in Women." In *Toward an Anthropology of Women*, ed. Rayna Reiter, 157–210. New York: Monthly Review Press, 1975.

Rudrappa, Sharmila. "Disciplining Desire in Making the Home: Engendering Ethnicity in Indian Immigrant Families." In *Second Generation: Ethnic Identity among Asian Americans*, ed. Pyong Gap Min. Walnut Creek: AltaMira Press, 2002.

Said, Edward. *Orientalism*. New York: Vintage Books, 1979, c. 1978.

Santa Ana, Jeffrey. "Affect-Identity: The Emotions of Assimilation, Multiraciality, and Asian American Subjectivity." In *Asian North American Identities: Beyond the Hyphen*, ed. Eleanor Ty and Donald C. Goellnicht, 15–44. Bloomington: Indiana University Press, 2004.

Sasaki, R. A. *The Loom and Other Stories*. Saint Paul: Graywolf Press, 1991.

Sato, Gayle K. Fujita. "Ghosts as Chinese-American Constructs in Maxine Hong Kingston's *The Woman Warrior*." In *Haunting the House of Fiction: Feminist Perspectives on Ghost Stories by American Women*, ed. Lynette Carpenter and Wendy Kolmar. Knoxville: University of Tennessee Press, 1991.

Schlegel, Alice. "The Cultural Management of Adolescent Sexuality." In *Sexual Nature, Sexual Culture*, ed. Paul Abramson and Steven Pinkerton, 177–94. Chicago: University of Chicago Press, 1995.

———. "Status, Property, and the Value on Virginity." *American Ethnologist: The Journal of the American Ethnological Society* 18:4 (1991): 719–34.

Schneider, Jane. "Of Vigilance and Virgins: Honor, Shame and Access to Resources in Mediterranean Societies." *Ethnology: An International Journal of Cultural and Social Anthropology* 10:1 (1971): 1–25.

Schwartz, Barry. "The Sociology of the Gift." *The American Journal of Sociology* 73:1 (1967): 1–11.

Sklair, Leslie. "Social Movements and Global Capitalism." In *From Modernization to Globalization: Perspectives for Development and Social Change*, ed. J. Timmons Roberts and Amy Hite, 340–52. Malden: Blackwell, 2000.

Smart, Alan. "Gifts, Bribes, and *Guanxi*: A Reconsideration of Bourdieu's Social Capital." *Cultural Anthropology* 8:3 (1993): 388–408.

Smith, Sidonie. "Filiality and Woman's Autobiographical Storytelling." In *Maxine Hong Kingston's* The Woman Warrior: *A Casebook*, ed. Sau-ling Wong, 57–83. New York: Oxford University Press, 1999.

So, Christine. *Economic Citizens: A Narrative of Asian American Visibility*. Philadelphia: Temple University Press, 2007.

Song, Miri. *Helping Out: Children's Labor in Ethnic Businesses*. Philadelphia: Temple University Press, 1999.

Storhoff, Gary. "Even Now China Wraps Double Binds around My Feet: Family Communication in *The Woman Warrior* and *Dim Sum*." In *Reading the Family Dance: Family Systems Therapy and Literary Study*, ed. John V. Knapp and Kenneth Womack, 71–92. Newark: University of Delaware Press, 2003.

Strecker, Trey. "Oriental Girls Desire Romance." *The Review of Contemporary Fiction* (March 22, 1998): 246.

Su, Karen. "Jade Snow Wong's Badge of Distinction in the 1990's." *Critical Mass: A Journal of Asian American Cultural Criticism* 2.1 (Winter 1994): 3–42.

Suh, Grace Elaine. "Gifts of the Magi." In *Making More Waves: New Writing by Asian American Women*, ed. Elaine Kim and Lilia Villanueva, 12–19. Boston: Beacon Press, 1997.

Sze, Julie. "Have You Heard?: Gossip, Silence, and Community in *Bone*." *Critical Mass: A Journal of Asian American Cultural Criticism* 2.1 (Winter 1994): 59–69.

Tan, Amy. *The Joy Luck Club*. New York: Vintage Books, 1989.

Ting, Jennifer P. "The Power of Sexuality." *Journal of Asian American Studies* 1.1 (1998): 65–82.

Tyrr, Tanith. "Sacrament." In *On a Bed of Rice: An Asian American Erotic Feast*, ed. Geraldine Kudaka, 89–96. New York: Doubleday, 1995.

Van Den Boogaart, E., and P. C. Emmer, eds. *Colonialism and Migration: Indentured Labour before and after Slavery*. Boston: Martinus Nijhoff Publishers, 1986.

Vietnamese American Student Publications, University of California, Berkeley. "The Stained Handkerchief: A Conversation about Chastity for the Vietnamese Woman." *Across the Sea* issue 4, "Speaking in the Feminine Tense" (1993): 2–6, 30–35.

Weber, Max. *The Religion of China: Confucianism and Taoism*. Hans Gerth, translator and ed. Glencoe: Free Press, 1951.

Williams, Raymond. *Marxism and Literature*. New York: Oxford University Press, 1977.

———. *The Long Revolution*. Canada: Broadview Press, 1961.

Williams, William Carlos. *In the American Grain*. New York: New Directions Books, 1956.

Wong, Jan. "Evelyn Lau Gets Perfect Grades in School of Hard Knocks." *The Globe and Mail* 3 April 1997: A11.

Wong, Jade Snow. *Fifth Chinese Daughter*. Seattle: University of Washington Press, 1989.

Wong, Nichole. "A Quarter-Life Crisis: Asian American Life Coaches Help Clients to 'Quit Being Chinese.'" *Hyphen* 19 (Winter 2009): 15.

Wong, Sau-Ling Cynthia. "Denationalization Reconsidered: Asian American Cultural Criticism at a Theoretical Crossroads." In *Postcolonial Theory and the United States: Race, Ethnicity, and Literature*, ed. Amritjit Singh and Peter Schmidt, 122–48. Jackson: University Press of Mississippi, 2000.

———. "'But What in the World is an Asian American?': Culture, Class and Invented Traditions in Gish Jen's *Mona in the Promised Land*." The Invention of Traditions: The Third Conference on Chinese American Literature. Institute of European and American Studies, Academia Sinica. Taipei, 11 April 1997.

———. "'Sugar Sisterhood': Situating the Amy Tan Phenomenon." In *The Ethnic Canon: Histories, Institutions, and Interventions*, ed. David Palumbo-Liu, 174–210. Minneapolis: University of Minnesota Press, 1995.

———. *Reading Asian American Literature: From Necessity to Extravagance*. Princeton: Princeton University Press, 1993.

———. "Ethnicizing Gender: An Exploration of Sexuality as Sign in Chinese Immigrant Literature." In *Reading the Literatures of Asian America*, ed. Shirley Geok-lin Lim and Amy Ling, 111–29. Philadelphia: Temple University Press, 1992.

Yao, Souchou. *Confucian Capitalism: Discourse, Practice and the Myth of Chinese Enterprise*. New York: Routledge, 2002.

Yee, Jennifer. "Ways of Knowing, Feeling, Being, and Doing: Toward an Asian American and Pacific Islander Feminist Epistemology." *Amerasia Journal* 35:2 (2009): 49–64.

Yep, Jeanette et al. *Following Jesus without Dishonoring Your Parents*. Downers Grove: InterVarsity Press, 1998.

Yezierska, Anzia. *Bread Givers*. New York: Persea Books, 2003.

Yin, Kathleen, and Kristoffer Paulson. "The Divided Voice of Chinese-American Narration: Jade Snow Wong's *Fifth Chinese Daughter*." *MELUS* 9.1 (1982): 53–59.

Yoshihara, Mari. *Musicians from a Different Shore: Asians and Asian Americans in Classical Music*. Philadelphia: Temple University Press, 2007.

Yuan, Yuan. "Mothers' 'China Narrative': Recollection and Translation in Amy Tan's *The Joy Luck Club* and *The Kitchen God's Wife*." In *The Chinese in America: A History from Gold Mountain to the New Millennium*, ed. Susie Lan Cassel, 351-364. Walnut Creek, CA: AltaMira, 2002.

Zelizer, Viviana. *The Purchase of Intimacy*. Princeton: Princeton University Press, 2005.

———. *Pricing the Priceless Child: The Changing Social Value of Children*. New York: Basic Books, 1985.

Zizek, Slavoj. *The Sublime Object of Ideology*. New York: Verso, 1989.

In Gratitude

These pages are bound by the time, faith, and generosity of wonderful people.

This project would be unthinkable without the guidance and influence of Abdul JanMohamed, Sau-ling Wong, and Colleen Lye. They are embedded here too thoroughly to footnote.

Berkeley is wrapped up in my memory with home-baked chocolate soufflés, hand-cut noodles, and my friends Trane Devore and Misa Oyama—who read each early page.

Friendship comes in no kinder yet diabolical form than Jim Lee, who cared enough to threaten me with worse things, even, than not finishing a book.

Because they form that most priceless of academic homes—a warm, supportive department—I am blessed to have as colleagues Diane Fujino, Xiaojian Zhao, John Park, and Celine Parreñas Shimizu.

The following people may not be entirely aware of how much their time and touchstones have done: Sameer Pandya, in assuring me that the revision was not, in fact, going all wrong; Dolores Inés Casillas, Carolyn Piñedo-Turnovsky, and Ben Zulueta, in turning the solitude of writing into an occasion for good company; Steve Sohn and Mimi Khúc, in their words of amen; and Julia Bader, in teaching a graduate course of lasting impact.

Moreover, this book has truly benefited from the insight, care, and thoughtfulness of its reviewers, whoever they may be.

I am grateful for the fellowship support—and further, the votes of confidence—from the following organizations and institutions:

the American Association of University Women, whose incredible members raise the funds for their fellows even if a dollar, or a cookie, at a time;

the University of California's President's Postdoctoral Fellowship Program and my mentor Rachel Lee, who put credence in a literary scholar's attempt to save lives; and

UC Santa Barbara's Interdisciplinary Humanities Center; Institute for Social, Behavioral and Economic Research; and Dean Melvin Oliver, of whose support an assistant professor is most appreciative.

For meeting me there, for taking me home, for bringing me saline solution: Alfred Lee, Grace Foster, Charles Chang.

For hearing me out: Donna Moriguchi.

For fighting our common battles, and her own: my sister.

For having become my advocates, my confidants, my friends: my parents.

For operating under a wholly different, sun-filled sky: my husband.

My editors and this press, thank you for putting *Ingratitude* on shelves and in hands. Emily Park, for starting me off; Ciara McLaughlin, for so carefully seeing me through. Eric Zinner, how glad I am you asked me at the MLA that day, whether I had a book project.

Index

education: of daughters, 91; in Lau and Liu, 106; musical, 108–10; rates of, 92. *See also* math; the model minority

Eng, David, 4–5

envy, masochistic, 114–15

escape and confinement, 96–99, 118

"Ethnicizing Gender" (Wong), 143, 183n8

ethnic nationalist criticism, 120–21, 122

extravagance, narrative, 83, 89–90, 111. *See also* narrative and structure

fairy tales, 55, 78, 173n2, 181n25. *See also* cautionary tales

familial economics, 23–27. *See also* child as capital investment; debt, filial; the model minority

families, Asian immigrant: adaptive practices of, 21–22; as capitalist enterprise, 2; cost of becoming American, 36–39; in defense of, 3–5, 119–22; narrative impulses in, 145–47; prestige and, 135–36, 153, 161, 163. *See also* child as capital investment; the model minority; sovereign power and law

Fa Mu Lan, 77, 78

female sexuality. *See* sexuality, regulation of female

femininity: Bartky on, 45, 133, 138; construction of, 128–29, 141, 182n5n5; normative, 148

feminist theorists, 63–64, 134, 182n3. *See also* Butler, Judith

Fifth Chinese Daughter (Wong): "At the Western Palace," compared to, 50, 51; autonomy in, quest for, 27, 30, 39–40; child as capital investment in, 91; classical liberalism in, 25, 26–27, 30; conclusion of, 51–54; cultural adaptation in, 21; familial economics in, 23, 24–26; filial debt in, 33, 34–35, 36, 39–40; introduction of, 19–20; Lau and Liu, compared to, 85–86; narrative in, 22, 47–48; Necessity in, 28–29; overview of, 2–3; passionate attachment in, 105–6; power in, 123; propriety in, 46; reading

in, 96n16; sovereign power and law in, 43–44, 45; surveillance in, 137; *Woman Warrior*, compared to, 49, 79

filial guilt, 42–45, 107, 147

filiality, perfect, 46, 75, 76, 77–79

filial obedience: attainment of, 45–46; capitalism in relation to, 38; economic aspects, 23; filial debt in relation to, 35; in *Woman Warrior*, 75–76. *See also* debt, filial; disobedience; sovereign power and law

Foucault, Michel: *Discipline and Punish*, 16, 41–42, 130, 136–38, 141, 143; *History of Sexuality*, 128, 132, 156; subject formation and, 11–12

Fox, Alan, 35

gender: child as capital investment and, 88, 90–92, 93; roles, 25; sexuality and, 128; surveillance and, 134. *See also* femininity; feminist theorists; sexuality, regulation of female

ghosts in Woman Warrior, 62–63

gift, theory of the, 103–4

Glenn, Evelyn Nakano, 23n4, 25, 30, 37, 171n12

Godelier, Maurice, 103

gossip: as a disciplinary technology, 129; gendered aspects, 134; significance of, 131; subject formation, role in, 142–43; as surveillance, 132–33; truth in relation to, 136–37

Griffiths, Jennifer, 64, 175n12

Guillory, John, 86, 93–94. *See also* New Class

guilt, filial, 42–45, 107, 147

Han, Shinhee, 4–5

harm: incommensurable, 113–16, 117; phenomenology of, 58; racial grief and, 60–61, 62; sovereign power and, 101; of threat, 63–65. *See also* self-destruction; suffering; trauma

Hattori, Tomo, 15, 120–21, 123

Hawaii, 37

symbolic capital, 60, 93, 94, 108–13
Sze, Julie, 131

third person narration, 47–48, 49, 50. *See also* narrative and structure
time management, 40–42
trauma, 63–64, 69, 73, 115, 177n22. *See also* harm; suffering
tropic economy, 23, 29, 169–70n4

ultimatum of sovereign power: effectiveness of, 104; gift theory and, 102n22; in *Woman Warrior*, 65, 66, 67. *See also* disownment
Unequal Freedom (Glenn), 25

violence. *See* harm
virginity. *See* sexuality, regulation of female
virtue, perceptions of. *See* sexuality, regulation of female

Wadhwa, Vivek, 13, 167n9
wage labor, 25, 27, 30
Williams, Raymond, 14
Williams, William Carlos, 49, 177n16
The Woman Warrior (Kingston): ambivalence in, 74, 79; child as capital investment in, 91; *China Men* and, 55n1; conclusion of, 80; discipline in, 42; discursivity vs. reality in, 56, 58, 64–65, 78; disownment in, 65, 66, 67–68; *Fifth Chinese Daughter* compared to, 49, 51, 77; filial debt in, 74, 75; gossip in, 131; illness in, 62, 63; compared to Lau

and Liu, 83, 178n3; math in, 91, 179n8; misogyny in, 56–58; narrative in, 49, 68–74, 83; perfect filiality and, 46, 76, 77–79; power in, 123; Sau-ling wong on, 27; sexual anxieties and, 69, 70; significance of, 56; sovereign power and law in, 44, 45; subjectivity in, 148; suffering in, 59–60, 62, 114; surveillance in, 132, 133–34; trauma in, 63, 64, 69; violence in, 59. *See also* Brave Orchid; "No Name Woman"
Wong, Jade Snow. See *Fifth Chinese Daughter*
Wong, Jan, 119–20
Wong, Sau-ling: cannibalistic motif of, 88–89; "Ethnicizing Gender," 143n8; *Fifth Chinese Daughter* and, 16; on Necessity, 33, 89; *Reading Asian American Literature*, 27
"The Word Love": cautionary tale in, 130; gossip in, 131; self-punishment in, 153–55; sexuality in, 143n7, 153; subjectivity in, 148
writing and reading, 94–100, 118

Yao, Souchou, 22, 173n3
"Year of the Dragon" (Chin), 92
Yellow Peril, 20n1, 60
"The Yellow Wallpaper" (Gilman), 53, 172n20
Yezierska, Anzia, 12
Yoshihara, Mari, 109

Zelizer, Viviana, 23–24, 35–36

About the Author

ERIN KHUÊ NINH is Assistant Professor of Asian American Studies at the University of California, Santa Barbara.